Psychic Diaries

Also by Lysa Mateu

Conversations with the Spirit World
(under the name Lysa Moskowitz-Mateu)

LYSA MATEU

HarperEntertainment
An Imprint of HarperCollins*Publishers*

Psychic Diaries

*Connecting
with who you are,
why you're here,
and what lies beyond*

FIRST EDITION

Designed by Renato Stanisic

Printed on acid-free paper

Library of Congress Cataloging-in-Publication Data
    Mateu, Lysa
        Psychic diaries: connecting with who you are, why you're here, and what lies
        beyond / by Lysa Mateu.
           p. cm.
        ISBN 0-06-055966-7
        1. Mateu, Lysa. 2. Mediums—United States—Biography. 3. Psychics—
        United States—Biographies. I. Title
        BF1283.M66A3 2003
        133.9'1—dc22   2003062475

03 04 05 06 07 WBC/RRD 10 9 8 7 6 5 4 3 2 1

This Book Is Dedicated to . . .

My husband, SATORI— We work, live, love, create, play, and spend every single night and day of our lives together and still, when you leave the house, I miss you. When you come home, I cheer. Your love nourishes and inspires me to go beyond where I ever thought I could go. Your fearlessness teaches me to love fully, holding nothing back. I love you with every ounce of my being, and then some. I thank you for uttering the two words that gave me the guts to do what I do. "Trust yourself."

My mom and dad, LINDA and LENNY— They say we get to choose our parents before we get here, and with that said, I must've been first in line because I chose the best parents ever! I love you both with every ounce of my being and it is an honor to call you Mom and Dad. You exemplify everything parents are supposed to be and because of you both (literally) my life has been and will continue to be blessed.

My brother DAVID— Growing up, nearly every photo is of us hugging, laughing, and hiding in suitcases, hoping Mom and Dad will get the hint and take us on vacation. You are my rock solid inspiration, a brilliant father to Amanda, a wonderful husband to Brenda, an outstanding son to Mom and Dad, and most of all a kick-ass big brother to me!

Contents

Thank You . . .

Nothing I have accomplished in this life was done by me alone. Even those things that appear to be of my own fruition are never far from the influence of others. Words people have said, passages I have read, images seen, experiences encountered, all play a role in the web of my life. With that said, I give enormous gratitude and appreciation to the following people:

The HarperCollins team, including, but not limited to: Josh Behar, my editor at HarperCollins, thank you for reminding me life is not only as I see it. Thank you for continuously asking me to probe deeper to uncover what I really want to say. Michael Morrison, for having the cojones to take on a project of this nature and for being a visionary. David Brown, creative PR genius, I thank you for all the enlightening brainstorming sessions and kick-ass phone conversations. Thank you to Debbie Stier, for your excitement and passion, to Susan Sanguily, for doing whatever it takes for as long as it takes to create this amazing book cover, to Kim Lewis and Susan Kosko, for your dedication and commitment to making this book happen, to Libby Jordan, for believing in this book, to Judy Degrottole, for your time and patience explaining things to me, and to Kyran Cassidy, for your enlightening conversations and outstanding legal expertise.

A huge thank-you to: Julie and Jonathan Uman, Liz and Ron Gilligan, Dagmar, Anders and Jennifer Wallin, the Russell Family, Scott Simons, Kellie Harmon, Anne Lepore and Frankie, Dawn, Jesse and Cassandra Gregory, Manova Lowman and Sarah, Rita, Peter and Jamie Murphy, Cheryl and Eric Tennant, Jason, Harry and Tiffany Bean, Marsha Tomilson, Donna and Charlie Quinter, Jennifer Rouse, Jeff Kasunic, Andrew Beauchene, Chandra, Susan and Robert Levy, Ashley and Angela, Stacey and Steve Almond, Charley, and all my clients around the globe, thank you for opening yourself up to what is possible. You are a gift to me, and to this world.

To the Spirits, for coming through to the people you love every single time they ask for you, and for teaching me to see without my eyes, to hear without my ears, and to trust what I feel at all times.

Noah Lukeman, for seeing potential in a postcard. I am grateful to you for being my champion and for leading with passion, persistence, and patience.

Dina Shapiro, for believing in me, for being my friend as well as my agent, for always putting our friendship ahead of business, and for being there from the very beginning . . . I love you.

All the radio and TV stations who let me do my thing. Plus, a big thank-you to Star 98.7 with Ryan Seacrest and Lisa Foxx, the first radio show where I did channeling on the air. KRQ's JohnJay and Rich, George Lopez, Richard Garner, Howard Stern, Fox News, Entertainment Tonight, Michael Doyle, David Moye, Detective W. C. Ward, Sergeant Corrigan, Keen. To Barnes & Noble, Borders, Bookstar, and Brentanos for allowing me to do channeling at your stores, to the CRMs who helped make each event outstanding, and to Marriott, Radisson, and Embassy Suites for generously donating rooms for our tour.

To John Miller, Jessica Samet, and Lauren Dolgen at MTV Networks, for believing in *Breakthrough* and having the guts to open your mind to what I do, and embrace it.

Some people teach you things, yet have no idea they've been your teacher, while others know the impact they've had on your life. To the teachers who paved the way for greatness, I thank you: Anthony Robbins, Richard Bandler, and Werner Erhard, John Edward, James Van Praagh, Stephany and Peter Hurkos, Arthur Ford, Ena Twigg, Edward Burns, Antwone Fisher.

Michael Moskowitz, for giving me insight, inspiration, and your expertise to know when something is good and when something sucks, big time. Thank you, bro!

Siobhan, my golden retriever, you have been with me for over eight years, sitting by my desk as I write, snoring in the car on tour, wanting to play at all hours of the night, reminding me that the most important aspects of life are a good night's sleep, lots of affection and love, and playtime all the time.

Last, but not least, I would like to thank myself for never giving up on me. For waking up each day and facing the computer, ready to write from the depths of my soul. I thank me for eliminating quitting as an option and for being courageous enough to not only stand for what I do, but for putting it out there for you to read.

To the Reader

Everything in this book is true. All of the readings, experiences, and connections with those who have crossed over occurred in the exact manner in which they are presented.

In all instances which full names and detailed stories are used, I have done so with those persons' written consent. In a few instances, at the request of individuals, I have changed first names and minor details that might give away their privacy, but what took place and what came through all remain true to form.

I am grateful to my many clients who took time to type transcripts from their recorded session tapes, and gave their signed permission to have their story told, including their own personal feelings about how, specifically, connecting with their loved ones transformed their life.

This book is based on the actual experiences and documented facts from the spirits, the people for whom they came through, and the medium in the middle.

The words from spirits are always written in italics.

All the TV and radio interviews you will read about here are available for you to view and hear on my website at **www.channeling spirits.com** or **www.psychicdiaries.com.**

Whatever your feelings are about channeling, remember, this is my journey as experienced by me. My intention is only to inspire you to discover what is possible for yourself, to remember who you really are and why you are here, and to always know that even in the midst of an emotional storm, you are never, ever, alone.

Psychic Diaries

Introduction

*T*his is not a book about death.

It's about life.

Your life.

My life.

The lives of everyone around us.

I am often amazed that people who have just lost their whole family in a plane crash are able to speak coherently, or that a ten-year-old boy who has just found his dad with a bullet through his head wants to know if his daddy will be at his baseball game on Saturday.

I do a phone reading for this little boy, and his dad comes through speaking a secret code language only he and his son know. He tells me what it felt like to die:

"The moment I put the gun to my temple, the moment I pressed my finger against the trigger, I forgot . . . How much I love my son—how much life is worth living—how tomorrow could have been better. If the image of my son had entered my mind, even for a moment, I could not have killed myself. I had to completely block what was good, and focus solely on my pain."

He had to go into the darkness. He had to block out the light.

"The moment I died—the light came on, and I remembered. . . .

"I love you, son.

"I miss you.

"I'm sorry . . . so sorry, for the pain I've caused.

"I'm grateful to have known you. I will be around you and see you grow.

"You don't have to make excuses for me, and it's okay to be angry. It's okay to yell.

"I wish I would have known. . . .

"I wish I could have shown you . . . I love you."

The next day, my phone rings. I hear a familiar scratchy voice. "I came home from school today, and guess what? Dad moved my baseball glove," my new ten-year-old pal tells me. "Mom couldn't have 'cause I locked my door to give Dad privacy, and know what? For the first time since my daddy died, I didn't feel so alone."

We have all felt alone.

We have all come home to find a big fat zero on our answering machine and a hollow emptiness in our soul. We have stood in front of the refrigerator, opening and closing it, knowing we're not hungry, yet settling on food to fill us instead of reaching out to a friend.

We have all felt surrounded. Alone, but not lonely. Comfortable in our skin.

And sometimes we're feeling great, then BAM! we feel like shit. We walk in the front door, and the shit hits us in the face. What we might not know is that our spouse just had a fight with their boss or that our roommate is pissed off because their date stood them up.

Our feelings are not always our own. We sometimes pick them up from others.

Emotions leave a residue.

They affect every person with whom we come in contact, every place we visit, every conversation we have, or fail to have. What we don't say, what we withhold, creates energy all its own. Our thoughts and emotions are living, breathing extensions of our soul.

Just ask your five-year-old how it feels when you're yelling at the slow driver in front of you. No matter how upset you get, the cars won't speed up, the traffic won't part, and when you finally do get to your destination, will all that bitching have been worth it?

How about using the time to talk with your kid? How about using it to sing at the top of your lungs or remind yourself that although you can't control some things in life, the way you choose to respond . . . to traffic, loss, love, pain, and life . . . is always up to you.

Too many people don't believe they'll ever have what they want in life. Whether it's an ideal career; a loving, committed relationship; a healthy, fit body; a perception of themselves that creates more joy than pain, people feel they can achieve these things short-term—find the relationship, make the money, get into shape, feel happy—but to have them consistently, they feel, is impossible, unrealistic, wishful thinking.

Not when you're a kid.

When you're a kid, you believe.

You believe you can be anything, do anything, have anything you want; there's no limit. I'm going to be a movie star! No, I'm going to be a doctor! No, I'm going to be an artist! Okay, I know—I'll be a movie star and a doctor and an artist!

You believe it until someone tells you to get your head out of the clouds and take a solid job, to stop being so picky about dating and settle down already.

For many of us, growing up means letting go of the dreams we had as kids.

Although we may think about what we'd love to become, experience, and achieve, to do these things takes commitment and focus, and who has the time these days? We've got bills to pay, e-mail to answer, calls to make, meetings to attend.

A man on his deathbed once told me, "I was so busy. I missed my life."

He spent his final days pondering the meaning of his outwardly successful, yet inwardly bankrupt existence, and came to the conclusion that he'd missed the point of his life. He hadn't stopped long enough to enjoy his success, to spend quality time with the people he'd worked so hard to support, and it wasn't until he crossed over that he finally understood what life is about.

When we're born, our inner voice screams, "I'm here! I've arrived!"

As we get older, the voice gets quieter . . . and quieter . . . until seemingly . . . it disappears.

Our journey is about getting that voice back, about listening to what it has to say, and about allowing it to be heard.

When someone we love dies, suddenly all of that stuff doesn't matter. It doesn't matter that we ate too much pie. It doesn't matter that our kid left the house a mess. It doesn't matter that we didn't check our e-mail. All that matters is the person we love is no longer here in the way they once were.

If I could invent something that made people we love never die, I would. I hate grief. I hate loving and losing and not being able to bring back the people I love.

I hate not being able to change death.

We can change so many things in our lives. We can change our jobs, our relationships, our bodies, our beliefs, our education, our looks, our surroundings, our cars, our religion, our income, our clothing, our sexual preference, even our gender, but we cannot change death.

It doesn't matter how much we pray and beg and plead and try to imagine what would've happened if she didn't take the car that night or he didn't get on the plane. It doesn't matter how much we replay what happened. Death just doesn't register. "What do you mean they're dead? They were sipping coffee in my kitchen an hour ago, how can they be dead?"

It's too painful to comprehend or digest, so we push it away, shut down, hide out, and end up feeling as though we're dying, about to split open or go insane.

Until you've lost someone, you cannot truly know how excruciating it feels. You can imagine, but it's not the same thing. You have to go through the experience to know.

When people we love die, we immediately regret scolding, insulting, judging, or being harsh with them. I believe that if we never insulted or judged another person, there would still be plenty of judgment and criticism left in this world because we inflict so much on ourselves.

We need to know that who we are, as we are, is okay.

We need to remember that the world does not change without us.

We change.

The world.

We all want to know we're more than flesh, bones, and organs. More than the grades we receive, the income we earn, more than our looks, our status, our material possessions.

We all want to feel significant, to know our presence in this world matters, to know that who we are makes a difference, and that when we are gone, people will miss us.

I remember being at this pool party when I was nineteen and thinking that if I were to leave the party, no one would notice. No one would miss me. I decided to leave, and as I was heading for the door, I heard a voice shout, "Hey, Lysa, where are you going?"

Even though someone noticed me, I felt like the celebrity everyone loves who goes home to drink a bottle of booze because they feel empty inside. Although I didn't drink booze, I felt just as empty. I didn't feel safe connecting with others until I learned to be comfortable within myself.

This world teaches us—life is not safe.

Don't go out after dark. Lock your doors. Gate your house. Install alarm systems. Check your windows. Don't talk to strangers. Don't carry your purse in your hand; strap it across your chest. Don't dress too sexy. Don't trust men. Don't trust women. Don't go on airplanes. Don't trust Jews, Muslims, African Americans, Asians, Latinos, Italians; don't trust anyone who isn't exactly like you.

It gets me crazy when I hear a news reporter say, "There will be another terrorist attack . . . sometime . . . soon . . . somewhere . . . in a big city . . . so watch out."

Watch out for whom? When? Where? What is the point of scaring us by giving us vague information just so we can be on high alert with our hearts pumping adrenaline at such an intense pace that we live in a state of panic?

Too much uncertainty makes us edgy, irritable, anxious, and fearful.

We look to calm ourselves. We overeat. We drink. We date. We marry. We have kids. We divorce. We have more kids. We marry again . . . and again. We have hope. We give up hope. We find "the one." We discover the one we'd thought was the one wasn't really the one at all, but the next one will be.

We reclaim hope.

We feel tired, but we don't stop. We can't. We're too busy accomplishing, doing—our days and nights filled to the brim. Every second of our life is jam-packed, so why, then, do we feel so empty? Something is missing, and we don't know what.

Our friends tell us we should be happy. We should feel grateful for what we have. It's not that we don't, it's just this nagging feeling of, "Is this all there is? Is this what my life is going to be? Is this what I came here for?"

We're afraid to admit how dissatisfied we feel at times. We hope nobody finds out that who we appear to be isn't close to who we really are and how we say we feel isn't at all how we really feel. We don't know if our journey is taking us to the destination we desire. We're afraid if we stop, even for a moment, everything we've worked so hard to achieve will disappear.

We all have a need for spontaneity, for variety; to not know what's going to happen, when it's going to happen, how it's going to happen every single moment of the day. We have a need to love others and be loved by them, to connect, to grow and contribute beyond ourselves.

We all want to know: Will I live the life I am meant to live? Will I get what I want? Will I meet and spend my life with a person who loves me as much as I love them? Will people recognize and celebrate my talents? And if I do get what I want—meet a person who loves me as much as I love them, and have people recognize and celebrate my talents—will these things make me happy? If they make me happy, how long will my happiness last? How do I know I won't end up broke, unfulfilled, and alone? How do I know all my hard work will be worth it?

How do I know I won't die without having truly lived?

How do I know I won't leave this world without people knowing I was here?

My work as a psychic medium is about much more than connecting with your loved ones who have crossed over. It's about rediscovering our purpose for living, even when it doesn't feel as if there is one. It's about moving forward when everything inside of you wants to stop. It's about having an awareness of death so you don't have to wait until a tragedy occurs to realize how important someone is to you.

I do not have the handbook to your life.

You do.

You got it when you were born, although some of you may have misplaced it, and some would swear it was never there in the first place. . . . Oh, it's there! Maybe it's buried under a huge stack of crap, then I come along, yank it from the pile, dust it off, and read it to you. "Hey, remember you wanted to be a rock star? Yeah, you wanted that before your dad told you to find something stable. You listened to him and stopped listening to yourself."

If you don't know what you're meant to be doing, here's a hint: It's what makes you feel good.

It's the same as saying, "How do you know you're in a great relationship?"

Because you smile when you see the person, instead of cringe. That's a clue, a sign!

Your life is about taking the dreamer in you and fiercely protecting it. It's about focusing on what you have rather than what you don't and remembering what you've shared more than what you've lost.

Dr. Milton Erickson, a brilliant psychiatrist, once said, "There is so much you know that you don't know that you know." When I heard that, I thought, What's the point of knowing if you don't know that you know?

Then I realized the juice of life is about rediscovering what's already there, what you know that you don't know that you know.

I believe that right before you're born, all the lights are on and you're glowing with the knowledge of who you are and why you're coming into human form.

Then, as you're descending to earth, about to make your way into this world . . . a whooshing sound blasts through your ears as you begin swirling. Whirling. Upside down.

Faster and faster on the ride to your life.

You're so excited!

Only five seconds until you're born!

Four.

Three.

Bring it on!

Two seconds to go.

One.

BAM!

You're Born!

All the lights go out.

Your journey is about turning the lights back on.

About discovering what it takes to keep your light shining, brightly.

We all fall asleep.

We all wake up.

The key is to spend most of your life awake.

GROWING UP NORMAL

The first time I saw a dead body I was seven years old.

It was sprawled out on the beach, like a whale, in Acapulco, Mexico. A group of people had gathered around this immense object that had washed ashore.

I wiggled my way to the center of the crowd and there he was—a naked man—lying on his stomach—three hundred pounds of solid flesh.

My dad quickly yanked me away.

It was an automatic reaction, an irrational fear of what might happen if I came too close, as if the man might suddenly wake up, as if that would be a bad thing.

I managed to break free from my father to get close enough to touch this man's flesh.

It felt like rubber.

Then, I heard it: the sound one hears when confronted with death—a scream so loud, so piercing, more like a sick animal than a human voice.

It showed me this man wasn't just a spectacle. He was a father, a husband, a brother, a son. His entire family came running toward the shore, shrieking with pain, cursing at the sky, falling into one another's arms, collapsing with grief.

I became paralyzed.

I watched as his mother slapped his hands, yelling, demanding him to wake up!

When he didn't, she cursed God, cursed the voyeurs of her pain, and then she did the most awful thing I have ever seen—she ripped off her shirt and went charging into the ocean shouting, "Take me, God! Take me now! Take me, you bastard!"

People didn't seem shocked when she ripped off her shirt, or when she ran toward the ocean, but when she called God a bastard, that shocked the hell out of them.

Not me.

I didn't recoil from this woman's uncontrollable display of grief.

I ran with her.

She looked at me, tears rolling down her cheeks, shaking her head at the unfairness of it all. I must have done something because the only thing I remember is her smile—this slow smile that crept up the edges of her lips and spread outward. A smile filled with tenderness and pain.

"Your son won't leave you. He'll always be around."

I said these words without opening my mouth.

She nodded and smiled as her husband wrapped a towel around her.

Her eyes never left mine. Not as she hugged her family. Not as paramedics carted her son away. We stared at each other—two souls who meet for only a moment and connect on a level that comes when we are fully present for another human being.

At age seven, I knew how to do this really well—to be there for someone without having to stop their pain or put a lid on what they were feeling.

As I got older and more protective, I became less comfortable with being and more comfortable with doing. Then, when someone was in pain, I had to fix it.

So, at the ripe old age of nine, I made my new post in life official. I became the Dear Abby of my third grade class.

Every Friday, a group of girls would write down their problems and put them in my cubby at school. Over the weekend, I would ponder how to help Diane get over a crush on our teacher, or how to help Kerry deal with her parents.

At age ten, I fell in love for the first time with a boy named Jimmy Delmonte. His dark hair, almond eyes, and rugged body were enough to make me want to quit third grade and run off with him forever. Every Wednesday, he'd come to my house and we'd sneak down to my basement where, between eating oatmeal cookies and drinking chocolate milk, we'd tell each other scary stories and stare into each other's eyes.

On my birthday, Jimmy presented me with a heart pendant, told me he loved me, and promised we'd be together forever.

Forever lasted approximately sixty-four days.

"I need to be free to explore my options," I told him. "It's not about you, Jimmy. I've gotta get focused on what I want to do with my life." I was a serious kid with serious goals.

I told my dad: "When I'm older, I'm going to live in California on the beach, drive a Porsche 911, marry a man with brown hair, have a little boy, and leave a mark on the world bigger than Freud."

I knew about Sigmund Freud because my mom took me to enlightenment courses where people cried over stuff that happened to them when they were young.

The first seminar was called EST. It took place in a big room in New York City. I was thirteen.

All I knew was they didn't let you leave the room to pee. This bothered me because I had to pee a lot. Not every five minutes a lot, but being restricted felt like torture. We also couldn't snack between meals. Not a piece of gum. Not a soda. Not a sucking candy. Only water. Nothing else.

Oh, and once you committed to staying for the weekend, you couldn't leave. They didn't lock you in or anything, but you know how uncomfortable it feels when you get up in the middle of a lecture to leave? Well, add to that having the instructor shout what a loser and coward you are if you go.

"What are the benefits of doing this course?" I ask my mom.

"Happiness," she tells me. "Inner peace."

"You took the course, right, Mom?"

"You know I did."

"Does it only work on some people?"

"Don't be a smart ass."

"I'm serious. Are you a portrait of happiness and peace?"

"Happiness is a process, not a permanent state."

"How do you know?"

"Because I've never permanently experienced happiness. It comes and goes. The key is to make sure it comes more than it goes."

So there it was: The beginning of a belief system that claimed happiness was something outside of me; it came and went, just like the mailman, just like nice weather. Happiness was something to be found not created. It existed when everything was exactly the way I wanted it to be.

It would take fifteen years before a wise sage by the name of David Adams, age five, would answer a question that would forever change my life.

We'd be sitting together, waiting for his mom to pick him up from the karate school my future husband, Satori, and I would own.

I would turn to him and ask, "David, what is the meaning of life?"

He would look at me, shaking his little blond head with disgust, as if I'd just asked a question to which the answer is painfully obvious.

"To be happy," he'd say, raising his eyebrows.

Of course, finding that answer far too simplistic, I would repeat the question. "No, really, David, tell me. What is the meaning of life?"

He'd smack his tiny hand against his forehead, completely flabbergasted that we adults just didn't get it, and he'd repeat, slowly, as if comprehension were my problem. "The meaning of life is to BE happy. Just BE happy now, ya get it?"

I did get it, for glimpses at a time: When I was riding the train to New York City eating Chicken McNuggets and reading the latest Betty and Veronica comic book. When I entered acting class on Saturday morning and the students cheered because I was there. When my brother and I put Jell-O in our hair and made funky hairstyles, laughing hysterically in the mirror.

Happiness.

When it would come, I would try to hang on to it.

I thought happiness was elusive and fleeting, something to be captured and contained. I did not yet realize that happiness was in my control, that it was something I created inside myself and had access to no matter what life presented.

For too many years, I searched for happiness . . . in food, in men, in making sure my body looked perfect, in finding ways to stand out, be witty, smart, talented and beautiful. I thought people would cheer if I shone. I thought my friends would be thrilled if the cutest guy asked me out or if I aced my exams. But instead of being thrilled, they were mean. Vicious mean, the kind of mean that makes you remember details of your childhood you'd best forget.

Like when Emily, Lauri, and Dina came to my house and Emily and Dina were in my bedroom shoving my jewelry, clothing, and makeup in their purses while Lauri distracted me downstairs. When they arrived at school the next day wearing my stuff, I learned the meaning of the word "betrayal."

But I remained strong. Even when Marsha Snyder punched me on the playground, even when David Capella spit a hamburger on my head at Iris Barzvi's birthday party. These people, who were my best friends one week, my enemies the next, eventually drove me to my father in tears. "Dad, what do I do when they push me?"

"You tell them you love their shoes."

"What do I say when they call me names?"

"You thank them."

The next day, Emily followed me home, taunting, "Lysa is a pussy girl! Lysa buys clothes at the Red Balloon. She's a big fat buffoon!"

"Emily, where did you get your shoes? I really love them."

"I'm not telling you, stupid idiot. . . ."

I bit my lip. I really wanted to slug this girl. I remembered my father's advice and repeated it, "Emily, it takes courage to speak your mind. Most people talk behind someone's back, but you're nasty right to my face, and though what you're saying hurts, I do admire your boldness."

Emily never bothered me again.

$\mathcal{A}$lthough talking to spirits wasn't something I did as a child, looking back, there were things I knew that I had no way of knowing how I knew, like who was on the other end of the phone and what was going to happen before it happened.

As a kid, I played in my room a lot. My mom would knock on my door and ask, "What are you doing in there, Lysa?"

"Nothing, Mom."

"Who are you talking to?"

"My friends."

She'd open the door and see me sitting on my bed. Alone.

She must've thought I created invisible friends to keep me company and there was no harm in that. I felt surrounded by people who weren't there, at least not physically. I could describe them to you in detail. How they looked, how they acted, their style of dress, quirks, habits, families, even their names, which I sometimes took on.

"Lysa, it's time for dinner!" my mom would yell from the bottom of the stairs.

I wouldn't answer.

She'd fling open my door. "Lysa, dinner."

"My name is Robin today."

"Okay, Robin, time for dinner."

I'd skip along behind her and always make sure to stop and say hello to my grandfather, who'd be sitting in his favorite black leather chair in our living room.

"Hello, Grandpa, how are you feeling today?"

He wouldn't answer, of course.

He couldn't.

He was dead.

"Don't you see him?" I'd ask my mom.

"Sure, we see Grandpa," my older brother, David, would say

rolling his eyes, "and the Easter Bunny and Santa Claus and the Tooth Fairy. . . ."

I saw Grandpa, and that's what counted. He knew a lot about me, especially how much I loved surprises, all kinds of surprises, until I learned the difference between a good surprise and a bad one.

A good surprise is when you enter your home to hear people cheering, "Happy Birthday!" A bad surprise is when you go out for dinner with your family and your whole world turns upside down. I was seven and a half years old when I received the worst surprise of my life.

It was 1974. My mom, dad, David, and I went for dinner at Young's restaurant in Port Washington, where I grew up. We'd go there each week and afterward get mint-chip ice cream at Carvel and drive through Sands Point to look at beautiful homes.

I cannot recall my parents ever fighting or yelling at each other. I'm sure they did but it must've been rare. The only time my dad spanked me, he cried. He couldn't do it. As a child, my most vivid memories are of throwing parties at our house, taking trips to Jamaica and Acapulco, making pancake Frisbees on Sunday mornings, and feeling lots of love and support from my family.

"How did you know dad was 'the one'?" I'd ask my mom many years later.

"He was my date at my Sweet Sixteen. He put an engagement ring on top of my cake. I said yes. We got married. You and David came along. We loved each other. I never questioned it."

It sounded so simple, so easy. Nothing like the drama people go through these days to find a mate—dating services, personal ads, blind dates, singles bars, speed dating.

Back then, you met, you married, you had kids, you got antsy, you wondered why you got married so young, you wanted more . . . you got a . . .

"Pass the mushu chicken, sweetie, your father and I are getting a divorce," I heard my mom say and I raced to the bathroom and immediately threw up. The news made me feel so sad and confused. How could they do this to my brother and me? How could they just up and quit on each other?

A week later, Dad moved out, and I made a pact with myself that no man would ever leave me again. **I** would leave him first.

"Your mom and I are good friends," my dad would say. "Some parents hate each other, which makes it hard on the children, so, in fact, this is a good divorce."

To a kid, there's no such thing.

This taught me that although bad things could happen, I wasn't allowed to feel badly about them.

I didn't care about my mother's new boyfriend and I definitely didn't care about Eileen, the woman with the flaming red hair who would, within two years, become my stepmother.

The first time I met her I refused to sit next to her. I was eight years old.

"Trust me, Dad. She's evil," I said. "Look at her hair, it's red like the devil."

"Eileen is not evil, honey. Get to know her. You'll see."

I didn't want to see. They didn't consult me about their breakup, so why should I care about whom they brought home or how they felt. I didn't want to have anything to do with the new people in my parents' lives.

I heard of a young boy losing his father and his mom telling him that although his Daddy had died, he was still in the little boy's heart, to which the boy cried out, "I don't want Daddy in my heart! I want Daddy in my home!"

That's how I felt. I wanted Daddy in my home. I wanted things back the way they used to be. I wanted to have a say. I wanted them to know divorcing was a mistake they'd later regret.

It wasn't up to me. I was powerless to change their decision.

We had fun together. We were a family. What went wrong? Why didn't I see it coming? Why hadn't they given me a clue?

"Next time," I told myself, "I'll be on guard."

So, I built myself a suit of armor to protect me from the pain that could, without warning, knock me to the ground. I learned life could change instantly, drastically, sometimes for the better, sometimes the worse; which would come first, I did not know.

No one did. I asked around.

People gave me pat answers like, "Only God knows the plan for our lives," or "Everything happens for a reason," or "It was meant to be."

If my parents were meant to be divorced, why did they ever get married?

Adults had an answer for that one, too.

"It was right at the time. What's good for you today might not be good for you tomorrow."

Breathing is good for me now, but it might not be good for me tomorrow? Food is good for me now, but it might not be tomorrow? That was the silliest thing I'd ever heard.

I went around to my neighbors, my teachers, my friends' parents. I even called one of those prayer hotlines and asked the lady, "Why do people change the way they feel about each other? How can you love someone, not imagine being apart, and then poof—your love is replaced with, 'You promised you would pay for the kid's clothing and give me the house!' "

"Let us pray," the hotline lady said.

We prayed.

Daddy still got remarried.

Mommy still got the house.

I still wanted things back the way they used to be. Prayer didn't seem to change anything.

But then I got to thinking, maybe prayer isn't supposed to make things the way I want them to be. Maybe it's supposed to teach me how to accept them the way they are.

I tried it. Acceptance. I felt better, and shortly afterward, I met Bruce.

His moves were like butter, gliding across the concrete floor. His body a chiseled masterpiece. His mind quick and alert. His humor infectious. His discipline to be admired.

Bruce Lee was the new man in my life, and I don't think he minded I was only nine.

Each weekend, my dad would take David and me to Manhattan's Lower East Side, where we'd sit in a theater with torn seats and popcorn that tasted like Styrofoam, waiting for Bruce to ignite our world. We'd come out throwing jabs, showing off kicks, and I'd brag to my dad, "I'm going to be a karate champion someday and then I'm gonna kick David's ass!"

"Yeah, right. In your dreams, sis," my brother would laugh.

If I said it, I would do it. Not necessarily kick his ass, but become a karate master just like Bruce Lee. I had big dreams. Dreams to help people and act in movies and write books.

In fifth grade, I challenged myself to read a book a day, every day, for an entire year. I cheered when I accomplished my feat. I'd handwrite stories that my brother's friend, Steven Abramowitz, would type. I loved leaving this world, daydreaming and fantasizing about places I'd never been, people I hoped to meet, experiences I'd one day have. Books were my savior, writing my sanctuary.

As a child, I felt happy most of the time. My only memory of anything "inappropriate" was an incident with a psychiatrist whom my parents took my brother and me to see after their divorce.

During my sessions, we'd paint, tell stories, and play board games, until one afternoon, my love of therapy came to an abrupt halt.

It happened quickly. I felt his wrinkled hand slither up the front of my shirt, fondle my tiny breast and then slip out, hopefully undetected.

I didn't tell anyone. I don't remember thinking I should.

Years later, whenever a boyfriend would touch my breast, my knee-jerk reaction was to push his hand away. I didn't know why until the memory of the incident returned, and when it did, I began to doubt the inner voice that once seemed so certain and began to lose touch with a vital part of my soul.

It was a slow and insidious process. Similar to when a kid tells their mom, "Uncle Benny kisses me weird. I don't like it." Their mom says, "Be nice, dear. There's nothing wrong with the way he kisses you." And slowly, you begin to ignore your intuition, ignore what you know, and instead, listen to what others tell you.

The first time I witnessed it, I was at my friend Kerry's house playing in her room. All of a sudden, we heard yelling and screaming from the kitchen, and we raced downstairs to find her parents fighting.

Kerry shouted, "Mom! Dad! Stop fighting!"

Kerry's mom shielded her swollen eye and took on this syrupy-sweet voice, "Oh, sweetie, we're not fighting. Go back to your room."

"But . . . but . . . I just heard you yelling."

"It was the TV, now go to your room!" her dad shouted.

Kerry didn't move. She fixated on the broken glass in the middle of the room. Her mother's eyes pleaded with her to go, and in that moment Kerry learned she didn't hear what she heard, see what she saw, and feel what she felt. In that moment, she began to discount her soul.

If we go through life having enough people tell us we don't see what we see, hear what we hear, and feel what we feel, if that goes on long enough, we tend to believe it.

I figure, by the time we're twenty, at least half the shit roaming around in our brains isn't even ours. It's the junk our parents, teachers, friends, and society spewed in our head.

Then one day, we get sick and tired of making decisions based on what someone, somewhere, sometime in history, told us was right—like staying in a job we hate because it's secure, or putting up with a less-than-satisfying relationship because no one else will love us. On that day, we change.

I don't think there's anybody on this earth who wakes up in the morning and says, "Let me see. . . . How can I under-perform, make very little money, eat crap that makes me feel like shit, and surround myself with people who remind me of how worthless I am?"

We all want a life that matters.

We all want to have a life where we can look back and say, "I'm really proud of myself."

It's not always the big things. Sometimes, it's simply saying no when you would normally say yes, or taking a stand when you would normally cower. For me, it was calling a guy when my friends told me not to, or being nice to those people my "popular" friends said were nerds.

Everywhere, I saw people living by rules that didn't make them feel good. I saw people in abusive relationships dishing out marital advice, parents telling their kids to do things they, themselves, did not follow.

I decided that living happily means kicking out the voices taking up space and not paying rent. Being free means choosing the life *we* want, because if we don't, someone will gladly choose one for us.

My life turned around when I enrolled at French Woods Festival of the Performing Arts in upstate New York and discovered a boldness I hadn't known was there.

I also discovered I knew things, like when I saw Jeff Laska, the cutest guy at camp, walk across the lawn. I turned to my friend Amy Connolly and said, "He's going to be my boyfriend."

"What do you mean he's going to be your boyfriend? You don't even know him."

"He's going to be. You'll see."

The next day, Jeff introduced himself and asked me out on a date. Being only fourteen, a date consisted of walking around eating marshmallows while impersonating our favorite actors.

Jeff was the second person I ever kissed.

The first was Matthew Burkhart. We met at Camp Pontiac, and just as with Jeff, I told my friend that Matthew would ask me out the very next day. Our date took place on the roof of my cabin, where I received my first French kiss, and then became obsessed with everything French.

For years I was consistently able to "predict" my boyfriends. I'd say to my pal that the gorgeous guy on the dance floor was going to be my next love. (His name was Bob and we went out for six months.) Anne

Hennessy and I would be driving down the Fort Lauderdale strip. "Stop the car!" I'd tell her, and when she did I'd yell, "Hey you!" to this gorgeous guy, Norman Lippiat, with whom I'd spend the next three years.

I'd tell my mom, "Wouldn't it be convenient if a sexy guy showed up at my front door?" And after smearing a mud mask on my face, the doorbell would ring. I'd answer it, green mask and all, and a cute guy named Chris would ask me to sign a petition to save the environment. Two weeks later, he'd come live with me in Los Angeles and stay for over a year.

One could say I have a knack for meeting great men or that I'm just lucky, but I know it's because I follow my instincts. Whenever I do not, pain is nearby.

I believe everyone has an inner voice they may call intuition, or psychic ability. Whatever you call it, what matters is that you listen and follow what it says.

I felt the healthiest and happiest during my acting school years. I enrolled at Manhattan Theater Workshop and would invite the entire class to Bagel Nosh for lunch and have sleepovers at my friend Julia Greenberg's house and practice improvisations with Amy Margolis.

But then, my dad said acting was interfering with my grades and I'd have to stop, just for a while. I stopped permanently. I stopped expressing who I was and became whoever I thought people wanted me to be. I made sure never to be too happy, too pretty, too talented, and too successful for fear people would be jealous. I couldn't stand anything being too perfect. My parents would buy me new sheets and I'd take a pen and write on them, just a quick dash to make them a tad imperfect.

"It's not okay to shine," is what I told myself. It's not okay to stand out.

No longer did I feel driven to do much of anything. I felt totally and completely alone.

I was always the well-behaved girl, while my brother got my parents' attention for messing up at school. It didn't take long for me to piece together the formula.

If you're happy, you'll be ignored. If you're sick, you'll be loved.
So I got sick.

It began on February 14, 1982.

The routine went like this:

I'd walk through the door.

Throw my schoolbooks on the counter.

Swing open the fridge.

And begin to eat.

Fried chicken, salami, cold soup, rice cakes, peanut butter, bread, chocolate-chip cookies, leftover Chinese food, Diet Coke; whatever was available I'd quickly shove down my throat.

I'd lock the bathroom door, pull back my hair, drink five glasses of hot water, and glance at myself in the mirror with disgust. I'd kneel by the toilet and forcefully shove two fingers down my throat. Once . . . twice . . . If nothing came up, I'd shove harder. Faster. Until I threw up everything . . . Until there was nothing left.

After, I'd stare at the blood vessels that had burst around my eyes, analyze the deep gashes in my hand where my teeth had dug in, and feel the soreness in my gut from my fingers pressing so hard. I'd promise myself, "Never again . . . I'll never do that again."

But deep inside a haunting feeling would come over me, a feeling of fear that someday, soon, there would come a time when I'd lose control again.

Binging was such an angry act. I didn't calmly open a box of cereal. I ripped it open and shoved the contents in my mouth at record speed. At night, food would call to me, "Lysa . . . I know you want me . . . just a tiny nibble," a chocolate cake would taunt me from the fridge.

In my journals, I captured the hell I put myself through.

When I turned fifteen, I moved to Florida, graduated high school a year early, and was honored as salutatorian of my class. I never showed up for the ceremony, never showed up for the prom. Instead, I got accepted to the University of Southern California just shy of my sixteenth birthday and headed out to California to begin a brand-new life.

Even in the land of sun and fun, bulimia was kicking my ass. I'd throw up in the dorm bathrooms, trying to hide my activities from my five roommates. The final straw came when one of them put laxatives in the ice cream to find out who'd been eating it. I spent the entire day on the toilet, and they knew I was the culprit.

Being found out made me think of the time I swallowed a hundred laxatives and my dad told me he used to think David messing up in school was important, but now this was so much more important. I remember thinking I'd finally gotten Daddy's full attention. I nearly destroyed myself in the process, but I got it nonetheless.

In that moment, I saw two distinctive paths.

To the left was the road of bulimia, a road filled with bloodshot eyes, swollen glands, shredded knuckles, embarrassment, loneliness, shame, and pain.

The road to the right was the road of health and self-honesty. It was clear, bright, unfettered by my past, and filled with possibility. It was a road of uncertainty, one that took a lot of courage, but on which I could create anything I desired.

I chose the road of health and self-honesty, and my stepmom suggested I attend Overeaters Anonymous (OA) for bulimics to get some extra support.

As quickly as I walked into the meeting in the Federal Building in Los Angeles is as quickly as I turned to walk out. It looked like a casting call for *Baywatch* rather than a meeting for bulimics and anorexics. As I backed out the door, a girl took my hand and whispered, "Stay. I'm new here, too."

I stayed, and I never binged or threw up again.

I am now in my eighteenth year of abstinence, and although OA meetings are no longer a part of my life, I know they are what saved my life. For that, I am grateful.

2

ONE THING LEADS TO ANOTHER

*S*ometimes we don't know why we're led to a meet a particular person, or go through a certain experience, until much later, when we can look back and say, "Now, I understand why I had to go through that."

My life had definitely taken some twists and turns. After four years, I dropped out of USC only one semester shy of graduation. I moved to New York for a year and then back to Los Angeles without having a job or much money.

I had just turned twenty-four years old, and I remember lying on the floor of my unfurnished apartment, reading *Star* magazine, coming across an ad for reporters. I'd written for several spiritual magazines in New York, done interviews for an art magazine in San Diego; written movie reviews for *DramaLogue,* an acting trade paper; but I'd never done anything remotely related to tabloid journalism.

On a whim, I sent two relationship articles to the paper, and the next day found myself sitting across from a Scottish man with a foul mouth and a belligerent, yet oddly endearing personality, who gave me exactly two minutes to decide whether or not I wanted the job.

I said yes because the prospect of working as a reporter excited me, plus the pay was $120 a day, more than I'd ever earned. I was hired three days a week to start, not on staff, but as a day-rate reporter, which suited me fine because I looked at the job as a training ground for honing my writing skills.

Within a few weeks of working as a reporter, I got my first real assignment, which oddly enough, was to interview a love psychic. Although my psychic abilities were undetected at the time, they were strong enough to know that the only successful love connection this woman had made was between the fourteen cats roaming around her barely livable apartment.

I soon discovered my knack for "knowing" things transferred to being a reporter. I'd write stories about things that hadn't occurred, like when Alec Baldwin proposed to Kim Basinger, I had written about it the week before. And when certain celebrities were about to become a couple or have a baby, I'd always be first on the scene.

From the start, I told my boss I wanted to do only positive stories, "No bitter divorces, custody battles, cheating, or funerals. Nothing nasty or mean," I told him.

"You can't pick and choose! You eat whatever we feed you!"

He'd tell me to cover a funeral. "Go by. See how they feel," he'd say.

"How do you think they feel? Their kid just died. They feel sad."

"For fuck's sake, just do it!"

I wouldn't. I couldn't. I quit working exclusively for *Star* and began freelancing so I wouldn't have to do stories that went against my gut.

One night, I get a call that Julia Roberts is getting married to Lyle Lovett. The news chief says I need to get on a plane—immediately—if I want to cover the story.

"Where are they getting married?" I ask him.

"How the bloody fuck should I know?" is his response. "Indianapolis somewhere."

I get on a plane, meet with photographer Larry Kaplan, and land in

Indianapolis at the crack of dawn. There is no time for sleep. No time for planning.

I tell Larry to follow me in his rental car. I figure if I press the gas, the car will lead me to Lyle and Julia. As silly as that sounds, it is something I believed.

With no time to waste, I use my time wisely, taking off my T-shirt at a stoplight and putting on a blouse. In the midst of my changing regime, I suddenly have to pee. I spot a hotel down the road. As I'm walking through the lobby, I get this feeling in my gut, the same feeling that, years later, I will come to recognize as a psychic cue, a signal for me to sit up and pay attention.

Larry asks around at the hotel to see if anyone's heard about the wedding or seen Lyle and Julia. No one's heard or seen a thing. Just as we're heading out, I get the urge to call to my dad, which pisses off Larry to no end.

No sooner does my father say hello, do I see him—Lyle Lovett. He walks right past me. "Dad, I'll call you back." The adrenaline rush is like nothing I'd ever experienced, like going from zero to a hundred in 4.2 seconds flat.

After the wedding, we attend Lyle's outdoor concert and Julia comes onstage. Larry goes nuts snapping pictures. I look around, paranoid he's going to get caught. "Just relax," Larry tells me. "Security didn't see."

A voice inside me says, *"Take Larry's film. He's going to get caught."* My eyes scan the crowd for security guards. There are none. Larry is safe.

"No, he's not," I hear the voice say.

"Larry, give me your film," I whisper. He glares at me, shaking his head, continuing to snap away. **"Larry, give me the fucking film!"** I say, snagging the camera.

He hands me the film just as a security guard taps him on the shoulder. I quickly shove the film in a place they'd never dare look—My bra.

While most reporters prided themselves on approaching the news from a stoic, detached point of view, I became thoroughly involved in the stories and people I wrote about. I sat outside the Viper Room hours after River Phoenix died, my legal pad drenched with tears. I walked into actor Ray Sharkey's hospital room when he was dying of AIDS, and listened to his thoughts about life while on the verge of death.

Sure, I had fun staying in the nicest hotels, traveling the country and meeting all kinds of interesting people, but I was tired and wanted out. I was ready to put the tabloids in my past and begin doing something that made me feel proud.

I decided to go back to USC to finish my degree. Once I did, I felt alive again, ignited with possibility. School was completely different than when I'd attended in a bulimia-induced fog years before. After completing all my courses, needing one last class, geography, in order to graduate and get my sociology degree—I quit. Again.

I was here to do something important, and what I was doing definitely was not it.

Something inside me needed to leave, needed an out, and as I would soon discover, whatever we look for, we find.

I call it the domino effect—how one simple action, one infinitesimal decision, can change the course of your entire life.

It starts simply.

You stand at an intersection, not sure whether to study your French literature at the Coffee Bean or Starbucks.

You choose Coffee Bean and the reason is immediately apparent. Soft brown eyes, plump, juicy lips, a face like an Adonis. His name is Charley.

To me . . . He is God.

Whereas my previous boyfriends all had a passion to live, Charley had a passion to die.

The first time he tried to kill himself he took a Swiss Army knife, shoved it in his stomach, ripped it through his chest, and stopped less than a quarter inch from his heart.

He had open-heart surgery at age nineteen.

Next, he swallowed a handful of Lithium and was rushed to the emergency room.

Later, he drove his VW bug to Yosemite Park and after meditating for an hour, made the irrational decision to drive as fast as he could into a tree.

His car looked like a pancake.

Charley walked away without a scratch.

I guess you could say he was a tortured soul. Self-tortured. He was brilliant, relentless, comical, introspective, and according to several psychiatrists, completely nuts.

If you don't see what I see, something must be wrong with you. If your reality doesn't fit mine, we'll get you some medication and fix that right away. A teacher of mine once told me, "If you want to talk to a tree, make sure you get a group of friends to do it with you because one person talking to a tree is crazy, a group of people doing it is therapy."

After six months of being together, Charley's radical mood swings became intolerable. I ended our relationship, and my life went on.

As Charley would often remind me—His did not.

A phone number would flash on my pager. I'd call it. "Steinberg Funeral Home, can I help you?" I'd hang up and call Charley, "Why do you do sick things like that?"

"To get you to call," he'd laugh, completely unfazed by his manipulative tactics.

I needed something to break the cycle so I'd never return to a man whose self-destructive behaviors were bent on upsetting my life. My mom suggested the perfect anecdote—an adorable golden retriever puppy I named Siobhan, which means "sweetheart" in Celtic.

Siobhan shows her excitement by peeing on my lap.

The first time, it's adorable. The fifth, it's not so cute. To train her, I buy a dog crate, in which she cries all night. I return the crate and get a gate, which she promptly climbs over. My mom suggests puppy school.

After graduation, I am told I need a crate to finish training. My mom suggests I get a used one in the Recycler. The guy I call tells me to meet him at Public Storage and I'm driving and driving and I can't find the place. After twenty minutes of being lost, my inner voice is screaming for me to turn around and go home, and another part of me is saying, "Keep driving, you'll find it."

I turn the corner, and it becomes perfectly clear why I am there. The reason is wearing these teeny jean shorts with holes in all the right places. I take one look at this gorgeous man and am immediately aware of the pounding in my chest.

I thought I was going to buy a dog crate. My dog, apparently, had other things in mind.

The guy and I hit it off immediately. For some reason, I start asking personal questions—what's he doing in Los Angeles, where is he from, how was his last relationship, why did it end.

Before I leave, he hands me a karate flyer and tells me, "I've trained since I was six."

"I've always wanted to learn karate," I say, unable to wipe the grin off my face.

"You should train with me."

"Maybe I will. I used to be a Bruce Lee fanatic . . ."

"Me, too!" he says, his brown eyes melting me. "If you'd like to have dinner sometime . . ."

Four hours later, I call him. We meet and he ends up spending the money I paid for the dog crate on dinner with me. The only problem is, we can't eat. All we do is talk . . . stare . . . talk . . . stare . . . and we leave the restaurant and it's five in the morning and we're standing in the middle of the street and he does this karate form called a Kata, which turns me on so much, I kiss him.

Satori becomes my soul mate, my business partner, my best friend, and . . . my karate instructor.

We spend several hours in the park each day, with him teaching me the basics of Shotokan karate—how to stand, breathe, punch, kick, block, and Ki-Ai. I watch old videos of karate masters, stopping and rewinding to study their intricate moves. I learn the art of being prepared, of throwing off an opponent without ever throwing a punch.

I am not only learning karate. I am learning a way of life.

Gichin Funakoshi, Shotokan's founder, believed, "The ultimate aim of karate lies not in victory or defeat, but in perfecting the character of its participants."

When I earn my yellow belt, the level above white, Satori takes me to a karate tournament at USC, my college. Once inside the door, he says to me, "You should compete."

Immediately, I panic. "I don't have my uniform."

"You can borrow one."

"I don't have my yellow belt."

A few minutes later, he comes back with a uniform and a yellow belt, and I'm screwed.

Before I can object, the announcer calls my name.

Me, the kid from Port Washington who once dreamed of being a karate champion, is about to kick some ass!

I stand in the center of the ring. I silently call upon Bruce Lee for help. I begin my Kata. My kicks are sharp. My Ki-Ai's powerful. I'm on fire. Every move I've practiced, every hour I've trained, comes down to this moment where my skills must be at the highest level.

I walk off the mat feeling proud of myself, and thankful to Satori for pushing me way beyond where I ever thought I could go. The next thing I hear is: "First place in Kata goes to . . . Lysa Mateu."

I love this sport!

A week later, I ask Satori, "If you could have anything right now, what would it be?"

"A karate school," he tells me.

"Let's go open one," I say.

We find a beautiful space on Wilshire Boulevard in Santa Monica.

"The rent is thirty-five hundred a month," the landlord tells us.

"We can't afford that." I grab Satori's arm to leave. He doesn't budge.

"We'll make it," he assures me. "Plus, we can live in the back like they do in Japan."

I look at him like he's nuts. "Honey, we're not in Japan, we're in Los Angeles!"

I go on a tour of our new home: There's no kitchen. No bedroom. No bathroom. No carpet. No closets. No shower. "What about a shower, Satori? We need a shower."

"Trust me, honey. I have a plan."

His "plan" consists of two large buckets, a bar of soap, and a bottle of shampoo. We move into the studio and begin a daily ritual of taking "showers" in the bathroom of the adjoining office building, with one person standing guard while the other quickly gets clean. On weekends, we lock the main door and dump buckets of water on each other's heads. It's quite a funny scene.

We cook all our meals in an electric pot and sleep on a ten-dollar futon on the cold cement floor. I oversee the karate school, write and design monthly newsletters, and train as a student, my husband's student, a task that comes harder than cooking all my meals in one pot.

You see, in order to be a student, I had to learn to leave my ego at the door. On the mats, I was like everyone else, which was hard because my ego wanted special privileges. I wanted to come and go as I pleased. I wanted to be treated differently.

Then one day, I dropped it—my ego—left it at the door. I discovered that the more I surrendered, the happier I became.

I was happy without a shower, a comfy bed, a stove, and a private bathroom. I had students I adored, kids who would look at me with big, curious eyes, hanging on to every word I said, ready to absorb new information or challenge me when I was wrong.

One day I asked the students, ages four and up, "If you could do anything with your parents, what would it be?" Their answers surprised me.

"Spend more time with my dad." "Hang out with my mom." "Talk about stuff we never talk about." "Make my dad leave his cell phone at home." "Buy me Super Mario Brothers for Christmas." Except for the last one, all the kids wanted something that didn't cost a dime—more time with their parents, more time hanging out with the people they loved.

Satori and I created Family Action Camps where kids taught their parents what they needed to feel loved, and parents taught their kids what they needed to feel respected, and Satori and I taught everyone, including each other, how to communicate our needs without it turning into an argument. We held karate sleepovers where we'd watch martial arts films with the kids at night and take them on samurai treasure hunts during the day.

We got involved in the community, speaking at school board meetings and hosting karate demonstrations at local fairs. We picked up kids from school and watched them long after class was over. We saw kids stop throwing tantrums and start using words to get their messages across, and we noticed how the older students did anything and everything to piss off their parents.

Case in point: Daniel, age fourteen.

According to his mom, Daniel was looking at porn on the Internet and had an apathetic, bad attitude. She called us to do an intervention at her home.

Satori and I felt like "Emotional Busters" driving over in our beat-up old van. Before we arrive, Daniel tells his mother that if she lets us in, he's going to call his lawyer. When she brings him breakfast in bed, he pushes away the plate, shouting, "I'm not eating this shit!"

We tell her to leave and head into his room. I immediately notice the empty breakfast tray. "Go throw up, Daniel," I tell him. He looks at me like I'm some nutjob and just turns away in the bed. "You told your mom you weren't going to eat."

"Big deal, I was hungry," he says still not looking at me.

"Don't talk to us!" Satori snaps. "Your mom said you weren't going to talk to us."

He smiles for a moment, then quickly resumes his apathetic glare.

We begin looking through his stuff, taking books off his shelves, rearranging his clothes, until he finally sits up and says, "Okay, fine, what do you want me to do?"

"Nothing," I tell him. "You do nothing around here except look at porn and lie about it."

"I do things. You have no idea what it's like being in this hell."

I look at his thin-screen TV, stereo system, and a framed letter from his parents saying how proud they are of him, and I wonder how a kid who's got it so good feels so bad.

"If you hate this place so much, move," Satori suggests.

"I'm fourteen. I can't just move. Don't take everything so literally." He shakes his head.

"How should we take it?" I ask.

"I don't know. People say things they don't mean sometimes."

"Like calling your mother a bitch?"

"I get frustrated. It just comes out."

"It's beyond your control?"

"They rag on me. They never let up."

"I want you to do something simple, fun. I want you to bock like a chicken," I tell him. "Satori will demonstrate." Satori gives a quick bocking demonstration. "See, it's easy."

"It's stupid," he says.

"Stealing a pack of batteries when you had a twenty-dollar bill was stupid. This is fun."

"I'm not bocking like no chicken. You can't make me."

"Of course not. Nobody tells you what to do," Satori says.

"What would make you bock like a chicken? If you had to, what would make you do it?"

"If you held a gun to my head, I'd do it," he laughs, arrogantly.

"A gun," I say eyeing the water gun on the table behind him, "would make you bock?"

"Yeah, sure, whatever." He shrugs.

I pick up the water gun, and I swear to you, I have never heard such an exceptional chicken bocking in all my life.

You see, once he got off his position, away from his need to be right, he was ready to change. The bocking was just a way to interrupt his pattern by having him do something silly.

After he bocked, we blasted his favorite music and asked him to write what he loves about his parents. By the end, he was no longer the aloof, unaffected teen we'd met hours earlier.

"I love my parents, okay, but I still hate when my mom tells me what to do. I don't want her in my room. I don't want my dad asking twenty questions when I get home. I don't want my brothers tagging along. I don't want—"

"You don't go to the store with a list of what you don't want to buy, do you? I don't want pickles. I don't want the cheap toilet paper that feels like sandpaper on my ass. You go with a list of what you do *want*, which makes finding it easier. When you know what you want, you move toward it," I tell him. "When you focus on what you *don't* want, you get more of that, too."

Daniel proved that anyone could turn around.

No one is a lost cause.

*M*onths later, Satori and I formed a karate team with our students ages five to fifty-five, and won local and national competitions competing with the best of the best. We were thrilled when all our students, including Satori and me, competed in the state championships and came in first and second, moving us forward to the U.S. Nationals for a spot on the U.S. National Team.

During the weeklong competition, Satori and I meet Sensei Motokuni Sugiura, the seventy-two-year-old head of the Japan Karate Association, who is the happiest man I have ever seen.

During his techniques seminar, he doesn't follow the official outline. He puts us through a Jean Claude Van Damme–style mental, physical, and spiritual training. He giggles as we sit on our knees, pulling out one leg, kicking rapidly, then tucking it back underneath without falling over.

One evening, I spot him reading a book in Japanese. I approach him, cautiously. He smiles and puts down his book, pointing for me to sit.

"Sensei . . ." I begin.

"Motokuni," he corrects me. "My first name."

"Motokuni, how do you get so happy?"

He belches out a laugh that ripples through his body. "I live by one rule. Do what you love. Forget what people think. People always think something. No good. Shouldn't do that. Not proper," he laughs. "Forget proper. Life better that way."

I take his advice and forget proper. I forget being how others expect me to be and start being myself. The transformation continues when Satori and I attend an Anthony Robbins seminar and, on the first night, walk across twenty feet of twelve-hundred-degree hot coals—Barefoot!

Walking on hot coals was just a metaphor for doing something thought to be impossible. If we could walk across hot coals, what else could we do?

Tony tells us to charge across as if our life depends on it, as if everything we'd ever wanted was waiting on the other side. When we get there, we are to cheer, not timidly like most adults, but like a kid, wildly, frantically, as though we'd just broken through our biggest fear.

Tony tells us to pick a partner, someone we don't know. I pick a girl with a cast on her leg, who hops across on one foot hanging on to Tony's arm. It is a profound testament to what's possible when we put our minds toward accomplishing a goal.

The firewalk was the first of many "unusual" tests we went through. Climbing up a fifty-foot telephone pole then jumping toward a trapeze (wearing a harness, of course) was another. Charging across forty feet (double the amount) of hot coals came after Satori and I enrolled in Tony's leadership academy, where we learned to be a coach to others, was still another. All of these "tests" were simply microcosms of life, designed to push us beyond our comfort zone and destroy our protective, yet suffocating, old suits of armor.

Times when I thought I had nothing left to give, I ended up giving the most.

But as much as I loved Tony's work, I felt confused about why humans had this driving need to fix, alter, and change themselves and others. I knew happiness wasn't about hyping oneself with rah-rah motivation. I knew for some people, like me, it didn't take much to get excited and feel passionate, but to be still and silent was a challenge. To each person, progress is unique.

We knew Tony would never give away the "secrets" behind his work, so we went to the one man certain to know everything about what Tony did and how he did it. He'd know because he taught him. The man was Dr. Richard Bandler.

If you can imagine the child of a mad scientist and a hippy, you'll get a sense of Richard Bandler. He's totally unorthodox, completely adventurous, and beyond brilliant. Thirty years ago Bandler set out on a journey to explore how to help people be happier and more effective and he cofounded, along with John Grinder, NLP (neuro-linguistic programming), one of the greatest developments in human potential.

To some, Bandler is a God. To others, a raving lunatic. Many warned Satori and me about Bandler's unusual approach to psychology. Being two who make decisions about people based on direct experience rather than secondhand gossip, Satori and I sign up for Bandler's seminar and buckle up for the ride of our lives.

When we return from Bandler's seminar, I drive by Charley's apartment, just to see how he is doing. I stop my car in the alley and see him sitting on his porch, smoking a cigarette, just like always. I don't go up to say hi because I know Charley will make a pass at me. He's not big on boundaries, and I don't want to put myself in a compromising position. I silently wish him well and drive away.

3

CHANNELING SPIRITS

On November 1, 1996 . . . as I am eating breakfast,
Charley is riding his bike to the Lincoln Boulevard Overpass of the Santa
Monica Freeway.
As I am clearing the dishes,
Charley is climbing over the ledge.
As I jump in the shower,
Charley jumps.
And my life as a psychic medium . . . begins

a year would pass before I'd be walking along Montana Avenue in Santa Monica and bump into Charley's dad, Jonathan, sitting at a café. "I went by your place about a month ago," I'd tell him. "I saw Charley smoking on the terrace, but didn't want to go up because, well, you know Charley, he's not one to keep his hands off." I laugh.

He doesn't. He stares at me as if I've said something horrible.

"You couldn't have seen Charley."

"Well, maybe it was a month and a half, but I stopped the car. I saw him sitting there."

"Charley committed suicide . . . a year ago . . . I tried to contact you, but—"

"I got married, new last name," I blurt out and immediately feel stupid for saying it.

All the way home, I think of the first time I'd heard news as devastating as this. I was in college and received a phone call from Florida police saying they'd found credit card receipts for packages my friend Jon had sent me.

"He sent me gifts, what's the big deal?" I asked him.

"He shot himself in the head last night," the cop replied.

Like Charley, Jon was a bit unconventional. He used to talk about things like science and the sky and the beauty of life, the words tumbling off his tongue with fervor. He'd take aerobics classes and do these grand movements in the opposite direction of the rest of the class. He'd smile and shout, "Woo-weee!" as the rest of us silently plodded along.

Jon said the full expression of oneself was the key to creating a heaven on earth and to suppress anything within his soul was to die, one breath at a time.

I did not know Jon well enough to know why he chose to kill himself. All I know is that he must have forgotten who he was and why he was here, if only for a moment. And so did Charley.

I return home in a daze, thinking of Charley's death. Sorting through the mail, I come across an envelope with a note from my mom. "I received these photos in the mail today. I don't know who he is, but he's sure good-looking."

I open the envelope to see what's inside.

The phone rings. I don't answer it. I can't.

I am unable to move or breathe when I see the person staring back at me.

It is Charley.

I do not understand how photos I took to be developed nearly two years before get mailed to my mom, who no longer lives at the address I put on the envelope. They're Charley's old modeling photos, the reason why my mom didn't recognize him.

Photos arrive the same day I find out Charley is dead?

"What do you want me to know?" I ask the photos.

"Write," a voice replies.

"Write what?"

"Just write."

I lock myself in the back room of our karate school and spend the next eight months writing a film, *Journey from Within*, crying, grieving, laughing, remembering, exploring—myself, life, death, suicide, souls. The process brings up every conceivable question: Who are we? Why are we here? What is the purpose of life? What happens after we die? Do we even die? How will we know for sure?

I read nearly sixty books about mediumship, psychic phenomena, suicide, mental illness, psychiatry, souls, and guides. I don't only read modern works. I search the Internet for books written between 1900 and 1970 because I want to get to the root of this stuff, dig deep. On eBay, I pay $2 for a first-edition book about mediums and the development of mediumship written in 1946 by Reverend Robert Chaney. I quickly read the inscription signed by Chaney, "To Geraldine Pelton, with many thanks for your help." While perusing the table of contents, I gasp when I see the name—Geraldine Pelton—listed as one of the mediums Chaney interviewed for this book.

This was her book, her personal copy.

Strange things continue to occur.

One night, a translucent image with a blue glow runs across my mirror. It happens so quickly I question whether or not it is real. I call over my dog, but she won't budge. She just looks at the mirror and begins barking ferociously. Her tail stands straight out, then all the lights go off. Satori gets the lights back on, but the moment he walks out the door—Bam!—they're off again.

After days of nothing but writing, I am ready to take a break. One last time, I place my fingers on the keyboard and take a deep breath before I see "What were you thinking right before you killed yourself?" typed across the screen. I'm sure I typed this even though I have no recollection of doing so.

What follows is eleven days of typing 135 words a minute, whereupon I ask questions and receive answers from seventeen people who ended their lives.

One of them is Charley.

Alexy, a twenty-year-old who hung himself, reveals, *"We suffer when you do, but not in the same way. We don't feel actual pain, like physical pain, we just find it difficult to move on when you're in pain."*

These souls let me in on the most personal details about how they lived, why they died, and what they would have done differently if they'd known life continues.

Each morning, I awaken eager to discover what new insights these souls will reveal. The process uplifts, renews, and absorbs me in a way I have never known.

When I'm done, I leaf through the 364-page manuscript, feeling exhausted and exhilarated, as one does after a vigorous workout. I read Satori a few chapters then toss it in the drawer. A few weeks pass and this thought won't go away: What if these people died in the way they said? What if everything I just "channeled" is true?

I don't just receive first names. I get full names, addresses, pertinent details that would easily be identified by friends and family members. I decide to research what I've received.

I begin on the Internet, looking up the names, researching the addresses, going to posting boards of suicide survivors.

The first validation shocks me.

It is from Jay Moloney—a talent agent who hanged himself while I was writing the book.

I found myself writing details about Jay's memorial service, then a week later, reading the words I'd written in the newspaper. I needed to find someone who knew Jay—a friend who could validate much of the personal information that came through. I decide to post a note on a message board where people have been chatting about his death. Maybe someone close to him would read my note and contact me. I receive a letter from a girl named Jaide who says she attended USC with Jay. I send her the transcript of Jay's words and include my phone number. An hour later, she calls and invites me to her house. There, she shows me photos of her and Jay.

She was having a really hard time with his death.

Two words in Jay's transcript catch her attention—"Blue Jay."

"I called him that," says Jaide. "My nickname for him."

On a suicide site, I contact friends and family members of several of the people who had spoken through me. A week after I complete the book, my mom, who did not yet know of my writing experience, asks me, "Honey, what have you been doing?"

She thinks I've been hiding something from her. I know this from the tense look on her face.

"I've just been writing, Mom, why?"

"I went to this spiritual workshop tonight and the instructor tells me, 'Linda, you have many spirits in your house. Your daughter has something to do with this.' "

An hour later, Satori comes home and plops himself on the couch. He looks bothered, weighed down. Unusual for his normally upbeat, optimistic demeanor.

"I feel awful," he tells me. "I spoke to my friend Gary, and he tells me, 'You know, Satori, your feelings may not be your own.' He tells me there are many spirits around me with unfinished business and if I want to feel better, I need to ask them to leave."

So there we were—left with the dilemma of how to get the spirits out of our house.

Since I was new at this and had no idea how to get rid of spirits other than what I'd seen in moves like *Ghost,* I relied on Whoopi Gold-berg for inspiration and ran through the house, shouting, "Spirits, be gone! Shoo! Go away! Get outta here!"

Satori did a special, "Spirit-Be-Gone Dance" made up on the spot.

The next day, Satori and my mom are restored to normal.

I, on the other hand, would never be the same again.

$\mathcal{S}$everal months later, I am standing on line at Bed Bath and Beyond, waiting to pay for some sheets, when this guy nudges me and says, *"My name is Troy. I'm twenty-seven. I died a year ago. My sister is the cashier."* I'm thinking, That's nice. I'm leaving!

Satori takes my cold and clammy hand. "Are you okay?"

I shake my head no. "A twenty-seven year-old dead guy named Troy told me his sister is the cashier."

"Ask her," Satori says, as if it's the most obvious thing to do.

"I am not asking her. You ask her. You know what, I don't even like these sheets. I'm going to get a different set—"

"It's not about the sheets, Lysa," he says, yanking away the package.

I look at him, defeated. He was right. It wasn't about the sheets. It was about my fear of being wrong, judged, thought of as weird. It was about venturing into an arena of which I knew nothing.

"Her brother came to you so his sister would know he's still around," Satori says.

"How do you know?"

"He wouldn't be here if he didn't have something to say."

We're next in line. The cashier scans our sheets. "That'll be fifty-six dollars," she says. I hand her a hundred-dollar bill. Satori nudges me. I quickly blurt out, "Do you have a twenty-seven-year-old brother named Troy who died a year ago?"

"You knew Troy? It's his birthday today. Baby brother would've been twenty-eight."

I bolt out the door.

In the parking lot, I am shaking. "What the hell just happened?" I ask Satori.

"Come on, this is a good thing," he says, hugging me tightly.

"If it's so good, why does it feel so weird? Why here? While I'm buying sheets?"

"Why do you think they call it **Bed, Bath, and B e y o n d**?" he laughs.

Two weeks later, I am at the Theological Society hearing a lecture by spirit medium James Van Praagh. In front of the crowd, I ask him why faces of people I've never met keep popping into my head and why I channeled seventeen people who killed themselves.

"You are a gifted medium," James assures me. "You have been a medium for many lifetimes with enormous abilities to tap into the spirit world and help people with your gift. You are advanced and ready to do this work. . . . Oh, and you were a dressmaker in your last life."

Satori nudges me, "Maybe that's why you almost never wear dresses. You're sick of them from your last life."

Less than a month later, I attend a John Edward seminar and during the questions section, I ask him, "How do you turn spirits off? Not turn them off, like piss them off, but . . ."

He laughs. "You're in charge. You say when you're ready to channel them. You give the go-ahead."

During his channeling section, I do an experiment to see if I'm able to channel the same spirits he is channeling. When he begins a reading, I mentally ask spirits to identify themselves, and when they do, I write the details before John brings them through. It works, until John busts me, calling out, "You must be buzzing with energy right now, having all those spirits around you."

When the seminar ends, John leaves the room.

I do not. I can't. People are lined up to have a reading with me. "Do you see my boyfriend?" "Is my mom still around?" "What does my aunt Rochelle say?" "Will I win today's Big Pick Lotto?"

My mom stands there, smiling. My eyes plead for help, and then—WHAM! A basketball player flashes in front of my face. I grab a teenage girl just as she's about to walk away. I ask her, "Did your boyfriend play basketball?" The number 42 flashes.

"His number was forty-two," she says.

On the way home I think about the moments of my life that led me to right now: from seeing my dead grandfather to playing with invisible friends to knowing things before they occurred to having this innate sense that my life was guided. I ponder whether this channeling/psychic ability has been there all along; if it is one of those things I didn't know that I knew, but now that I know I can't ever go back to **not** knowing. Same as in a court of law when a judge instructs the jury to disregard the last statement; jurors can't do it. That statement is stuck in their minds forever. They can never **not** hear what they just heard.

I decide to move forward, check out if I'm really meant to do this work. I make a bunch of flyers about being a psychic medium; Satori and I put them in coffeehouses all over town.

Within days, the phone rings. A man wants to have a session with me. "When is your next opening?" he asks.

"Let me see . . ." I say, flipping through my completely empty schedule, pondering whether to pretend I'm in high demand or to just tell the truth, "I have an opening today," I blurt out.

I hang up the phone and shout, "Holy shit! My very first client!"

Okay, he's going to be here any minute.

Vanilla candles are lit.

Curtains are closed.

Lights are dimmed.

Tape recorder is set.

There's only one thing missing.

My mind!

I am out of it.

Frantic.

Can I do this? What do I say?

Okay, Lysa, get a grip. You know how to do this.

TRUST YOURSELF.

Listen to a meditation tape. Open your chakras. Be one with the light.

It's so dark in here. He's going to think it's a séance. You need more light.

I open the curtains. There—much better.

The doorbell rings.

Oh my God!

He's here!

*M*y first session led to my second session and to my third, and to tell you the truth, I felt like I was winging it. I had no idea whether I was doing it right, saying what the spirits wanted me to say. All I knew is that people understood what I was bringing through—the names, how their loved ones died, details about their life—everything.

But things seemed too easy. I put out flyers and people called. I was suspicious of how smoothly my life was sailing and decided to shake up a storm. "I can't do this full-time," I tell Satori. "I need a job that's secure." He looks at me as if he doesn't know me. This attitude of fear definitely has no place in my head. But I am determined to get another job, just in case the spirit thing stops working.

I send out more than seventy-five résumés to production companies looking for assistants. Yet even though my résumé states that I type between ninety and a hundred words a minute, know Macs and PCs, and have great people skills, I don't get one call, not one speck of interest.

Instead of seeing this as an obvious sign to go back to channeling full-time, I muster up some more self-will and sign on at a temp agency.

Little did I know when I arrived for my first day of work as assistant to the vice president of domestic television at Paramount that the spirit world had a plan for me.

As I was arranging the daily trade papers, a man taps me on my shoulder, and says to me, *"Tell Bobbee to take a break. She's needs a vacation, to get some rest."*

"With all due respect. This is my first day on the job. What can I say? Here are your faxes, Ms. Gabelman, and your deceased father thinks you need a vacation. Have a great day."

Her dad wouldn't leave me alone. He was stubborn, distracting, and relentless. I decide to confide in Nancy, the regular assistant whom I'm prepping to cover for, during lunch.

I ask, "Do you know what a spirit medium is?"

She looks at me, dumbfounded. "Like that kid in *The Sixth Sense*?" she says.

"Exactly," I tell her and go on to describe things she can confirm about her boss.

The next day, I am fired.

The excuse? I stepped over the line, the invisible one that says, "You're only a temp, you have no right to reveal personal details about the boss. Just answer our phone, get the coffee, and keep your mouth shut."

I knew the universe had given me the boot.

The boot is when you get fired from a job you hate, or when the guy or girl you've been wanting to break up with breaks up with you first.

The boot wouldn't allow me to do something that wasn't my mission. It closed doors and bolted them shut, forcing me to no longer allow fear to rule my decisions.

I thought about my friend who blew up her car because she knew it was the only way she'd buy herself a new one. As long as that piece of shit ran, she'd drive it. Destroying the car forced her to buy a new one. It's the same with keeping clothes you know you'll never wear but hold on to "just in case." Just in case what? Leopard boots come back in style in thirty years? Buy yourself new boots if they do.

The universe was teaching me I had to "clean out my closet" and make room for the new me, which felt scary because, who was this person who could channel the dead and tell people intimate details about their life without knowing them? How would people who'd known me all my life react to my newfound "ability"?

I would never know by pondering. I had to take action that forced me out of my shell.

Doing stuff you know you do well is easy, but doing stuff you've never done, stuff you're a bit unsure about, that's the challenge that stretches you and makes you grow.

As fate would have it, the moment I tell Satori I'm taking on chan-neling fulltime, the universe sends me an assignment to put my bravado to the test.

It comes in the form of a phone call from Star 98.7 radio station in Los Angeles, where the program director tells me she received the e-mail I'd completely forgotten I'd sent.

"We'd like you to be our guest on Halloween," she tells me. "It's the number-one drive-home show, with hosts Ryan Seacrest and Lisa Foxx. You'll be doing readings for listeners on the air and can choose to come to our studio or do it from home; it's up to you."

I decide to do the show from home instead of making an ass of myself in their studio.

An hour before going on the air, I find myself repeating a mantra that's anything but spiritual. "What if nothing comes through? What if I'm wrong? What if I make a fool of myself in front of hundreds of thousands of listeners who will know my name, my phone number, and my website address!"

My fear had nothing to do with any deep-seeded issues or insecuri-ties from my past. It had to do with my fear of screwing up in the pres-ent. I wanted these callers to hear from their loved ones. I wanted to do this work at the highest level, and since nothing in life is 100 percent, my fear was that small percentage of chance I may screw up.

"What if everything comes through?" Satori asks me. "What if the connections you make change people's lives for the better? What if you inspire them? What if you bring through their loved ones more clearly than ever? What if—"

"Don't use that self-help shit on me!" I laugh.

I could just as easily focus on what could go right as what could go wrong. I knew thoughts impacted experience and told myself I didn't need to prepare myself for failure by starting off in the dumps.

Seconds before going on, I have a quick chat with the spirits. "Okay, you guys, I'm about to go on the number one drive-home show in Los Angeles, so if you don't show up, you're out of a deal."

I was willing to do my part and they had to do theirs. I wasn't about to say, "I think I see a cat. Anyone have a cat? What about a dog?" No way.

When the first caller, a guy named John, comes on the line and asks to connect with his mom, I go forth full speed ahead. "Your mother crossed from cancer and she's saying baby boy, she called you baby boy, a nickname, before she died."

"She always referred to me as her baby boy because I'm the only boy in the family."

"Did she die of cancer?" host Ryan Seacrest asks.

"Yes, she did."

Next caller. A woman's grandmother comes through, and then a guy's buddy, and a wife, and one after another, the spirits speak clearly, accurately, and precisely, making me feel so excited this stuff actually works; channeling the dead is not only real—it can be done on the spot!

Finally, I channel the grandfather of the rather skeptical Ryan Seacrest, telling him, "Your grandfather is showing his ring that was given to you, and he says happy birthday to your sister."

"I got chills right there," Ryan replies. "My father gave me my grandfather's ring, and we just celebrated my sister's birthday."

Before the show ends, our home phone is ringing off the hook. Call us naïve, but we had no idea we'd receive more than two hundred phone calls from listeners wanting to sign up for a reading. It was insane, with Satori answering phones while I took messages from the answering machine, which was filling up faster than I could write.

The response confirmed I was on the right path, but I knew I would have to wipe the slate clean and start from square one. If I wanted to do this work at the highest level, I'd need to learn how spirits speak from my own experience.

Looking back, I see that if I'd abided by the rules set forth by others, believing that giving single letters is acceptable, that you can't ask for specific spirits, or even promise anything at all will come through, if

I would have made this my truth, I never would have taken the steps to discover what was possible.

Don't get me wrong, I love John Edward, I think he's the greatest. But at the beginning I believed what he and many other mediums said about not being able to ask for specific spirits was true. Now, whenever I hear a medium tell people this, I get a knot in my stomach because it's just not true. "What, are you too busy?" I asked the spirits early on. "If your loved one took the time to call the radio station, the least you can do is drop by to say hello."

They did. They do.

When mediums say they can't guarantee anything will come through, they're giving themselves an out, a way to blame it on the spirits if nothing shows up.

I didn't want an out. I knew that as long as someone had a need, a desire to connect, the spirits would come through. Unless they were reincarnated (which happened once with a dog) there was no reason other than my blocking myself for why they wouldn't come. I couldn't make them speak or force words or images to come through, but I could train myself to be the best receiver and giver of messages I knew how.

From the get-go, I spoke to the spirits the same way I spoke to everyone else. I treated them like regular people. They weren't saints, at least not the ones I met. Their messages were poignant, personal, and oftentimes hysterically funny.

When someone was shot, I'd feel an impact. If they were alcoholic, I'd feel tipsy or start slurring my words. I'd see a car coming at me or feel my body smashing through a windshield if someone died in a vehicle accident. Whenever I saw a mime or Charlie Chaplin, I knew that person couldn't speak before they died. When I saw tubes coming out of someone's arms, I knew that person died from a disease.

It was like watching a movie, or seeing photographs flashing before me at rapid speed.

I also smelled spirits, strongly.

"Old Spice. He puts on too much Old Spice," I tell a woman about her son.

"Yes," she laughs. "He'd shake the bottle all over his back. Stink up the entire house."

When I'm channeling, my hands sweat, become freezing cold, wet and clammy. It's quite attractive.

The cold clammy sweating thing started when I was seven. My brother used to tease me, "Lysa, your hands are crying!" My feet would do the same. I thought it had to do with nerves or overactive sweat glands until I began doing this work and noticed a correlation between channeling and sweating.

I've heard many psychics and mediums speak about struggling to come to terms with their gift, often fighting it or wishing it would go away. I've never felt that way. I've felt more curious and fascinated as to why and how these spirits suddenly appeared.

I began to ponder: If I can tell someone details about a person I've never met who is dead, and details about people still living, about their future, past, and present, what does this mean about the boundaries of the human spirit? If we don't die, that screws up our entire belief system. It means everything we've been taught about death being the end is false. If we can connect with people no longer in a body, what else can we do? What else is possible?

I didn't come up with the answers alone.

The spirits taught me only as much as I was ready to learn.

To strengthen my ability, Satori tested and challenged me. I'd tell him, "Come on, honey, hide something; let me see if I can psychically find it."

I'd walk into the bedroom and a can of soup would flash in front of my face. I'd mentally zero in on it, and voila! Behind the curtains, the can of soup was revealed.

"Hide more stuff; come on, make it harder."

I trained myself as an Olympic athlete would, strengthening my mind, body, and spirit while improving my speed, accuracy, level of detail, and clarity. I wanted to push the limits. I wanted to live by the saying we'd printed on our karate school T-shirts years before. "One who has attained mastery of an art, shows it in every action."

From Tony Robbins, I learned the importance of constant and never-ending improvement and the power of immersing oneself for a period of time to reach a particular goal. I likened it to seeing a movie. We don't take two weeks to watch a movie, viewing it five minutes each day. We watch it in one sitting, totally immersing ourselves in order to get the full experience.

To become the master of my art, I immersed myself by creating the *Rocky* of psychic trainings—doing readings for anyone, anytime, anywhere.

My martial arts training taught me I needed to be ready at a moment's notice, like the surgeon who learns his craft at medical school and is fully prepared when called upon in an emergency. If a patient with a shotgun wound to the heart is wheeled into the ER, the surgeon can't tell the staff, "I need fifteen minutes to meditate before I save this guy's life." He needs to be ready, on the spot, for action.

I'd heard about this service where people could read my web page and be connected directly to me whenever I made myself available to receive calls. Since there were no scheduled appointment times, it meant I had to be ready to give a reading at a moment's notice. I'd be making lunch or cleaning the house or even in the shower, and the phone would ring. BAM—I'd start channeling or doing a psychic reading.

I was amazed when people from not only the United States, but from China, France, England, and even Iceland called. It took skill, alertness, and trust to do readings at this kind of pace. I had sixty seconds to bring through details to let the person know it was their loved one coming through. Some people didn't want to get off the phone, and I'd be telling them, "You've had enough now. Go spend your money on some new clothes."

During my first call, I heard, *"Peter, Peter, Peter,"* but I was afraid of being wrong. Then the lady on the phone says, "I miss my Peter so much," and I'm like, "Shit! I should've said it first!"

More often than not, I trusted what I saw, felt, and heard from the spirits and from my psychic self, but this was only after learning how to shut off the negative voice, the one that policed my every word and went over things a zillion times before acting.

I finally had to learn how to quiet the Bitch with a whip.

Oh, you know the Bitch.

The Bitch is the voice that stops you from expressing who you are and berates you for saying and doing something you cannot go back and change. It nags and nags and nags you.

I first met the Bitch many years ago at a club called Limelight in New York City. I'm with some friends when I see this gorgeous guy on the other side of the room. I happen to be feeling sexy that night, so I decide to walk right up to the gorgeous man and ask him to dance.

I start walking, no, strutting, I'm halfway there when the Bitch with a whip shows up and starts getting on my case, telling me, "He's probably got a girlfriend. He won't be interested in you. What if he blows you off big time; that'll scar your ego. Is he really worth all that pain? NOOO!! Don't go!! Don't risk rejection!!! STOP!!!"

I walk right past the guy.

The Bitch wins.

I've since learned how to handle the Bitch. Now, I send her to Starbucks before I do a reading, and she's not allowed to come back until I'm done; even then, she's only allowed to give constructive criticism, not blatant insults.

It's the same with doing creative work and having your editor present at the time of creation. If you're writing a book and your editor is present, that book is going to be a pain in the ass to write. The editor will keep coming around saying, "You should change this, add more of that."

Here is how mediumship would sound if my editor (Bitch) were present:

"I hear a Jacob."

What if it's Mike?

"I see a fireman."

He could be a cop.

The Bitch tells you everything you're not capable of doing, being, or achieving. It says, "Don't show people how much you love them—they'll take advantage of you. Don't shine—people will be jealous. Don't express what you feel—it may piss someone off and if they're pissed off they won't love you and if they don't love you, you'll feel empty and then you'll start drinking and overeating and be fat and drunk and no one will ever want to be with you, so just keep your mouth shut and walk the other way."

After I realized I was in control of whether I listened to the Bitch or not, she stopped coming around. Being ignored pissed her off so much she left my mind for weeks, sometimes even months, at a time. Just as flowers wilt when their needs are ignored, the Bitch got quiet when I no longer listened to and followed every word she said.

Mediumship is not about analyzing. It's about relaying exactly what I see, hear, feel, smell, and experience, the moment it occurs, without first turning it over in my mind. Without pondering, "Should I or shouldn't I say this?" It is about speaking so quickly my rational mind doesn't have time to get in the way.

I got really good at channeling spirits by doing it. Not by thinking about it, planning on doing it someday when I was "ready," but doing it to the tune of five to six readings nearly every day for an entire year. I trained myself to hear, see, feel, smell, and taste at a level beyond what I normally perceived and become aware of the things I used to ignore.

The sunshine blazing through the side of my curtains bothers me. I fix them. They separate, sunshine beaming in my eyes. I ask the woman sitting across from me, "Did your mother have a problem with sun shining through the curtains? I keep wanting to tape them shut."

"My mom worked the graveyard shift at a diner and would yell when we forgot to tape the curtains to stop the sun shining through while she slept during the day."

I have a session with an eleven-year-old girl. My nose starts to bleed. I excuse myself to wipe up the blood. In the bathroom, her father tells me he died of a cocaine overdose and that his nose used to bleed, which his daughter later confirms.

As I'm in the shower getting ready to do my first ever channeling seminar, this guy named Harry shows up wearing a tux, looking all dapper, and he says to me, "Make sure to call on my wife tonight. She'll be wearing a red dress. I'll try to get her to sit in the front row, but she'll probably opt for the third. She's got a thing about third rows."

"Thanks, Harry, I'll keep that in mind, now please get out of the shower."

At the seminar, there she is, Harry's wife, in the third row. She laughs when I describe where Harry came through. She tells the group how Harry would always open the shower door and speak to her while she was showering and he was getting dressed.

At that same seminar, I did something I'd never done before—I gave readings to every single person in the room, sixty-five readings back to back. My dad, who flew from Florida to be at the event, and my mom, were sitting with their jaws open, wondering how their little girl who wanted to become a sociologist ended up helping people by connecting them with the dead.

It's rather funny my parents didn't freak out or send me to a shrink when I told them my new vocation because, you know, there is a fine line between channeling spirits and going nuts. If I didn't know myself as well as I do, if I didn't have the training of all those seminars my mom took me to as a kid, I don't think I would've been prepared to handle this and use it the way I do.

Channeling did sometimes become a bit freaky, especially when spirits started influencing my behaviors and moods without letting me know. I'd be sitting on the couch watching TV and feel this sudden voracious urge to clean. I'm not talking a little dusting and vacuuming; I'd resemble a cleaning lady on speed. The phone would ring, and a woman's mother would come through telling me I could've done a better job. The woman would confirm it, saying her mom inspected with a bleached white glove.

During an event in Santa Clarita, California, my eyes keep darting to the African Studies section of the bookstore, toward a book called *The Psychedelic Experience* by Timothy Leary. I ask the man I'm doing a reading for if the book has any significance, and he says, "Well, yeah, I've just read every book by Leary. He's a God. The whole drug trip, theory on life, I dig it all."

Okay, so maybe spirits can move books, or maybe it was just shelved wrong—that happens, right?—But next to a guy I'm doing a reading for who's just read every book by Leary? Don't think so.

I know to mention the book because it illuminates itself, just as a good-looking person does across a crowded room. They "shine" more brightly than those schleps in the corner.

I become fascinated by the details spirits bring through; the baseball card shoved in the casket, the exact words spoken before they died, the vacation to Bermuda where the luggage was lost. These tidbits, more than anything else, prove their continuing existence.

I keep finding new ways to test and stretch myself. On a message board for a show called *Beyond Chance,* a mother writes that she wants to find a psychic medium to connect with her dead son. I start typing. "I see a car smashing into a pole. I hear J.R. I see a giddy, joker type. There's ice. Slippery." The next day, the woman responds, "Yes, my son died in a car accident. The roads were icy. His name was Jamie Robert (J.R.) and he was a prankster."

I do free chat readings on Friday nights for the Excite search engine chat room. I do e-mail readings, phone readings, in-person readings; any kind of readings I can think of, I do.

I even toy with remote viewing, calling my dad and telling him what color pajamas he is wearing. I test and push myself in every way I can.

What comes through is the raw, naked truth.

Secrets are revealed. Lies, admitted. Mistakes, owned up to.

The experience, from what clients tell me, is nothing short of a mental, spiritual, and physical cleansing. Once the truth is revealed, the burden is lifted. People, both living and crossed over, no longer walk around feeling horrible and filled with regret.

So why then, with everything I know, everything I've learned, do I still fear losing the people I love?

"There is a death," a spirit reveals. *"The death of a certain form of relationship, death of the body, of the convenience of being able to speak, to touch and feel in the manner which you've been accustomed. Connecting doesn't stop you from missing us. It just has you know we're still around."*

The connections are a healing salve, able to draw out whatever still needs to be expressed and heal it to move forward. I start wondering: How can connecting with spirits help us? What can channeling the "dead" teach us? What do spirits want us to know? Through them, can our life purpose be revealed? Can we learn from their mistakes and from what they discover after they've "died"? How can we use that knowledge in our life?

The first answer comes from the mother of a man sobbing hysterically about how much he misses her. *"Interrupt him already!"* his mom tells me. *"Then, he'll definitely know it's me."*

I do, and he laughs, "I never could get a word in."

His mom was eighty-nine years old. She'd mothered five girls and a boy, outlived three husbands, and *"Enough is enough, already!"* she tells me.

"I chose the moment I would pass, 7:04 P.M. Right after Larry."

"She's saying she died after Larry," I tell him.

"Larry King. She never missed a show." Her son smiles. "Taping it was out of the question. She even made us change hospitals because they didn't get CNN."

I am not merely channeling this woman. I am literally with her. I silently ask why she feels so close to me, and she says, *"There is no other side. It's not—you're in California and I'm in Miami. It's all here, just a different level of here. Some spirits get closer than others. I happen to like close. I'm good at it."*

"What about that place depicted throughout history as being an oasis for the soul?" I ask.

"We're not in the sky and not in a fire pit below, although some could benefit from a little heat. You can't see us the way we can see you. If you could, you'd never feel alone. You'd be spooked at how close we are. We can touch you. We go with you to the movies (only when we like the picture). You think of us and we're by your side. We're nagging you to get out more, to stop kvetching about your problems. We're yelling at politicians, which I absolutely adore. We hear all the lies, secrets, tomfoolery people do."

I go over her words several times: The spirits are here, just on a different level of here, and within their level, there are many levels. Just as within Los Angeles, there are many neighborhoods. **Spirits go where they resonate, which is determined by the life they led.**

"We still want you to listen, follow our advice, and quit being so darn stubborn. We still like to be right. The difference is, we now see what we weren't willing to before. We're braver, in a sense, more willing to accept personal responsibility. Not all of us, but most."

I've never heard a spirit say, "You know that argument we had right before I died? I'm still pissed off at you!" Spirits don't waste their time blaming others or complaining about the past. They own up, get honest, and face themselves, sometimes for the first time in their lives.

I think about how easy it is to feel spiritual when everyone is being nice or when life gives us everything we need. The challenge comes when something horrifying happens: Our child dies. Our husband or wife gets cancer. Our parents are killed. Our world shatters. Our foundation is destroyed. We want the pain to stop, but we don't know how to stop it.

Hearing the endless wailing of a wife wanting her husband back or seeing the confused look in a child's eyes when they're told mommy won't be coming home again breaks our hearts.

"When will my wife stop grieving her mother's death?" a husband asks me.

I tell him of a conversation I had with my dad when I was seventeen. It took place on a pay phone at Red Lobster in Marina Del Rey. I was bitching about how adversely their divorce affected me and how its impact still lingered on, when my dad cuts me off and says, "It's been ten years since our divorce, when are you going to get over it?"

Without thinking, I tell him, "I'll be over it when I'm over it!"

A few weeks later, I was done feeling badly about something I didn't have the power to change. It was painful enough when it happened; to replay it meant to relive it and I no longer wanted to relive my life. *I wanted to live my life.*

"It takes what it takes," I tell the husband regarding his wife's grieving. "It takes what it takes to get over the pain, to learn new ways of being, to complete what we didn't get to complete before they died. Connecting with them speeds the process, as does allowing ourselves to feel exactly what we feel when we feel it, no holding back, no putting a cork in to stop the pain."

The spirits tell me connecting isn't just for us. It's for them. They need to connect with us sometimes more than we need to connect with them.

"For many of us, speaking to you is as new for us as it is for you," a spirit tells me. *"We need to learn how to send messages the same as you need to learn how to receive and relay them. People think we are the same. We can communicate with our mouth as we did in a body. It isn't the same. Until you die, you cannot know how much energy it takes to relay even the simplest of messages. We are sending you words, impressions, feelings, and thoughts that you then have to process, comprehend, and relay. You want us to communicate clearly with you when you don't even communicate clearly among each other."*

I think about how often misunderstandings occur because someone says something that is misinterpreted by the other; how one simple conversation can turn into a fight.

"Now take this into the spirit world where we no longer have vocal cords to speak, a body to make gestures, a face to show expressions, and a tonality that lets you know what we mean, and you expect us to still come through exactly as we once did? Please!"

I thoroughly enjoy these "private" conversations with the spirits, several of whom were psychic mediums when they were "alive." Some were famous, some unknown, all were wise, witty, and wonderfully gutsy.

After reading several books about famed psychic Peter Hurkos, I make it my mission to get in touch with Peter's wife, Stephany.

Within days of writing her a letter, she responds, inviting Satori and me out to dinner. We show up at her apartment. I'm barely inside before she says to me, "Show me whatcha got. Let me hear what you can do. Go on now; I want to know if you're psychic."

I am caught off guard. I came for dinner and conversation, not a psychic test. But I can't turn down the wife of a psychic I admire so much.

I tell myself to treat it like any other reading, not to put extra pressure on myself just because it's Peter Hurkos's wife. The moment I think this, I am pulled toward the wall. "Peter is telling me about one box with his things behind that wall."

"Go have a look." Stephany grins.

I walk behind the wall, open the closet, and there it is: one box filled with Peter's things. Across the hallway, Peter urges me into another room. Stephany opens the door and I am thrust into psychic medium heaven. Rows of file cabinets filled to the brim with Peter's life work and boxes of his most personal possessions take up the entire floor.

"Go on . . . open one," Stephany says, noticing my eyes glued to the cabinets.

I run my finger along the battered tin, relishing the moment as long as I can before opening the file, slowly, carefully, my heart pounding as my fingers touch the papers from Peter's most famous cases—the Boston Strangler, the Manson murders—all at my disposal.

Just imagine you are an aspiring filmmaker standing in Steven Spielberg's private office after he crosses over, and you touch and look through the archives of his creations, the items he once held dear. You get a rare glimpse into the man who created the magic.

I want to be left alone with Peter, to read through his cases, sort through his notes.

I touch a green shirt stuffed in a file, and wonder if it belonged to the victim or the killer. I touch a lock of hair, newspaper clippings, photos—items that, Stephany later reveals, belonged to missing persons, murder victims, or murderers.

Peter used psychometry, which means he obtained information about a person or an event by holding something they owned or by touching an object connected to the event, like something from the crime scene.

"What are you getting?" Stephany asks, knocking me out of my trance. She sits on a small bed against the wall and starts taking notes of everything I say.

"Someone uses Peter's first and last name, saying he's his son. It's a scam." My hands glide up and down along my shoulder as if I'm playing violin. "I'm playing Peter's violin. Now he laughs and says you've already cleaned out his stuff and this mess is the cleaned-out version."

Stephany doesn't say a word.

I make a circle with my fingers and hold them to my eye. I'm looking through them. "His magnifying glass is under the desk, in one of those boxes." Without warning, my hand clutches my chest. I feel dizzy. "He died quickly. You found him on the floor. His heart gave out. He led to his own demise. Drank too much. Liked to be left alone while he ate. He's gruff."

Finally, she puts down the pad and says, "You are correct. I did find Peter. How he died was never in the news, so you got that correct. He definitely drank too much. Using his name, yes, a man had been using Peter's name claiming to be his son. His violin, his daughter has. This is the cleaned-out version of the room, absolutely. His magnifying glass is in one of those boxes. Peter used it to locate missing persons on a map."

My stomach growls, and I laugh. I feel nervous around Stephany. Not at all at home. We go back into the living room where Satori has been waiting patiently and I begin to hear a loud ticking sound, as if the room is suddenly filled with grandfather clocks. I look around but see only a small digital clock on the shelf. I tell Stephany what I hear. Satori says he hears it, too.

"Peter used to have a collection of old grandfather clocks that filled an entire room," she tells us, then picks up the phone and starts dialing. "During the 1994 earthquake, the clocks broke so we threw them out." She signals for me to wait a second while she whispers, "I'm ready," into the phone. She covers the receiver and hands it to me. "The person on the phone isn't going to say anything but hello. Tell them everything you pick up. I'll write down what you say."

My stomach growls in protest. I don't want to do this. I want to go eat!

I look at Satori, begging for help. He blows me a kiss.

"Peter used to rub the phone cord," Stephany adds. "Said it made the messages stronger."

I take the phone. A soft voice says, "Hello." And I begin: "I'm seeing a writer. Hearing the name Patrick. Someone close to you had problems with pregnancy, getting pregnant. You're on the big screen. I hear a singer. They're close with you. I'm seeing plastic surgery around the eyes. You have brown hair. You ate pasta for dinner. You're in a dark room now. I see divorce, recently. Okay, I'm done." I hand Stephany the phone.

She goes over her notes with the mystery caller, hangs up, and says to me, "The person has brown hair, was in a dark room. She is a film actress, hence, seeing her on the big screen. She does write. There is a Patrick. Her sister had problems getting pregnant. Her boyfriend is the singer. She just went through a divorce and had plastic surgery on her eyes, and yes, she ate pasta for dinner, and by the way, you were talking to Sean Young."

At dinner, Stephany bursts my bubble, telling me I did "just okay."

"What are you talking about? I got everything right," I tell her.

"True, but we'll have to see how you do the next time."

After dinner, we go to pick up her friend, Dina Ousley, from the airport and the moment Dina gets in the car, Stephany says to me, "Do her."

No! I'm digesting my meal! I'm off duty! I don't want to!

"Put your hand on Dina's shoulder and tell her what you get," Stephany insists.

Why can't I say no to this woman? What needs to happen for me to put my foot down?

I place my hand on Dina's shoulder, "I see you teaching others your methodology, a male close to you playing classical piano. I hear El, like Ellie. Your father crossed from a heart attack. I see you running your own company; you're doing it already."

Dina applauds. "I teach a unique methodology of makeup application. I run my own company. My boyfriend plays piano. I was in the play *Ellie*, and my dad died of a heart attack."

Can I go home now? Take a break? Rest?

Stephany offers some pointers before I leave. She tells me never to interpret what I receive. "If you see a woman with a black eye, don't interpret it to mean the woman is being beaten. Just say you see a woman with a black eye."

She tells me about a woman Peter trained who is better than me. My first reaction is to get angry and defensive, but I say nothing and just nibble on my lip.

"You got everything right, Lysa. That's fine . . . for starters. Peter was as close to one hundred percent as anyone could get. This woman I'm putting you in touch with is eighty-five to ninety. I don't want you to have a blown-up ego so I won't say where I think you are."

Why do I feel so overpowered and intimidated by Stephany's strong personality?

"This is not a competition," a spirit whispers. *"Let the information speak for itself."*

Since I've never experienced a reading before, I feel excited getting one from Stephany's friend. She insists I give her a reading first and then she'll do me. I record both, with my telling her details, like being involved in a home shopping network type of deal, that she validates as true.

To say I feel disappointed after her reading is an understatement.

She tells me, "You have three kids."

"No. I don't have any kids."

"You will."

"When?"

"After you get married."

"I'm already married."

"Your husband needs to stay home more."

"My husband and I never spent even one night apart."

"He's away all the time, travels for work."

"He works from home."

I hang up the phone, click off the recorder, and promise myself I'll find a psychic medium who knocks my socks off, someone I can share with, learn from, and grow.

begin to have memories that are not my own.

Imagine saying to a buddy, "Remember the time we went kayaking in Thailand?" Then you say to yourself, "Wait a minute. I've never been to Thailand."

That's what was happening to me. The combination of recalling events that had never happened to me, hearing voices that were not my own, and feeling pain experienced by another soon became part of my normal life.

"Why me?" I asked the spirits. "Why don't you just go directly to the people you love?"

"We do," a spirit informs me. "We always go to them, first."

The spirit explains it's the same as when a kid asks mommy for something and mommy says no, so the kid goes to daddy to try again. In this case, the spirit comes to me, "Hey, Lysa, could you get the message across? Could you tell them we're here?"

"People think they're calling you for a session on their own, when in reality, we're the ones nudging our loved ones because we want to connect with them. We'll send them thoughts or make them turn on a certain radio station so they hear you channeling and call in and connect."

A woman looking for a Thanksgiving book discovers my flyer stuffed between How to Make a Winning Turkey and Cooking Tips for People Who Can't Cook. She has a cup of coffee and notices a sign advertising my appearance at the store that night. The woman arrives just as I say, "There's a stubborn man who feels embarrassed about losing his hair. He shows himself spraying it with this black dye stuff, the kind you see on TV."

The woman tells me I am channeling her father.

The spirits have their ways to get through to you, but they need you to know they don't automatically become Buddha when they cross over. They don't necessarily access the inner workings of the universe, but they do grow and learn.

If your mom was a loud, pushy woman before she died, she's not going to come through all dainty and quiet. If she was filled with years of unexpressed anger and resentment, I can promise you she's dealing with her shortcomings now.

Many books say that once we cross over, it's all sunny days and bright-colored fields of love, forgiveness and eternal peace. No more pain, angst, or worries. No more sadness or tears.

I've heard spirits cry, sob, express anger toward themselves, feel pain and regret, so when people ask me if their loved ones are okay, I cannot give the pat answer of, "Yes, they're wonderful," because they're not always fine.

Sometimes they're upset about the way things were left. They feel frustrated because they want to come back and have things back the way they used to be, but they can't and that frustrates them.

I've had many people come through who, right after pulling the trigger or swallowing pills, wish they hadn't. They were so damn angry they didn't stick around to handle what they falsely believed dying would erase. Then, they crossed over and had to deal with it anyhow.

You can't kill your spirit, put a gun to your problems, or swallow pills to erase your pain. You must go through your situation and deal with it in order to move past it.

There are no shortcuts.

I've heard spirits give thanks for the life they led, the people they loved who loved them just as much, and the experiences they had the privilege to share.

But sometimes my patience was tested. Not by spirits, but by the people who came to see me.

When Amy Buetell walks into my office wearing hot pink shorts, a barely-there T-shirt, and funky green sandals, and says, "Go ahead, do your thing," I know I am in for a treat. "Don't tell me names or details," I begin. "Just ask for a person by the relationship . . ."

"Rob. I want to connect with Rob."

Great. I just told her not to tell me names and she tells me a name. Okay, Lysa, chill out.

I begin licking my lips. "I feel like I'm choking on my own saliva, swallowing pills. I see a college, looks like Harvard. He gave you a silver ring, tells me to say page, doodled on notebooks, drawing cartoons. He shows a belt. Wrapping it around his neck. Threatening to die. You talk him out of it. He promises to live. He OD's anyway."

After an hour of channeling, Amy proceeds to rattle off validations like reading a grocery list. "Rob went to Harvard, threatened to hang himself with my belt, gave me a ring, doodled." She pulls a cartoon-covered notebook from her knapsack and tosses it on my lap. "His mom is Paige. He OD'd on pills, sure, right, perfect, whatever, but come on, Lysa, be real with me, how do I really know it's him?"

I thank God self-control is one of my more refined qualities or I'm certain the next words out of my mouth would make the Osbournes proud.

"Unless you know some other guy named Rob who died of pill overdose, went to Harvard, bought you a pinky ring, threatened to hang himself with your belt, drew cartoons in notebooks, and has a mother named Paige, I think you can rest assured that it's him."

At the door, she gives me a hug, thanks me for the session, turns to leave then looks back and says, "You can never be sure about anything in this world. It may not be him."

I'm sure the door left a nice red mark on her ass.

I know it's not spiritual to say, but I felt pissed. I couldn't understand how someone could deny what was so blatantly obvious. I guess we see only what we choose to see. We don't acknowledge what is right in front of us because of what it would mean if we did. It might require us to rethink our beliefs about who we are and what happens when we die. It might interfere with religious beliefs we've been taught since childhood. It might mean letting go of feeling so much grief.

Whatever we resist—persists. Whatever we deny does not go away.

It wasn't about convincing her. It was about relaying exactly what I received and then letting go of opinions, difficult attitudes, and the need to always please everyone.

Satori reminded me time and time again, "This isn't about you, Lysa. It's about speaking what the spirits tell you to say."

I needed to trust what came through, even when people did not understand it. "Check it out," I'd say, not wanting to waste their time trying to get them to remember what, at the time, they might not even know.

As my client Marsha Tomilson wrote me after her session, "You started with a reference to William Tell and mentioned it was like an arrow piercing the heart of Phil, the man who was murdered whom you were channeling. You said there was a hole in his heart. I didn't know about this. Much later, the autopsy report revealed Phil had a very large hole in his heart—large enough to cause blood to flow in the wrong direction. This was not anything anyone knew, as he hadn't had any symptoms."

When I am a guest on the radio show "Opie & Anthony" in New York, a guy calls in asking me channel his son. I keep saying, "You're pulling the wool over my eyes."

I'm sitting on my bed, shaking my head no. Opie and Anthony start ganging up, telling me the guy's son was murdered. It was in all the papers.

I don't budge.

I remembered how Peter Hurkos always stuck to the information he received, never allowing himself to be thrown off by anyone.

Opie finally says, "You're good, Lysa," but doesn't admit it was all a lie. The listeners write to me after I get off the air, saying that Opie admitted it was a fake, a test to see if I'd fold.

In Jacksonville, Florida, a woman asks to connect with her deceased sister, but I keep seeing her sister sitting next to her. I tell her I don't feel her sister is dead. I go on about the girl's life, bringing through information about her writing scholarship and plans for her future. After the event she comes up to me, says she feels really bad, and then introduces her sister, who was sitting beside her the entire time.

Channeling isn't a game. It isn't a show. It isn't to convert people to "believe." It's to help those who truly want to connect with the people they love.

When a guy asks me, "What do you think about skeptics, Lysa?"

The truthful answer is, "I don't."

I think about possibility and love and exploring who we are and what we're about. I think about getting close to people, connecting, sharing, creating, and breaking through fear and pain. I think about how people often tell me they're afraid of intimacy, afraid of falling in love, of getting too close, and I tell them, I don't think it's love we fear, but loss of love that scares us the most.

Thinking of Satori dying makes me sick inside. We are each other's world. We choose to have it this way, to love each other so completely and disengage the protective walls that go up whenever we give of ourselves, expose who we are, and love without restraint.

Loving takes courage. Letting people know how much you need them, how much they matter to you, how if they were gone, you don't know what you'd do, takes guts.

Not taking the people you love for granted takes awareness.

The kind of awareness Loretta Dubliner has the day I am channeling her daughter, when, in the middle of her session, she turns and stares at the clock on my wall. I mentally ask her daughter what her mom is doing. She tells me to just wait. So I do.

Then at precisely five o'clock, Loretta lets out a wail so loud, it shakes me to the core. I don't know what to do.

"You don't have to do anything," her daughter tells me. *"Just be with my mom."* Okay, I can do that, be with your mom. We sit, being in a moment of silence.

You see, at 4:59 P.M., Loretta's daughter is breathing.

At five o'clock, her daughter is dead.

Loretta knew, "I've got sixty seconds left with my daughter.

Twenty seconds more. Ten. Nine. Eight. Seven. Six. Five. Four. Three. Two . . . "

That's it.

She's gone.

She had sixty seconds left to live.

Loretta takes a pink note wrapped in blue tissue paper from her purse and hands it to me. "Shelli wrote it when she was twelve," she says, nodding for me to read it. "Dear Diary, I'm gonna die before mom. Saw it in my dream. Mom was alone with a cake and 26 candles, I counted."

Shelli died on October 23, 1992, one month shy of her twenty-sixth birthday.

"She lived life," Loretta tells me. "Packed a lot of life into her short one."

Death Awakens Us.

It sweeps us off our feet, throws us on our ass, and reminds us of what's truly important, as Loretta Dubliner reminded me that day.

4

YOUR VOICE IS MEANT TO BE HEARD

*H*ave you ever been in the Grand Canyon of human thinking? You know, that place between "Should I or shouldn't I?" where you ask all your friends for their opinions then finally decide to take their advice so if it doesn't work out, you can always blame those schleppo jerks who told you to do it in the first place.

My Grand Canyon dilemma had to do with the manuscript gathering dust at the bottom of my underwear drawer. The spirits who came through in the manuscript were getting antsy, pushing me to get their message out, saying it wasn't about me. It was about them, what they needed the world to know. For a long time, I held back, unsure of how people would respond to their words. I did nothing.

"Stop screwing around," Alexy, one of the spirits, tells me.

"You've been given this gift to share with others," Kimberly, another spirit, says. *"The bigger the risk, the bigger the payoff."*

"Yes, and the higher the jump, the harder the fall," Charley laughs.

They assure me this isn't about spoon-feeding the public ideas to which they are already accustomed. It is about giving a voice to those who no longer have one through which to speak.

Charley lays it out. *"People have opinions. If you're quiet, you're aloof. If you speak your mind, you're arrogant. Some foolish foe will always find a flaw for the sole purpose of having something to say."*

I take out the manuscript, blow off the dust, give it a name, and decide to get it out there.

Satori tells me not to get a publisher, that we can do it ourselves for the experience and challenge. I submit the book to one publisher, just in case, and then tell Satori, "All right. Let's go for it!"

I call the book *Conversations with the Spirit World,* design the cover, and print a whooping fifty-five copies for $13 a piece. "Fifty-five copies, that's going for it?" Satori asks.

"If we sell out, we can always print more."

I guess the universe had a bigger plan, because, a week later when we pick up the books, I leaf through a copy and a page falls out. Satori shakes another, and another, until thirteen pages are scattered on the floor. The shop owner shoves a page back in the book and smiles as if he's solved the problem brilliantly. "See. Perfect. No one will know."

Sure, buddy, reprint the books. Two days later, we pick them up, praying this time they'll be perfect. I shake a few copies. The pages are intact. I go to pay the man, and hear, "Uh-oh."

"The title on the spine is upside down," Satori says, holding it next to a hardcover book.

Next stop: Kinkos.

They give us the bargain price of $11 a book, so we up the amount to a hundred copies.

Five days later, they deliver the books, and I swear to you, they resemble the Leaning Tower of Pisa. The top of each one is cut diagonally, chopping off the words on the last twenty-three pages.

I force myself to laugh it off, dreaming that someday I will recant this story on *Oprah* and let millions of viewers know how much these little books went through in order to be read.

I could have easily used the screwups as an excuse, even a sign, not to publish the book. But with each screwup, a spirit reminded me, *"It's not about life becoming easier. It's about you becoming stronger."*

Finally, we hire a professional printing company and up the ante to ten thousand books.

"The bigger the risk, the bigger the reward."

We take out a sizable loan from my dad and promise to pay every penny back. I notice this split second when my rational mind confronts my creative spirit and asks, "What the fuck do you think you're doing? Are you crazy borrowing so much money from your dad?"

Two months later, ten thousand books arrive, as does a letter from the only publisher to whom I submitted the manuscript, saying they want to publish my book. "Nice going. Perfect timing!" I shout at the spirits.

I look at the boxes piled to the ceiling of my living room and I wonder how we're ever going to distribute all these books. I think about how I'd wanted to remain hidden, in the background, living on my own terms without having to listen to people's opinions and receive too much input from the outside world. I'm a homebody who loves my privacy. I didn't want to give that up.

"Your life is bigger than you," says Vertitude, a higher spirit who came through in the book. Vertitude says I can't keep my foot on one base while checking out another.

"Thinking what you thought yesterday and taking the same action won't lead you to your destiny. You can sit in your room and pray all day, but the spirits help those who're willing to play in, and not be a spectator of, the game of life."

How do you speak up when you've been silent? Change what's been ingrained in you?

"You make a decision that cuts off all other options. You decide your life."

Everywhere I look, I see people allowing themselves to be pulled along by the dictates of others or by the pressure they place on themselves. I decide to define myself by the love I share, the hurdles I over-come, the inspiration I contribute to others. I don't want to look back on my life and see volumes of should'ves and if only's. I have to take a chance.

So when my friend suggests I call her publicist to put together a plan to launch my book, I am surprised to hear, "You're an unknown, a nobody," from Suzanne, the publicist at a prestigious Beverly Hills firm. She tells me right off the bat. "Can't get you on top radio. Forget the networks. Barnes and Noble, Borders, out of the question. None of the big chains give self-published authors the time of day. It'll cost you three grand a month, but here's what we can do. We've got to think small, petite. . . ."

Petite is a dress size—not a business plan!

"Lysa, trust me. I've been in this business twenty-one years. You cannot do it on your own."

Her lack of faith in me causes me to involuntarily slam down the phone.

Satori looks at me, "What happened?"

"She wanted us to pay her three grand a month to remind us what we couldn't do."

He laughs. "Well that's just crazy, honey. Why would we pay her to tell us what people will gladly tell us for free?"

Instead of being crushed by Suzanne's words, I feel like Muham-mad Ali, who with every blow, hurled back, "That all you got? Bring it on! I'll show you what I can do!"

Once again, two roads appear before me, just as when I gave up being bulimic.

The first, the road of Playing Small, leads me to silence my gifts, ignore my abilities, and listen to others who tell me all the reasons why something I passionately want to do will never work.

The other road, the one of Big Cojones, promises freedom, self-expression, contribution, the chance to live on my own terms, inspir-ing people, challenging myself and living my dreams. Certainly the road of Big Cojones takes guts to follow, but that's why they call it Big Cojones.

I think about Bill Gates starting Microsoft from the back of his station wagon and indie bands touring the United States selling CDs town by town. I choose the path of Big Cojones and tell myself that no matter what I encounter, I'll never quit.

Satori and I kick into high gear, contacting bookstores across the nation, radio and TV programs, and friends and family members about my new book. I leave copies in public places with a note inside saying, "If you found this book it means you are meant to have it. Take the book and enjoy it."

I e-mail every rock-and-roll and top-forty radio station in the country, staying awake most nights way past four in the morning. I begin living by what Steve Tyler, the lead singer of Aerosmith, says: "Anything worth doing is worth overdoing."

If I'm going to do this, I must do it fully, completely, without reservation.

I relearn the meaning of "If you build it, they will come," the famous line from the film *Field of Dreams*. I had to take action and trust that people would love my book and attend my seminars; that I wouldn't be waiting, fearful no one would show up, like at my birthday party when I turned fourteen.

I'd planned this huge party at my house and was all excited until this kid, Scott Pittman, called two days before to say no one was coming to my birthday party.

I wanted to call the whole thing off. "Don't you dare," my brother warned me. "Tomorrow we'll tell everyone at school about the party, and you just watch how many people will come."

My brother and I invited the entire school.

Over two hundred people showed up, including Scott Pittman. You couldn't see from one side of the street to the other, that's how packed it was. People were crammed into every corner of my house, and it was my first lesson in "If you build it, they will come."

The second was when Satori and I opened our karate school with only five students.

The third occurred at Tony Robbins's event in Pasadena when, on the last day, Tony was speaking about healthy eating when I got an idea to write a cookbook. I raised my hand and told two thousand people about my nonexistent book: *Now You're Cookin'—Recipes for Success.*

After the seminar, people were shoving twenties at Satori, insisting on paying up front even though Satori told them the book wasn't finished.

Not finished? It wasn't even begun!

With the help of Satori and my dad, I wrote, designed, and printed one hundred cookbooks. My dad ran the inkjets. Satori organized the pages. Kinko's did the binding. Voilà! Mission accomplished in two weeks' time!

Taking this idea from thought to action to materialization felt exhilarating, just as publishing *Conversations with the Spirit World* did. Once we published it, we went full speed ahead, and boy, did they come! We earned enough money to pay back my dad within the first three months of publication.

I started doing lots of radio shows, sometimes three or four a day. On Mega 92.7, comedian host George Lopez gets choked up when I bring through details about the treatment he received from his dad.

On "Johnjay and Rich" in Arizona, Johnjay asks, "How is my wife doing?"

Immediately. "I feel highly emotional. Dizzy. She's been trying to have a baby and didn't. She didn't have the baby, something went wrong."

"Jesus Christ," Johnjay gasps. "My wife had a miscarriage yesterday."

"No one knew that," Rich adds. "We didn't even know till this morning."

Soon after, requests from radio stations and bookstores pour in. I do readings on the air and during commercials. Information comes through faster and faster. A woman asks for her sister. My hands go around my neck. "I feel like I'm choking, someone is choking me."

"Yes," she confirms. "My sister was strangled."

The letters I receive validate how right the spirits had been about allowing their voices to be heard: "Dear Lysa, I cannot put into words my gratitude for what you have done. Not only are you truly gifted, but are blessed with the ability to recognize an urgent cry for help. You saved Michael's life last night. He had even planned on how and where he was going to end his life. . . . Because of you, I won't have to go through life without my best friend. . . ."

"Dear Lysa, I am a 20-year-old from Minneapolis. I would like to say how much your book touched my soul and mind in ways I didn't even know could be touched. It saved my life a few times, to be honest. While feeling depressed or suicidal, I know if I sit down with it, I get something that makes me want to live again. If not for you and 'company,' I may have been dead by now."—Andrew Beauchene.

Satori and I decide to make our bookstore appearances true events, with music, inspiration, and fun. We buy our own speaker system, headset, cordless microphone, mixer board—the works—and lug it around California, many times having a blast until the store closed.

I discover if people raise their hand and ask one question, not telling me names or details, but simply saying, "I want to connect with my mom, dad, sister, friend," it calls the spirit to the front of the line.

One night, when a woman with no front teeth and bright red cheeks asks if I think fairies will stop ruining her life, her mother comes through telling me this is ridiculous. The woman tells me several psychics said fairies were sabotaging her life because of what she'd done wrong in her past, because of her karma.

"That's a load of crap," I tell her. "Karma isn't about punishment. It's about learning from what we've done and doing differently next time. Besides, we don't need fairies to sabotage our life. We're perfectly capable of screwing it up on our own."

The woman's mother tells me her daughter is abdicating responsibility. *"When all else fails, blame it on the fairies, and that sort of thing."* When I repeat this, the woman blushes.

"No more fairies, okay," I tell her. She nods and gives me the prettiest toothless grin I have ever seen. "And stop listening to psychics who tell you stupid stuff."

Many psychics tell people stupid stuff. I can't count how many times a person has said I was telling them the opposite of what five other psychics told them. Usually, it's related to relationship readings rather than channeling spirits, but just the same, the advice these psychics dish out is not only appalling, it's dangerous because it keeps these women waiting, hoping, desperate for prince charming to return.

I tell one lady that I don't see her getting back with her ex-boyfriend and she tells me three psychics said if she played hard to get, made the guy jealous by dating someone else, he'd come back. The psychics all said playing the game was the *only* way to catch him.

"First of all, he's not a fish, so you don't need to catch him," I point out. "If you play hard to get and get him back, you'll have to keep playing hard to get to keep him. You can't relax because then he'll leave since he wasn't interested in you to begin with; he was interested in the chase, the thrill of the capture, the game."

Game playing is the ultimate tug-of-war of human existence. I want you. You don't want me. I act like I don't want you when I really do, and since you think I don't want you, then you want me until you find out I really want you and then you pull away.

Many people feel just as devastated when a relationship breaks up as when someone close to them dies. Each person deals with loss and grief in their own way, in their own time, depending on the meaning they attach to what has taken place.

If they make a breakup mean they are unlovable, they're going to be in a lot more pain than if they make it mean it's time to move on and find someone new.

Spirits teach that no matter how devastating the circumstances, or how deep the pain, people's lives can turn around for the better, and it doesn't have to take years. By connecting with the people around them, the spirits, and themselves, and by changing the meaning they attached to what happened to them, people can change how they feel in an instant.

"There is a place where all is known, nothing is hidden. A place of self-honesty where who you are and what you have been through becomes clear. Hiding doesn't have a place in the evolution of our spirit, neither does lying, cheating, and fear."

Antwone Fisher once said, "You don't get better by putting your problems in a closet then standing in front of the closet door, going, "'Ain't nothing in there. I ain't got no secrets.'"

"So move out of the way and let me see what's inside."

"No, it's private stuff. I've got to guard this closet."

We sometimes do that. For years we guard the closet, oftentimes forgetting why we began guarding it in the first place. The guarding becomes automatic. Our emotional shield goes up without knowing what triggered it. Our reactions become ingrained.

The spirits help open the closet to reveal the raw, sometimes shameful secrets that hold us hostage to our pain.

"Freedom comes when shame goes away. Shame goes away when the truth is told."

I was quickly learning how much of a correlation there was to expressing oneself fully, cleaning up and releasing the past, and living a healthy, happy life. The more secrets kept, closets guarded, experiences denied, the more painful life a person would lead.

A mother admitts she protected a marriage in which her husband abused her child. She reveals she knew about the beatings but looked the other way.

"I saw the abuse. I allowed it to occur, did nothing to stop it, and I am so sorry."

Healing your relationships while you're still in a body makes crossing over much easier because you don't carry a load of shame from this life into the next.

Yet sometimes people feel shame over things that aren't their fault, like the woman who is raped, or the little girl who is abused by her father, believing she should've known better at age six. What could she have done? Tell on Daddy and risk breaking up the family? Push Daddy away and risk his leaving for good?

Spirits who were victims of abuse and those who were abusive say, *"The universe records every action, every thought, every intention a person has. There will come a time when this recording will be played for all to view and hear."*

Spirits heal themselves by helping us forgive, move forward, be free. *"Healing is a tandem act, not one we do alone."*

Though I was learning so much from the spirits and the people for whom they came through, I began to feel afraid I'd get caught up in the demands and needs of others and forget to refuel and take care of myself.

I got a clue how much time I was spending channeling spirits when my brother called and left a message with Satori, saying, "Tell my sister she spends more time speaking with the dead than with the living."

I'd heard stories about musicians and actors working themselves to the bone or allowing others to overwork them. I began to notice a fine line between driving oneself due to the need to express one's passion and being driven by the need for love and adulation. The line could easily blur if one was not careful to look at where one's self-worth was derived.

I didn't want to be like the man on his deathbed, saying, "I was so busy I missed my life." I wanted to enjoy my life. I wanted to be present for the ride. I didn't want to be the gerbil on the wheel, looking so industrious, working so hard, but going around in circles. Although I wasn't going around in circles, I was definitely spending more time working than enjoying the fruits of my labor. So in the midst of all my busyness, I decided to stop. Take a few weeks off and not do any readings, radio shows, events, or interviews.

"You didn't need to justify your right to exist on this planet. You are a human BEING, not a human DOING."

After my much-needed break, I came back feeling refreshed and renewed, able to see things in a clear light. That's when I began to notice the changes people made.

They'd be in therapy for years and then turn their life around, like Scott Simons, who wrote me:

> My partner and I had been in therapy for 8 months and I couldn't take any more talk without action. After my reading with you, I took action. We ended our relationship, and although I've gone through the normal neurotic feelings of being alone, starting over, yada yada, I know this is the best decision I've made in years. I've put my house on the market and will be living in Austin where I've always wanted to be.
>
> As you know, I'm an artist . . . a painter . . . I can already tell a difference in my work. It has become looser and less rigid, which, in turn, makes me less rigid.
>
> The other night, I was in my studio, alone, painting, when suddenly I stopped, put my tools down, and just looked at my work. Nothing was finished and it was all this big mess trying to come together, but even then, I had to stop and say out loud, "Look at what I can do."
>
> What a blessing. What a life.
>
> —Scott Simons

$\mathcal{T}$o be willing to step into the unknown, courageous enough to put your heart and soul on the line while having the guts to speak your truth and stand for what you believe while contributing to others—is the purpose of life.

Too often we quit and never see the amazing gifts we would've seen if only we'd hung in there. The love of your life was going to show up on Friday night, or the record deal was about to go through, but you canceled your date and blew off the gig where the record producer was going to sign you to a deal.

If you quit—You fail.

I'll say it again for those of you munching on Doritos.

If you quit, you fail; and quitting is often disguised. Holding yourself back is quitting. Playing it safe is quitting. Sabotaging your success is quitting. Sure, you may go through the motions looking as though you're succeeding, but your belief in yourself is long gone.

To quit and resign is death: the death of your goals, wants, needs, and passions. The death of your voice, which if silenced, robs the world of hearing what only you can say.

Living your entire life without ever doing what you love, without ever discovering what is truly possible is an insult to the mind, body, and spirit with which you were born.

My theory was confirmed a few weeks ago when I picked up a book called *Three Screenplays* by Edward Burns. In the introduction, Burns talks about starting out as a filmmaker and how he was bitching and moaning to his father about how Hollywood sucked and how they weren't giving him a shot at the big time, blah, blah, blah, and his dad says to him, "If you're a filmmaker, why don't you just make a film?"

Burns says he's got no money and it's so hard to come up with the money. His dad points out that since he'd already made a fifteen-minute film for $3,000, he could make a ninety-minute film for $18,000. So with his dad's help, Burns writes, directs, produces, and stars in *The Brothers McMullen*. He's proud, for about ten seconds, and then starts bitching and moaning about how unfair the film festival people are, how distributors don't give him the time of day, how he can't get an agent. . . . When he's done with his piss fest, his dad asks if he wants to take a test to become a cop, to which Burns responds, "No!" His dad asks if he enjoyed making *The Brothers McMullen*. Burns tells him, "It was the greatest experience of my life."

"Why are you bitching and moaning if making the film was the greatest experience of your life," his dad asks.

"I want to be a *filmmaker*."

"Did you make a film?"

"Yes."

"Then you're a filmmaker."

"It's not the same thing."

"Shut up. If you're doing this writing and directing because this is how you have to express yourself and because you enjoy it, why the fuck would you give a shit what those assholes out in Hollywood think about your work? If you really enjoyed the process as much as you say you did, go out and make another film, and if they don't like that one, go out and make another one after that, and keep making films until you have nothing left to say.

"But if you are making films because you want to be a big Hollywood hotshot and make a lot of money and go to parties, then I don't want to know you and I'll never invest in another one of your movies. But if you're doing this because you love it, write another script and we'll find a way to get you the money."

Burns continues to make films because he still has something to say.

ou can't hide the thing you love. You cannot obliterate your passion. You can ignore it. Deny and push it away, but it will not leave you.

I believe most of the pain we feel on a daily basis comes from our not expressing ourselves. People get diseases from harboring resentment. They get depressed, angry, and withdrawn from withholding emotions, walking around enraged, not expressing love.

If we love someone and don't share it, we pay the price of having our emotions come out in thwarted ways. We feel easily triggered or inexplicably afraid. We make sharing love wrong instead of beautiful. We make showing someone we care a sign of weakness instead of a sign of strength, especially when we're not sure if they'll give us love in return.

I wish more people, including myself, would stop expressing anger and irritation rather than love and affection. But anger feels safer to most people, which is why they fight on their way to the airport. It feels easier to slam the door and yell, "Good-bye!" instead of expressing how much we'll miss them. It's a painful kind of safe because beneath the anger is hurt and beneath the hurt is fear and beneath the fear is love.

The question is, "How do we get to that layer of love, faster?"

You do it by telling the truth and giving up your need to protect yourself.

When a person knows they're about to die, they often give themselves permission just to "tell it like it is" because they've got nothing left to lose.

You never lose the love you give. It comes from inside you and is replenished the moment you give it.

Many spirits say they would've been nicer to their family, given their kids more attention if they'd known their life, as they know it, was about to end.

Why does it take something as monumental as death to wake us up to change the way we speak to the people we love?

I remember hearing a boy at our karate school yelling at his mom because she forgot to pack his uniform. I said to the boy, "How do you think I'd feel if you spoke to me that way?"

"Oh, I would never speak to you that way, Lysa," he replied.

"I'd rather you not speak that way at all, but if you do, it should be to me instead of the person who's going to take care of your ass for the next twenty years," I told him.

Why are we nicer to strangers than to the people we love? Most of us would never bitch at a guy at the bus stop if he were jumping with joy, but we scream at our kids for doing that.

How differently would you treat people if you knew they were going to "die" in five minutes?

We don't like to think about death. We deny it and maintain our low standard of communicating. I used to be irritable toward Satori, then he'd say, "What if I died and you had to live with the way you just spoke to me?"

It's a wake-up call. Only don't let death be your alarm.

am doing a reading for a woman when her grandmother comes through insisting I tell the woman her mother will be dead in a month. "I'm not saying that," I silently tell the spirit.

Instead, I say to the woman, "You need to visit your mother."

"I haven't spoken to my mother in years. I don't want to see her."

I urge her to go. She tells me she'll think about it.

Months later, she writes to say that if she hadn't gone, her mother would have died. Alone.

Regret causes people excruciating pain. Regret over not telling someone how much you love them, over fighting about trivial things, over not speaking the truth. I know this from my own experience and from what others, like my friend Marion Redding, taught me.

It is Thanksgiving Day when Marion is trying to stuff an oversized turkey into a tiny pan but no matter how much she shoves, it just doesn't fit. Her husband, Hank, is on the couch eating pretzels and watching TV when Marion starts yelling at him to go buy a bigger pan. He storms out of the house cursing under his breath. He runs across the street, is almost to the curb, when a car speeds around the corner and hits him.

He flies into the air and lands on the cement.

"How do we know it was a person's time to die?" Marion asks me.

"All we know is—They died. We miss them. We want them back," I tell her. "How many times are you going to replay what happened?"

"Until I die of suffering," she says.

"You could do that right now, you know."

"No, I could never leave my kids."

"You leave every time you live in the past instead of being with them in the present."

"They haven't a clue what I go through. They're too young."

"They know more than you think."

"I'm sure of it; they haven't a clue."

In college, I took a child development class where I saw a film of an experiment that proved how, before we're even a year old, we pick up the emotions and thoughts of those around us. In the film, a mother is given the assignment of blankly staring straight ahead while thinking only happy thoughts. She is not permitted to smile or give any verbal or visual indication of how she is feeling. Her ten-month-old baby is then placed in a high chair beside her and she must continue staring, thinking happy thoughts, not paying attention to her child. In the film, the baby looks at her eagerly and then bursts out laughing, cooing, and smiling.

In the next segment, the mother's assignment is to blankly stare straight ahead, but this time, she is to think unhappy thoughts. Once again, giving no visual clues, they bring out the baby, who starts crying and reaching frantically for his mother. Through an earpiece, the mother is told quickly to change her unhappy thoughts to happy ones without changing her blank expression. The moment she does, the baby starts laughing and smiling again.

Lastly, the mother is told to look angry while thinking happy thoughts. It's incredible because at first, the baby stares at his mother's angry face and then starts laughing and cooing.

If a ten-month-old knows what his mother is feeling, imagine what our teenagers, family members, coworkers, and significant others know about us.

People often speak loudest without saying a word.

In Japan, many businessmen believe the one who remains silent remains in control. The one who remains silent is also the one to watch out for, because what people hide, what they fail to say, is often more telling than what they reveal.

After police caught serial killer Jeffrey Dahmer, many of his coworkers at the chocolate factory said, "He was such a quiet nice boy. Wouldn't hurt a fly." If Jeffrey had told them the truth, "Hey guys, I'm putting human remains in the batch today, you cool with that?" it would have blown his cover. Silence became his place to hide, as did lying.

If I had a quarter for every time a man or woman denied their gut feeling, I'd be a billionaire by now.

We know when a person is lying, but we may not always know what they're lying about.

People lie because they're afraid of what might happen if they tell the truth. We cover our ass, even if it means placing the blame on someone or something else. Our survival instincts tell us to protect ourselves at all costs, and we all do.

Anyone who says they never lie—is lying.

People lie about why they're late, why they had to break plans, what they were doing and with whom. They lie about their feelings, "Mommy isn't crying. The onions are making Mommy's eyes tear." We say we're not angry when we're fuming. We remain in miserable relationships, jobs, and situations, hoping no one will notice we're as unhappy as we are.

We sometimes deny what we know because of what the truth would mean. It may mean admitting the person we love is having an affair or our coworker badmouthed us to get a promotion, or, as with Scott Peterson's parents, our son may be a murderer.

We hide what we know is true because we're afraid people will pull away, leave us, or get angry for questioning their integrity.

Many people trust another before they trust themselves.

They trust what the other person tells them rather than what their intuition says.

I trust myself before I trust another.

I trust what my gut is saying before I trust what comes out of someone else's mouth.

Spirits never lie. Even those who lied like bastards while living come through telling the truth because, the moment they "died," they had to face themselves.

Until you've heard the cry of a husband coming through to his wife, revealing the affair he'd vehemently denied, admitting her instincts were correct all along and knowing his denial caused her to doubt herself, you have no idea how much pain a spirit can feel.

Spirits cannot move on until the truth is revealed. . . .

Neither can we.

It's like the pile of crap you throw in the closet when company comes over. Just because they can't see it doesn't mean it's not there. The lies we hide remain as invisible barriers in our relationships, unspoken shields, keeping us distant, pushing us away.

Thoughts and actions are energy. They're alive, and whatever we don't express drains us, slowly, insidiously, until we walk around feeling empty and have no idea why.

The moment we tell the truth we release ourselves. We are free.

But doing so takes guts.

Stop telling. Start asking. Stop complaining. Start changing. Stop talking. Start hearing—your voice—the voice of others. If your grandpa can shout without having a mouth, then you definitely have no excuse not to be heard. Say it like it is. Like you see it. Be bold and audacious in the face of fear. Tell the truth about lying. Tell the truth to yourself. Speak your mind. Mind your business. Allow all things to be as they are. Give yourself permission to be free.

What do you want to say?

What do you *really* want to say?

Come on. . . .

We're listening. . . .

5

CHANNELING CHANDRA LEVY

*S*he's dead."

Satori looks at me.

He's used to this sort of thing.

I am jumpy.

Sweating.

Scrambling for thoughts.

My body is shaking.

I cannot control the sweat pouring from my hands.

I move closer to the TV to get a good look at her face.

Yes. She is definitely dead.

I feel strange. I hear her voice speaking to me as if she is right here.

I am fixated on the image I see, the image we all saw plastered on the front page of every newspaper in the country: Chandra Levy. Missing Intern. Gary Condit. Sex. Politics. Secrecy. A soap opera of epic proportions, only this wasn't a soap opera. It was a young girl's life.

I quickly close the television cabinet.

"It's best if you turn off the TV first," Satori says, grinning.

Right.

I'm not thinking clearly.

I cannot get Chandra's face out of my head.

How do I even know she is dead? How do I know she's not just hiding out with some guy she met en route from D.C. to California? How do I know that any minute she won't walk through her parents' door and tell them she just saw the strangest thing on the news—herself—and then tease her mom about being such a worrywart?

I know because I see it: Wrapped around her neck, a thin wire, sharp enough to cut your finger. She's clawing wildly. Her survival instincts kick in. A sock shoved in her mouth. Duct tape seals it off. She whacks the bastard; her heel to his jaw. He punches her, hard. She passes out.

A voice, not mine, whispers, *"Rock Creek Park."*

Memories, not my own, flood my brain—dark glasses, sitting on a rock, bag slung across my chest, striking a pose. *"Take a picture already, Mom. I hate my hair. I want it to be straight."*

Are these Chandra's memories? I need to be sure.

One thing I know is that people who die suddenly, who never get the chance to say good-bye, come through loudest. Chandra is very loud. She keeps talking. She won't leave me alone. It's not that I want her to go, I just don't know what to do.

"Call the police," Satori suggests.

"What do I say?"

"What do you want to say?"

"I don't want to be mocked. I want to be taken seriously."

"Why?"

"Because, this is serious."

"Tell them that."

"What makes you think they're going to believe me?"

"What makes you think they're not?"

Good point. Okay. No more excuses.

I must do this.

I will do this.

I am doing this.

I dial the Washington, D.C., Police Department. I want to hang up. HANG UP!

Instead, I hear my voice saying, "I need a detective on the Chandra Levy case."

"You're speaking with one. Detective Durant here."

"I have some information you should know about Chandra Levy."

"You can fax what you've got or tell me now."

"I have a tape. I'm a psychic." Why did I just say that? WHY did I just say that?

"Send it, Attention Detective Durant. I'll have a listen and get back. You've got the address, right? Being a psychic and all . . . Just in case you don't do addresses, send it to . . ."

I hang up the phone questioning why I said I have a tape when I don't.

"Not yet," I hear Chandra's voice say.

I understand why detectives trained to rely on concrete facts and tangible evidence would doubt psychics. Many give fluff. "She's in a forest. She's alive, then again, maybe not."

What if I'm wrong about Chandra?

I don't want to waste anyone's time or be put on display. I feel like it's my first day of school and I want to make a good impression on the teacher. Maybe I should just forget this whole thing.

"Quitter."

I'm not quitting. I just need to know it's you, absolutely. I've channeled people who were murdered but never without someone to validate what I received.

Immediately, Chandra is next to me. It's comforting and strange. She is precise about how she wants things done. She tells me to type today's date—June 4, 2001—and points me toward Michael Doyle, a reporter at the *Modesto Bee,* to whom I write a three-page letter revealing details Chandra wants her family to know. I also write it so someone outside my circle of friends, an objective third party, can hear what Chandra is saying.

In the e-mail letter, I talk about Chandra's personality, her need for privacy, her not letting people get too close; about who she went with the day she disappeared, her middle name—Ann—and the names of Chandra's relatives, including details about her grandparents. I tell Michael to respect my anonymity and not publish this e-mail but to give it to Chandra's family.

Michael calls me. We play phone tag, but never speak. Although he doesn't print my e-mail, he does print the name of my book, my website, and the fact that I've connected with Chandra. Little do I know how much this simple letter will play a role in leading me to meet Chandra's mom face-to-face.

A month later, July 2001, I decide to record myself channeling Chandra.

I walk around my living room holding the recorder to my mouth, feeling wacko, on the verge of something miraculous and insane. I speak in first person. I do not think I am Chandra, but rather, I am allowing her words to come through unfiltered by me.

I press the record button and begin:

"She keeps showing dirt thrown over her. I feel like I'm in the woods and I'm trying to get out. She was going to be found so they dug her up and moved her. She shows a street, sounds like Green or Greenbrae or Greenborough. It feels like the person connected to this lives in Upper California, around there. Things got out of control. She was threatened to keep quiet. There is significance to 5/26, the date, May 26th and 5:26, the time."

"Things get out of control, they go horribly wrong. I'm strangled. Buried alive. Rock Creek Park, near the creek. My bracelet fell off. He took my ring. They will find me, but not in one piece. He didn't want me coming forward with what I knew, and what I knew was that I was going to have a baby."

"What happened on the day of your disappearance?"

"I came home, got a phone call from Gary. He wanted to meet with me. A guy with dark hair, bushy mustache, in a black sedan picked me up. No big deal, we're going for a drive, everything seems fine, cool. Things turn bad.

"I was strangled. Tied up. I kicked, tried to punch in the door. A gag in my mouth, my hands tied behind my back. Driven to a place I'd never been. My dad cannot comprehend I am gone. My mom they have on so much medication she wouldn't recognize me if she saw me right now. Dead, I mean."

I stop speaking. It feels too intense. Later, Satori and my mother listen to the tape. "It doesn't sound like your voice," my mom tells me.

Okay, now I'm *really* freaked out.

I mail the tape to Detective Durant and Chandra's parents. I leave a message for their lawyer, Billy Martin, but don't say I'm psychic. I mention only that I have a tape about Chandra.

I wait a few weeks. No response.

You would think that after hearing someone has a tape about Chandra, they would call, but no one does. I e-mail Billy Martin, mail him a copy of the tape, and, weeks later, there's still no response.

Chandra keeps driving me to do whatever it takes to get through to those who can help find what is left of her rapidly decomposing body.

I receive a call from Flash News reporter David Moyé, who wants to interview me about a psychic healing cruise I am doing. After we hang up, he calls back and asks, "Do you have any impressions about Chandra? Off the record, I'm just curious."

The next morning, there are fifteen new messages on my answering machine. *Entertainment Tonight* wants me for their cover story. KROQ's number one morning show, "Kevin & Bean," wants me to channel for listeners. Fox News wants a sit-down interview. Alan Colmes in New York wants an hour on the air. The list goes on. News stations and radio programs across the country want to know what the psychic who channeled Chandra Levy has to say. David apparently forgot the "off the record" part, as well as the psychic cruise, and instead printed this:

MEDIUM TAPES CONVERSATION WITH CHANDRA LEVY

LOS ANGELES (Wireless Flash)—A 60-minute cassette tape could blow the lid off the Chandra Levy case—but only if her family is interested in talking with her ghost. A spiritual medium in Los Angeles named Lysa Mateu claims Levy is dead and that she spoke with Levy's spirit last night (July 10). Mateu claims the Washington intern's apparition gave her specific names, dates and diary notes that could crack open the case. Although she taped the conversation, she won't release any of it to the media until Chandra's family listens to it first because of specific details only they will know.

While I'm still in my pajamas, I go on "Kevin & Bean." The first caller is Sierra, who asks if I can connect with her sister.

"Suddenly, I feel cold. I'm outside. Shivering. My bones are broken. There was a car accident. I'm hanging on for life," I tell her.

"Yes," Sierra cries. "She died in a car accident, my sister. Outside, they found her. She was shivering. Her bones were all broken, oh God . . . she was hanging on . . . she tried to make it."

An hour later, *Entertainment Tonight* arrives at my house. Kevin Gershan, the *ET* producer, asks me to channel Chandra. It's scary because my entire face changes. When I am channeling Chandra, my eyes shift from bright and vibrant to dull and sad. For over an hour, Chandra answers questions about her relationship with Condit, his wife, her parents, and what the police covered up.

Before we close, Kevin asks, "Does Chandra have a message for the public?"

"She's saying, *'If I came back right now, I would be so famous. Gone for a little period of time and I'm famous.'* She's making me feel like she would've thought that was cool.

"Chandra reminds me that all I need to do is focus on her parents; focus on the fact that they will not see her wedding. She makes me want to cry. They will not see these things. Chandra just keeps directing my focus, telling the public this is about a girl and a family that wants their daughter home, and she's not coming home, and how can we help her family deal with that, how can we help them deal with the fact that she won't be walking through the door."

On July 18, 2001, I do an on-camera interview with Fox News reporter Heather Nauert and tell her, "Chandra's around where the Rock Creek Park is, near a street in the park."

I repeat what I've told the twenty-six-plus radio and TV shows I've been on since Chandra first came through. Not one fact has changed, yet I feel tired of talking about it. I want to take action.

"I need help. Tell me what you want me to do," I beg Chandra.

The next morning, my wish is granted.

It comes from the most unlikely source.

Howard Stern.

Howard's people tell me they want me on the show—immediately.

I feel apprehensive because to put it gently, Howard is a dick.

Okay, maybe it's all an act, a persona to get attention, but I'm in no mood to become a spectacle in Stern's circus, especially after a friend informs me of a psychic Howard tore apart.

But at four-thirty in the morning, after staying up all night, I get the call.

Howard begins nicely. He asks where I am from and sings a Hebrew song for no reason other than to pay tribute to my heritage. "By the way, I saw you on *Entertainment Tonight,*" he says. "You're not a bad-looking broad. Once you knock out this nutty stuff, you could be Lysa Mateu-Stern. I'm going to put you in the same hospital as Mariah Carey when you're done. . . . Now, where are you buried, Chandra?"

Immediately, I switch gears. *"They moved me. They moved me twice already. The worse things get, the worse the heat gets the more they keep moving me. I will no longer be found in the full form I once was."*

"What part of you is where?" inquires Howard. "Where is your head?"

"How many pieces of you are there?" asks Robin Quivers.

"Four."

"Now, did Gary Condit order this, or not?" Howard asks.

"He didn't say, 'Go kill Chandra Levy.' What he said was, 'Take care of this.' He did not, under any circumstances, want me to have his baby."

Howard starts joking around, "I'm going to fly you to Washington, have you on the air on Monday as we search for Chandra Levy's breasts."

He's being an idiot. It takes everything not to hang up. Howard questions my abilities and my reasons for going on his show. He tries to get me angry, to make me defend myself.

I remain calm . . . sort of. I ask him, "Why, in front of millions of people, would I come on your show, give out my name and website, put my reputation as a psychic medium on the line if I couldn't back up what Chandra has told me?"

I wish you could know how it feels to have a murdered girl's spirit urging you to pass on her message while Howard Stern barks about how delusional you are.

"You are not here for the reason you think," Chandra tells me.

Next thing I know, I'm headed for Washington, D.C., with Satori, my rock of stability, by my side. On the plane, he tells me to relax, close my eyes, and ask Chandra to lead the way.

I lie on his lap and with one eye open, begin drawing a map of a place I have never been. I draw a fork in a road that turns into a bridge. I see a place resembling a scene in the film *Stand by Me*, where the kids find a dead body in a marshy area with an inclined creek surrounded by trees and rough terrain. I draw a mill. Miles above it, an energy plant. I draw a house up a winding road and write the word "Falls."

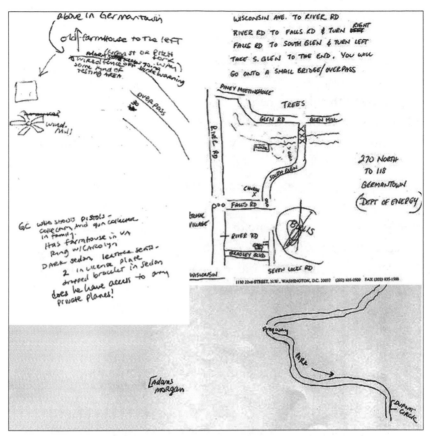

Maps I drew on the plane, plus one the hotel manager drew according to what came through from Chandra.

I am focused. I want to get this right. I want Chandra to be proud.

And then I get the same feeling I had when Lyle Lovett walked past me, the same feeling when I knew Satori was the man I would marry, an electrical impulse that zips through my gut and tells me I'm on track. I keep asking Chandra to show me the way.

We arrive at the Ritz-Carlton at four in the morning to find a note from Stern's people telling us we have to meet them in the lobby at 5:50 A.M.

Hotel employee Scott Jackson leads us to our room and asks why we are here.

"She's a psychic here for Chandra," Satori says.

Now I *know* I won't get any sleep.

"Show him the map you drew," Satori says. I take out the map, hand it to Scott.

"I know this place," he tells us. I look at him like he's nuts. What place? It's just a bunch of lines and words. "It's where I grew up," he continues. "You see where you wrote 'falls,' that's Falls Road. And the 'mill' is Mill Road, and . . ." His voice drones on, like in one of those movies where the person's lips move but no sound comes out. To think I drew a map that depicts a location someone recognizes feels surreal, but I'm too tired to celebrate this small feat when there are crisp white sheets awaiting my arrival.

The moment my head hits the pillow I'm out, at least for twenty minutes before the alarm blares and my journey begins.

In the lobby, a guy with tattooed arms and a huge belly, who calls himself Crazy Cabbie, greets us. "I've got my own gig at K-Rock," he says, shaking Satori's hand while giving me the once-over. "No disrespect, but, man, your wife has some nice set of cans. Real nice jugs."

Exactly what I love to hear at six o'clock in the morning.

E! cameramen Adam Carney and Richard Wilson arrive to film the day.

But still, one person is missing.

"Uh, Howard is sorry he couldn't be here," Cabbie says. "He had some important—"

"Don't bullshit a psychic," I tell him, following Satori into the van.

"Turn left at the corner, slow down . . . stop here," I tell them. We get to the place I drew on the map and I start feeling sick and I know we are in the right place.

Adam and Richard film every move I make, every word I utter, every feeling I receive. My heart is pounding. I feel nauseous. Distressed. "Chandra keeps showing me her hairs and a gold bracelet," I say to the camera. "The person living up the winding road is connected to this."

I plow through the heavily wooded area, my brand-new boots splattered with mud, my hair tangled in branches, my white shirt stained. I am a woman on a mission. I have no fear.

We get to the creek. We can't go in. A sign says it's toxic. I stand at the edge, sweating and disheveled, hearing Chandra's voice telling me she lost her bracelet in a black four-door sedan. *"A fist slams the back of my head—thin wire wraps around my throat—I am knocked unconscious, dragged through the woods, and dissolved of, rapidly."*

"Something was poured on her to make her flesh dissolve rapidly," I tell Cabbie as I begin feverishly digging through the leaves. "She was moved. She's not here, but the person connected to this lives here." We keep searching anyhow and find duct tape, an empty cement bag, and photos of kids on a ski vacation.

Cabbie pulls a T-shirt, twisted like a rope, from a hole in the ground. We find a woman's running shoe. Cabbie promises to pack the evidence as I go up the winding road with Adam.

As we walk, he films me as I say, "There's a black four-door sedan and blue umbrellas outside the house up this road. An associate or relative of the person who lives here was involved in Chandra's murder. The guy is a lawyer. Has several Social Security numbers. Evidence is here. The sedan was used to transport her." My gaze wanders to the woods. "They'll find her pants."

"Lysa, look!" Adam gasps pointing to the house.

A black four-door sedan is parked in the driveway.

Blue umbrellas are perched outside the house.

Richard, the other cameraman, comes running up the hill. He walks up to the black sedan and starts filming it. "Hey, you guys, it says sedan on it!"

"I've had enough," I say, backing away. "Richard, stop filming, let's get out of here."

Later Cabbie tells Howard what we uncovered: the cement, duct tape, photos, a shirt, a running shoe, the sedan, blue umbrellas, and the house.

Howard isn't impressed. He still wants a breast.

I've had enough of his shit.

So to get my point across to twelve million listeners, I do the unthinkable. . . .

I hang up on Howard Stern.

*B*ack at the hotel, I find five hundred new e-mails and eighteen thousand hits to my website since morning. Some are neutral, some disgustingly rude, most are supportive of what I'm doing.

Before our plane leaves the next day, there is one last stop I have to make.

Satori and I arrive at police headquarters at two P.M. and ask to speak with Sergeant Corrigan, whom I phoned the night before. We are led to a room that looks like it's straight out of a movie, with computers inserted into desks and a large screen showing CNN. Sergeant Corrigan shakes my hand, and says, "It's admirable you came all the way from Los Angeles."

"Yeah, either admirable or insane," I reply. "One psychic swears she saw Chandra locked in a refrigerator. I think she got that from an episode of *The Sopranos*."

He laughs. He likes that one, and apparently so does the man behind him who's looking at me in that way only police officers, detectives, and suspicious spouses do.

"Detective Ward. Call me W.C.," the guy says, firmly shaking my hand. "I'm a straight shooter, been on the force too long to not have heard and seen it all. A psychic who's accurate? You might be, but I've never seen it," he says, leading us into an interrogation room.

"Look, I don't know you, and you don't know me," I tell him. "So let's just begin with a clean slate. You forget your preconceived notions about psychics being loony tunes and I'll forget my preconceived notions about detectives being egotistical dicks."

All right, that's what I would have *liked* to have said.

Instead, I give the guy a reading. A five-minute tirade that turns his face so red, he abruptly excuses himself and leaves the room. He returns with Gerrard, the computer and records specialist in charge of surveying the contents of Chandra's computer and phone records.

I tell them what was found on Chandra's computer that wasn't made public. I speak about a phone conversation before Chandra's disappearance between Mrs. Condit and her. This conversation is later confirmed when phone records reveal a short call from Chandra's cell phone to Gary's apartment at a time when he was at a meeting and only Mrs. Condit was there.

W.C. repeats he doesn't normally believe in psychic stuff, but for some reason, he believes me. What I am telling him makes sense. Even so, I know the moment I leave, W.C. and Gerrard will unravel what I said so it fits into their logical, facts-based mind. Nonetheless, they promise to follow up, check out everything I told them and get back to me in a week.

I return home to find out Cabbie left the photos, duct tape, cement bag, T-shirt, running shoe, all the evidence, at the site. Howard's people call. They don't care about the evidence. They just want me on the show again. I tell them no.

Screw Howard Stern.

Has quite a nice ring to it.

Screw Howard Stern.

Could become my new mantra.

"You're not doing it for Howard," Satori reminds me. "People need to hear what Chandra has to say."

So for the third time in less than a week, I put on my insult-protection gear and spend an hour dodging obscene comments from Howard Stern. Gary Del'Abate, Howard's producer, suggests I give a reading to someone on Howard's staff and record it to play on the air. "Why doesn't she do it with one of our salesmen, someone she can't research," Howard cuts in.

"It doesn't even matter. I'll do it with anybody. Don't even tell me their name," I say.

"You know what's the difference between what you do and what I do?" Howard asks me.

"I make a profound difference in people's lives, Howard. What do you do?"

"I entertain people. I don't claim to have superpowers, which unfortunately, no one does."

"Just because you don't have them, no one does? You have an intelligent audience, so why do you insult them by—"

"I don't have an intelligent audience. My listeners are all idiots!"

He's dug his own grave.

I am finished with Howard Stern.

*T*he next day, I receive a call from Isabelle Hewitt, the community relations manager at Barnes & Noble in Modesto, California, where Chandra's parents live. She says she read about me in the *Modesto Bee* (so that's why Chandra had me write to Michael Doyle!) and wants me to do an event at their store.

I bet Chandra whispered in Isabelle's ear and led her to me. I bet she did the same with my mother's blind date, the one who turns out to be a private investigator. He checks out the guy with the black sedan and reports back that the guy is a lawyer and has four Social Security numbers. Information I promptly fax to Detective Ward.

"What do I do now?" I ask Chandra.

"I'll tell you when you get there," she replies.

On November 30, 2001, I am in Modesto. Our event at Barnes & Noble is packed. People stay for three hours. We leave when the store closes. The next day comes the reason Chandra sent me here. I am a few blocks away from the Levy home, feeling scared that if I knock on the door, I'll have it slammed in my face.

What is Mrs. Levy going to say? "Come in and have some tea and cookies."

"When you get near my house, my mother will come out with our dog and get the mail," Chandra tells me. I quickly repeat it to Satori and our friend, Michael Ames.

We turn down the next street. I hold my breath. We pass several houses until . . . there she is, Mrs. Levy. Walking to her mailbox. A fluffy dog by her side.

"I'm going to be sick, I can't do this."

"Go. Now. You can do it," Satori urges me.

"I can't."

"Can't is a matter of ability. Stop talking yourself out of it. Don't think. Just do it."

My life has become a Nike commercial.

I see Mrs. Levy look our way. "Hide!" I yell, ducking like a crazy person.

Satori and Mike shake their heads. I must do this. I have no choice but to do this. I get out of the car. Mrs. Levy has gone back in the house. I walk toward the front door. "Let your mom know it's okay, Chandra. Make her feel comfortable," I say inside my head.

I ring the bell. Chandra's brother answers, their fluffy dog runs out and starts licking my hand. Next thing I know, Mrs. Levy is standing before me.

"Can I help you?" she asks.

"I'm here in Modesto doing a channeling event, I mailed you a tape," I say in one breath.

"Oh, you sent that tape? I haven't been able to listen. I'm afraid," she giggles nervously.

"I spoke with D.C. detectives regarding your daughter, and I . . ."

"Would you like to come in?"

"What? Oh . . . um . . . sure . . . Okay."

"Are you in Modesto alone?"

"I'm here with my husband. He's in the car."

"He shouldn't sit in the car. Tell him to come in."

"Our friend is with him. He's fine, really."

I enter slowly, wanting to absorb everything. By the door—I see it. The photo we have seen so many times. The one of Chandra wearing a white tank top, leaning on one arm, her head tilted slightly, smiling. It is blown up and framed. Below it are two baskets filled to the brim with opened letters and cards.

"Would you like some hot tea and cake or cookies?" Mrs. Levy asks.

Okay now this is getting strange.

"Just go with it," Chandra tells me. *"Just say what I say."*

I sit at the counter and feel distracted by the newspapers and circulars in disarray.

"Straighten them," Chandra says. *"Sort them into one neat pile."*

No. I will not organize your parent's house.

"I'm normally an open person," Mrs. Levy tells me, placing a cup of tea and some cake in front of me. "Ever since Chandra has been missing . . ." Her voice trails off then abruptly comes back. "You won't believe who called me. Sylvia Browne! Ridiculous. Said she saw Chandra in a white tank top, can you believe? This was after the picture of Chandra in her white top had been on the news for weeks."

Mrs. Levy takes a seat opposite me. "I hung up on Sylvia. It was nonsense, really. Nothing she couldn't have read in the papers."

"I'm not going to tell you anything I could have read in the papers," I assure her.

"Tell me about my father, but wait a sec, I just need to make a call. I want to get someone here, my lawyer, to hear what you have to say, or maybe we could record it."

"I have a tape recorder in the car, I can get it."

"One sec," she says. She calls her lawyer. He's not in. She calls her other lawyer, Andrew Mendlin. He's stepped out. She calls her husband, not available either. She flips through her Rolodex. The phone rings. "Robert, you need to come home. We have a psychic at the house."

I can just imagine her husband thinking—My wife has lost it! The stress has finally taken its toll.

The phone rings again. It's one of her lawyers. "You've got to come to the house," she tells him then covers the mouthpiece, "Lysa, my lawyer is at the eye doctor, but he can be here at six-thirty if you can stay with me until then."

I look at the clock, it's five, and we have an event in Stockton at seven. "I can't," I say.

"Andrew, you need to leave the doctor now. The psychic can't wait." She hangs up the phone and claps her hands excitedly, "He's coming over!"

Her warmth and enthusiasm put me completely at ease, especially since she did not ask me to come here. She did not ask me to channel her daughter. She inspires me.

I do a reading about her father and she confirms what I am saying. During a powerful moment, the doorbell rings and in walks her lawyer, reeking of skepticism. The energy immediately switches from open and receptive to closed and confining.

I look at Mrs. Levy and feel like crying. I feel oddly connected to her.

"How do I know you're not taping this whole thing, that you don't have a hidden camera," asks Mendlin.

"You want to check me?" I say, raising my arms for him to pat me down.

He gives a lingering look and shakes his head no.

I describe everything I've told police about the man with the bushy mustache, Chandra's missing ring and bracelet, the phone call with Condit's wife, the black sedan, the creek, the woods, Chandra's not being in one piece, her being found near Rock Creek Park, and something about . . . I hesitate, glancing at Mrs. Levy, not wanting to upset her.

As if on cue, she gets up to fix some tea, and I whisper to Mendlin, "I got something about finding Chandra's head . . . not attached to her body. You can call E! to get the footage. Everything I said that day is on video."

Satori knocks at the front door and tells me we need to leave soon. Mrs. Levy invites him in and then decides to "test" me, put me through a series of twenty questions, which I explain is not how mediumship works. I tell her I can give only what I receive. I can't make them tell me anything.

"What was Chandra's favorite ice-cream flavor?" she asks, ignoring what I just said.

"My mouth feels like I'm chewing something, gum, it feels like, does that make sense?"

"Yes. Bubble gum ice cream!" Mrs. Levy claps excitedly.

She wants me to do more "tricks"—tell her where Chandra sat at the table, where her bedroom is. I do it, though it feels off. "It's not like that," I tell her. "It's not a game."

We go into Chandra's sparsely decorated bedroom. Remnants of her life: her clothing, a party bag with a blue bow, a few books on the shelf—Kahlil Gibran's *The Prophet* and Shel Silverstein's *Where the Sidewalk Ends*, books I own—a yearbook from University of Southern California, the same university I attended.

Mendlin turns to me, "Because the case is open, I can't confirm what you've told us, but I can confirm you're on track, scary on track." He leans in as if he's about to say something he shouldn't. "You think Gary murdered before?"

"No. It never went this far before, but let me put it this way, when Gary makes a mess, he calls a housekeeper."

Mendlin nods. "That's what I thought."

We're about to leave when Mr. Levy, Chandra's father, walks in the room.

Mrs. Levy runs to him. "Lysa is a psychic who says Chandra is talking to her."

Oh God. How awful that must sound.

"Can you come back tomorrow night?" Mrs. Levy asks us.

"We can't. We're traveling on tour. I really wish we could."

"Just a few more minutes then," she says. "A few more minutes."

We go into the kitchen and once again, Chandra tells me to straighten the messy newspapers. I tell the Levys what Chandra has told me, and Mrs. Levy laughs. "'Mom, you have to clean up this mess. I can't listen to you when it's a mess.' That's what Chandra would say."

I look at Mr. Levy. He is crying. I feel the urge to hug him, and I do.

Mrs. Levy touches my arm, "You know, we still have hope. We still want to think Chandra is alive. We need to believe that."

She didn't have to explain. I understood their need to believe their daughter is alive. I also knew that because of this belief, everything I'd told them would be ignored, denied. It had to be in order to keep their hope of Chandra's safe return, alive.

ONE YEAR LATER

WHAT I SAID IN 2001—WHAT POLICE DISCOVER IN 2002:

JULY 19, 2001   On-camera, I tell Fox News I see Chandra's remains in Rock Creek Park.

MAY 22, 2002   A man's dog finds Chandra's remains in Rock Creek Park.

JULY 30, 2001   I fly to D.C. finding a twisted T-shirt and a woman's running shoe.

MAY 22, 2002   Detectives find a T-shirt, twisted leggings, and a woman's running shoe.

JULY 30, 2001   I tell Howard Stern and E! Chandra is not in one piece, her head isn't attached to her body. Her remains will be found. I say this on over twenty local and national radio and TV shows.

MAY 22, 2002   Chandra's skull is found along with her scattered remains.

JULY 18, 2001   On *Entertainment Tonight* and Fox News, I tell them Chandra was strangled.

JULY 14, 2002   According to her autopsy, the *Washington Post* reports Chandra was strangled.

JULY 18, 2001   I tell *Entertainment Tonight,* "Chandra keeps showing me her missing ring." On the Alan Colmes national radio show, I say, "I see a missing ring, given to Chandra by her mother."

MAY 30, 2002   The *Modesto Bee* and several other papers report that Chandra's missing ring could play a role in solving her death and add that Chandra's mother bought her the ring.

JULY 30, 2001   I tell E!, Chandra keeps talking about her bracelet falling off in the black sedan.

MAY 30, 2002   The *Washington Post* reports police are looking for a gold bracelet Chandra may have been wearing when killed. Her aunt, Linda Zamsky, says Condit bought her the bracelet.

JULY 18, 19, I tell *Entertainment Tonight*, Fox News, and
AND 30, 2001 Howard Stern that Chandra's body has been moved twice, and they will move her once more before she is found.

MAY 22, 2002 A year later, police chief Ramsey would only speculate that Chandra's remains might have been dumped in Rock Creek Park; that it is not where her murder occurred.

couldn't shake the feeling something was fishy. Chandra's running shoe, leggings, and USC top, all found "conveniently" close to her body, as if to suggest a sloppy impulsive killer, not a hired professional.

Condit's lawyer, Mark Geragos, appearing on CNN's *Larry King Live,* said of Condit: "Now they'll be able to completely exonerate him. I believe now that her remains have been found, that it points to a stranger, that it was a predator in that park."

Chandra keeps whispering to me, *"If we put her remains in the park, it will look like she was murdered by a stranger, which will change the investigation from focusing on Gary Condit to focusing on those guys who attacked women in Rock Creek Park around the time I went missing. A perfect distraction."*

A big fat lie.

If I had to do it over again, I would have spent more time in Washington, D.C., searching on my own, following her lead without outside distractions. At the time, I honestly didn't think so much of what I said would turn out to be true. I thought speaking about her missing ring and bracelet and Rock Creek Park and the black sedan, maybe one or two things would prove true, but all of them? No way.

On May 1, 2002, the Levys held a candlelight vigil outside their daughter's former apartment in Washington, D.C., telling reporters they still have faith their daughter is somewhere out there and that she is still alive.

On May 22, 2002, Chandra Levy's remains were found in Rock Creek Park.

JANUARY 5, 2003.

I pick up the phone.

Hang it up.

Pick it up.

Hang it up.

I tell myself to stop being such a chickenshit.

I dial the number. A boy answers.

"Is Susan home?"

"Yeah, one sec, who's calling?"

"Lysa."

"Okay, one sec."

Hang up the phone. Hang it up. Do it while you still have the chance. HANG UP!

"This is Susan."

"Hi. This is Lysa. I came to your house, November of 2001. I did a reading for you."

"Are you Mateu?"

"Yeah."

"I don't really want to talk to you, I'm so sorry, but—"

"I just want to ask you something, and I won't call you again. At your house, when I did a reading about your father and about Chandra, I'm just curious why, when you went on Larry King, you joked about this psychic showing up at your home and talking about the messy newspapers, like it wasn't something Chandra would do, when you and Robert said it was."

"I'm sorry about that," Mrs. Levy says. "I was upset, out of it, not knowing if Chandra was dead or alive, and when I saw the video you sent me, I felt uncomfortable seeing you talk about channeling Chandra, about her being dead a year before her remains were found."

After ten minutes of chatting, out of the blue she asks if I've worked on the Laci Peterson case.

"After what I went through with Chandra, I'm not talking to any-one." I laugh.

"Has Laci contacted you? . . . Did you call the family? What did Laci say?"

I reveal what Laci has told me, and then tell her, "I don't pretend to know what you're going through, what you've been through, but I want you to know Chandra's love for you wouldn't let me walk away. Believe me, I wanted to. I didn't want to have her words bashed by Howard Stern. I didn't want to spend hours with D.C. police only to have them not follow up. If I wanted publicity, I'd work on these cases all the time because, sadly, there are enough to go around. I don't seek out spirits. They come to me, and when they do, I take their request seriously. Chandra had a mission to get through to you, and she wasn't going to give up without a fight."

6

WHAT HAPPENS WHEN WE DIE

Death Approaches.
Instinctively, you fight for your life. That is automatic.
Your body goes limp.
Your heart stops.
No more air flows in or out.
You lose sight, feeling, and movement.
Your ability to hear goes last.
There is no pain the moment of death.
Only silence.
Calm.
Quiet.
And still . . . you exist.

Most people feel afraid around a dead body.
Their first instinct is to panic—then scream—or maybe the other way around. Not many of us remain calm in the face of death, either our own or someone else's. We are taught to fear cemeteries and morgues and bodies that no longer move.

Teachings about burning in hell, skulls, darkness, and eternal damnation; movies depicting spirits coming back to haunt or possess us; being told communicating with spirits is against what God wants, and we've got a nation of people believing something so beautiful, so basic, is wrong.

Let me ask you something, "If God didn't have a problem with you talking to your mother before, why would God have a problem with you connecting with her now?"

It takes courage to question the beliefs we've been handed down.

I questioned the spirits when they first came through. I wasn't this woo-woo kid from New York who played with angels and Native American spirits. I was taught to believe in what I could see, feel, and touch, in the concrete not the invisible, in the obvious not the subtle. I didn't blindly believe. I needed proof the spirit was living long after the body was not.

Every day, people die.

Tragically. Unexpectedly.

They die on their way to the market, on their ride home from school. They die on a plane, a bus, a car, a boat. They die while crossing the street or going for a jog.

Every second in this country, innocent, beautiful, talented, honest, hardworking people who have every right to live—Die.

Death isn't something we speak of openly, either its eventuality or its actuality. Talking about death before it happens seems almost taboo, the way believing that telling what you wished for on a star automatically cancels out your wish. As if talking about our fear of someone dying automatically makes our fear come true.

It doesn't. We are not that powerful.

Yet we sometimes treat death the way we view an anorexic picking at her food. We see her doing it. We know there's a problem, yet acknowledging it would make it real and that scares us, so we remain silent.

We don't speak about so much. We tiptoe through life. We don't tell people they're obese because it would be rude. Instead, we allow them to eat themselves to death.

We don't ask a child whose hair is falling out if they've got cancer because it would be prying. But maybe if we asked they would feel grateful someone is willing to speak to them about it.

We bring pie to our neighbor whose six-year-old daughter was taken from her bedroom. We're worried about saying the wrong thing, so we tell them it's going to be okay when in our heart we know, it's not.

We need never be afraid of connecting with people, either in a body or in spirit.

It doesn't matter how many sessions I do, how much proof I have that people survive death, I still feel loss. I still miss people. I still hate that one day my parents will cross over and I'll miss talking to my dad, keeping him up past his bedtime, laughing about, "Just one more thing I wanna say . . ." I'll miss hanging out with my mom, sharing ideas, hearing her amazing insights about life.

There's this picture in my mind where I'm walking on stage to receive an Academy Award, and my parents, brother, and Satori are by my side. I want them here for it all, and though I know they will be, either in a body or in spirit, it's not the same thing.

I'd never pretend it is.

*S*ometimes we prolong a life. We keep a person on life support long after their brain ceases to function, or we beg them to take medications that make them feel horrible. It's not because the person wants to live, but because we don't want them to die. We're not ready to say good-bye.

A man speaks to me from a coma and tells me his wife is keeping him on life support to hold on to the illusion that breathing means living. She won't give him permission to leave and he no longer wants to stay. He doesn't want to hurt his wife, so he sticks around in a state of limbo, one foot in the material world, the other in the spirit world. I tell him *he* needs to make the decision because his wife never will.

That night, he dies.

Then he tells me how it felt to shed his body. *"I'm dead and I'm not. I shout, and no one tells me to be quiet. I dance, and no one comments on my lack of rhythm. You know how obsessive I was before? I'd rewash clean laundry, just to be sure. Laundry no longer matters, that's a relief, and I'm glad to be rid of that overweight mass of flesh. The suit came off and I'm light as a feather."*

Another man, who's been in a coma for two years, comes through from his coma and describes what happened to him and how much he hates his pajamas.

"They're brown and dirty. I need new pajamas. Yellow ones, with pictures. Bright. Happy pajamas," he tells me. *"She's gotten rid of my suits. My wife doesn't want me to come home."*

The man explains that he doesn't want to go back to fourteen-hour workdays and fighting with his wife. **He wants to live, but not that life.**

"Tell her to buy me bright yellow pajamas: neon. If she refuses, I won't wake up."

It has nothing to do with yellow pajamas. It has to do with feeling wanted and needed.

"I don't know where to buy these yellow pajamas you speak of; it's silly, a grown man in neon pajamas," his wife says.

Two years later, he is still in a coma, hoping his wife will change her mind and buy him yellow pajamas, which will mean she is finally ready for him to come home.

What do spirits do all day?

Are they around us all the time?

What can they see, hear, and know about our lives here?

Where do people go when they cross over? How does it look?

Do they have town houses and condos or do they all just crash on a fluffy cloud?

Can they see everything in our future? Can they change our destiny?

Do they get to meet their favorite celebrities?

Do they fall in love?

Or, as my brother once asked, "Grandma's not watching me have sex, is she?"

"No, David," I tell him. "Grandma didn't suddenly become a pervert when she died."

"I'll tell you when I get there," is what I tell people when they ask for specifics about what happens when we die because no matter what I tell you, until you cross over, you won't truly know.

Although you can instantly confirm your father's name was Ed, he died in a fire, and had a dog with one blue and one brown eye, whether "heaven" is this gorgeous land of vibrant colors, triumphant symphonies, and angelic beings comforting you in a white glow of love, this you cannot immediately confirm.

I've never heard a spirit speak of living on a cloud nine or chilling with the angels or being engulfed in the flames of hell or getting a prize for being a perfect Christian. Out of all the readings I have ever done, not once did a spirit show themselves as being anywhere but *here*.

Here—where we are—just on a different level of here.

"We live in wavelengths far in excess of the speed of light," a spirit teaches me. *"When we speak, it's not like ordinary speech of which you are accustomed. You need to adapt your hearing to connect with our speaking.*

Just as a dog hears a higher frequency of sound, you must begin to hear on many levels, begin to listen with your entire being.

"Listen to what others may not hear. You do this by quieting your noisy mind and jotting down the words that come to you. You may feel a buzzing in your right ear or a tingling on your cheeks. Listen and relay on a pad or into a recorder only what you hear, see, and feel.

"You must remember you are energy, a form of vibration resonating on a lower level than spirits. When you die, your body goes through a transition where your soul begins vibrating at a higher level, while your body, the dense matter, gets thrown away, and whether it's put in the dirt or cremated does not matter because your soul remains whole and intact.

"You cannot harm, destroy, or wound the human spirit. How your body looks at its final stage has no correlation to the shape your spirit is in when it crosses over. The shape of your spirit is always determined by how you lived, the kind of person you were, before you died."

Why do some people feel a loved one's spirit while others feel and experience nothing?

"No one is unvisited by their loved one's spirit—but all must learn how to know their loved one is around. Denial, and the need for big proof, stops many from experiencing a spirit's presence. 'It takes what it takes' also applies to how hard a spirit must work to get through to you."

When you're dealing with a devastating loss, the last thing you want to hear is, "I see a pink glow from a spirit behind you."

Whose spirit is it? How did they die? Come on. Don't insult me by giving me fluff when my heart feels broken. This is not about perfection. It's about honoring people by giving them a straightforward, integrity-filled reading with facts they can instantly verify.

I, like everyone else, expected things to be easier when we "died." I didn't want death to be a continuation of this life. I wanted to win this grand prize trip to paradise. Like if you missed the entire point of living, you'd get the Motel 6 version; but if you contributed to others, gave of yourself, loved, laughed, and learned, you'd get the MGM Grand.

"You people have a fantasy of heaven being a place where your soul is resting, eternally at peace. How boring! Who would want to hang out forever with nothing important to do?"

When I tell people that spirits are just on another level of here, they sometimes get upset, as though I'm ruining their idealized version of what happens when we die.

"It sounds so unevolved," a guy tells me. "My dad still going to basketball games."

If he loved basketball before he died, why wouldn't he continue loving it after?

The only reason we want life to get better when we die is because we're too damn lazy to make it better while we're here. I know that sounds harsh, but it's true. We need to rest when we die because we don't give ourselves permission to rest now. We need death to free us from our pain because we don't know how to do that for ourselves while we're alive.

Finding out life continues endlessly, indefinitely, brings up enormous anger for those who've been under the impression that once they died all their problems would go away.

Just think about it; if death were the end, it would be a horribly shitty deal. If we got three, five, twenty-five, seventy-five, or however many years on this earth and then—POOF—standing at the corner buying a bag of peaches, a car hits you, that's it, time's up!

No more you, never again, for infinity. That would suck.

I remember when I asked my Dad how long infinity lasted, and he told me, "Forever."

"How long is that?" I was only six, so he knew I was not gonna let this one go.

"Forever is . . . always, never ending. It's forever," he said, hoping the answer would suffice.

"Okay, Daddy, thanks," I said and went to Mommy to ask the same question.

"Infinity is my love for you," she told me. "It goes on and on and on and on . . ."

I used to drive myself crazy thinking that when you died you remained dead forever. I couldn't picture in my mind how long forever lasted. I couldn't comprehend it.

*P*eople are at the farmers market less than eight minutes from my house. I go there all the time. I could've easily been there yesterday. Ten minutes before closing, a man plows through the crowd, his car out of control, bodies flying, people shrieking; seconds earlier, a mother looks away from her two-year-old in the stroller to pay a vendor for some fruit. Next time she looks back, her baby is gone. Dead. Just like that.

She had no idea when she went to buy fruit that day it would be her baby's last.

And when a woman named Sara Anne thanked God for her blessings in the morning, she didn't know that before dusk she'd be cursing him out.

"I was thanking God while running on the treadmill," Sara Anne recalls. "I was thinking how lucky I am. My two daughters got into college. My son travels to Italy next month to pursue his dream of being an architect. My husband and I celebrated our twenty-third wedding anniversary. I'm forty-eight. I look like dynamite. I'm truly blessed."

Four hours later, Sara Anne's world fell apart.

Her eighteen-year-old daughter Kayla was killed by a drunk driver.

"I will destroy the irresponsible fool who took my child's life. I will obliterate whoever did this!" Sara Anne screamed at God.

Until she found out the drunk driver's name . . . and then she changed her mind.

The driver was her seventeen-year-old daughter, Lai, who'd drunk a little whiskey and swallowed a few pills before picking up Kayla from dance class. With Bon Jovi's "Blaze of Glory" blasting on the stereo, the two sisters belted out the song at the top of their lungs as Lai swerved around a sharp curve, lost control of the wheel, and rammed her brand-new Mazda into a telephone pole.

Kayla's body propelled through the windshield and plummeted into a ditch where Lai, unscathed, found her sister's lifeless body drenched in blood.

"I watched myself dying. I heard Lai scream. She looked at me and cried about how much she'd miss me, and please don't go, and I'm thinking, 'How can she miss me? I'm right here.' It was excruciating knowing I was right beside her and she had no idea."

Life can change in an instant . . . and spirits have to deal, just as we do, with not getting to say good-bye, with seeing people they love in extreme grief, and with not knowing what happens next.

"This sucks," Kayla tells me. *"I won't lie. At first, I hated being dead, hated going to college with other dead kids and seeing my family grieve over me being gone and me being right there and them not knowing it. The whole deal sucked, and for a long time I was angry. I didn't want to see my relatives who died. I didn't want to see people living, having a blast. I wanted to be left alone. It's been a while now and I'm used to my new body. Yes, I still have a body. It's not like you get to choose the model—5'8" blonde, big breasts—I should be so lucky. You have the one you would've had if you hadn't gotten stitches in your head or broken your leg skiing. And FYI,—time does not heal—not in spirit or in a body. What you do with your time either heals you or holds you back, I learned that watching my family. My mom is healing because she working on herself, but Lai is a total wreck, drinking, drugging, killing herself in so many ways. The passage of time did not heal my sister. It healed my mother because of what she did with her time to help herself heal."*

To heal is to make ourselves whole in spite of the losses we've endured. Instead of waiting for time to heal us, we can ask ourselves, "How do I want to feel about this person? How do I want to feel, period? How can I honor them? How can I live my life so they feel proud of me? How can I live so I feel proud of me? What can I take from their crossing to strengthen my soul? How can I be nice to me right now?"

To miss someone presupposes they're not around.

Spirits are around, but they still miss connecting with you in the way they once did.

They see what's going on in your life and hear your thoughts and know your joy as well as your pain, but they cannot interfere with your free will. Believe me, if they could, they would prevent a lot of people from doing a lot of stupid stuff.

"Life and death are like night and day, they occur one after the other, over and over again. We do everything we did while living except without the confines of the material world. We live by one basic rule in the spirit world, which I call Basic Decency 101—you treat people like shit, you feel like shit. You treat people kindly (including yourself), you get to have the whole shebang. What's the whole shebang? Living and dying a happy life."

"We still experience everything you do just not in the way you do. It's like having a vivid dream of being on vacation in the tropics. When you wake in the morning, you have to stop for a moment and think, 'Did that really happen? It felt so real.' The material world feels real to you, but once you die you will see how real the spirit world is. It's as real as everything you see, feel, touch, smell, taste, and experience. It's another world within this world."

The premise of the spirit world is: *"It's not what you had, but how you lived that determines the level on which you'll reside when you cross over."*

And ten Hail Marys do not instantly reverse a life of hypocrisy, judgment, and cruelty. You can't get better accommodations by shouting a quick, "Forgive me, Jesus" or giving a last-minute confession of your sins.

The one you'll have to face is yourself.

"When you cross over, you step into the shoes of those you've harmed and feel the pain you put them through. You also feel the love you shared and how it touched people's lives. You see the beauty inside your soul and cry at the self-doubt you fed yourself. When you take a good look at yourself and learn from what you see, then you are free."

Other spirits tell me what happens when we die. . . .

"We are the same in spirit as we were in a body, but each individual spirit is attracted to the conditions he or she prepared for while living. The

life we led, the actions we took, the love we shared or did not share, our deeds and the intention behind our deeds contribute to where we live when we die."

"The journey always continues. Time is continuous, as is life. Time only feels separated because humans need to put things in boxes, into seconds, minutes, hours, days, weeks, months, years, so they can manage their life."

"If, for example, you were a great musician on the earth, then you will be attracted to like-minded folk and spend your time learning and playing with them. If you were a murderer, you will spend your time reflecting upon, rectifying, and making amends for the pain you caused others. You know you've learned from your mistakes when you no longer repeat them."

"In the material world, there are locations one can choose to live based on economic status, but in the spirit world, souls reside based on their spiritual, not religious, growth and development."

"The universe is one. We are not in another place, but in another state of consciousness. We do not move aimlessly, back and forth between your world and the next. There is but one world and in this world, many levels of existence."

They tell me we don't automatically stay with the person we were married to before we cross over.

"Only if the love is real do you remain connected when you die. If you wanted a divorce but never got one, believe me, when you die you'll be divorced from that person and have to face what kept you in the relationship so long. Circles of souls are connected and reincarnate together, which is why you can feel as though you've known someone for lifetimes after meeting for only a couple of minutes. You have known them. You need to trust yourself about that. We fall in love just as you fall in love. We experience everything you do. The only difference is, without the material body."

"You can contact those who were famous in a body, but remember, spirits will not come if the intentions of the person are not pure. Why should they? You would not knock on an enemy's door only to have your face spat in and your existence denied. If you are an artist with an intense obses-

sion with Van Gogh, yes, calling upon Van Gogh for inspiration, guidance, even a bit of talent will assure his granting of your request. But if simply for ego gratification, you desire to just see if John Lennon will come through, of course, everything is possible, but why, dear God, would he spend his time speaking with someone whose desire is so trite rather than someone whose musical ability and desire to serve others calls upon his inspiration."

When an actor plays the role of a deceased icon, whether it's Val Kilmer portraying Jim Morrison, Jennifer Lopez as Selena, or Denzel Washington as Malcom X, I am certain the icon's spirit is around, influencing them, bringing their soul and essence to the role.

"For a famous person to come through to someone they did not know prior to crossing over, there has to be a link. Having something in common is essential. Whether you share a talent, a passion in life, or it's inspiration you need, as in the case of an actor's portrayal in a film, a famous person needs a reason to come through to you."

So if spirits can offer us insight and inspiration and help us tap into our gifts and abilities—if they can pass on what they've learned—then nothing is ever wasted. The cycle of life is continuous, and each evolution of the cycle is improved upon. At least, that's the goal.

"If you want to live in a world where kids don't have to worry about being shot during recess and murderers don't push heroes out of the headlines, you need to drastically change your thinking now. Energy is the source of life, and mental energy is wasted by fearing things that may never come to pass. By having an out before you're even in, by preparing for the worst but not for the best, and by waiting your entire life for the other shoe to drop, and then crossing over and realizing, 'There was no other shoe,' you'll have wasted all that time worrying about the goddamn shoe!"

As I listen to spirits, absorb everything they have to say, I notice a twinge of doubt in my gut. I'm feeling uncertain if everything they are saying is actually true. I should already know, right? Have no more questions or doubts about the spirit world being real.

I could say the same thing about Kurt Cobain. After performing to thousands of dedicated fans, he should've known how loved and important he was.

Instead, he took a rifle to his chin and blew himself away.

How can we have so much evidence yet remain so blind?

I dump forty-five video and audiotapes from my channeling events and TV shows on my bed, and I start watching and listening—one after the other—stopping, replaying, transcribing. I listen to my radio shows, analyzing every word. I listen to old session tapes, going over what I brought through and what the spirits said. And after endless hours of listening, viewing, digesting, dissecting, I can no longer deny what has now become embarrassingly obvious.

What happens when we die is that we don't.

7

September 11, 2001

*I*n late August, Satori and I fly to Stockholm, Sweden, where he was born and raised, for a much-needed summer vacation. I tell the spirits I will be available only for emergencies. To my delight, they oblige. A few days before we're set to return home, I start feeling sad for no reason. On the verge of tears. Edgy. Uncomfortable.

I have felt this way before, but it usually comes from things happening to me, inside me, things I can pinpoint, like getting my period or not getting enough sleep.

This feels like sadness has attached itself to me and won't let go.

I shop, hoping the sadness will get bored with my inattention and go away.

It doesn't. It follows me everywhere.

"I'm thirsty," I tell Satori. "I'm going to get some water at the candy store."

Inside, people are gathered around a small TV, watching an action film. A man runs for cover behind a car. A woman is choking. People are screaming. Their faces are covered with thick white debris. A building is burning. Total chaos.

"Is that the *Towering Inferno*?" Satori asks, joining me inside. "I loved that film."

"It's New York City," the man behind the counter tells us.

What is this guy talking about? He must be mistaken. That *cannot* be New York.

"Two airplanes hit the Trade Center—*on purpose*," he says.

It doesn't register. Not fully. It won't until I come face-to-face with those tragically affected by the events on that horrific day.

ovel.

Iced tea.

Sunglasses.

Bikini.

Fluffy towel.

I am all set to relax.

I lie on the chaise, inhaling the fresh air.

The sunshine renews me. It is going to be a great day.

I close my eyes and take a deep breath.

It is then—I hear it.

"I am on a plane, flying through the air. I see a city below . . . too close . . . the plane accelerates . . . faster and faster . . . people scream . . . I'm screaming. . . . Before we hit the building . . . I close my eyes, automatically. Next time I open them . . . I'm dead."

I open my eyes. Look around the pool. Satori is hanging out with my brother, chatting to him about our trip to Sweden. No one else but a little kid, and a grumpy-looking man, is seated around me. "Go away. I'm off duty," I whisper, and close my eyes once again.

A moment passes—and then . . .

"I am crashing, screaming, crying, praying—to God, Jesus, Mary, Joseph, I love you, PLEASE, NO, STOP, OH GOD, HELP ME, HELP US!! I DON'T WANT TO DIE!!"

I bolt upright. I look at my hands—soaked with sweat. There are goose bumps on my arms. I am freezing, sweating, freezing, sweating. I know a spirit is around. I desperately want him to go away. I am tired. I need a rest. Who is he? Why is he here? I have no idea.

To my right, I see a woman reading a magazine. All her stuff is laid out around her, but for some reason, I didn't notice her until now. She looks up at me. I get this zingy feeling in my gut, and I know . . . the man . . . is for her.

"Who are you?" I ask him.

He tells me he is her husband, tells me about why she's here on vacation, about what this place means to her, about how he died, tells me so much until I am left with no choice but to face the frightening task of approaching this woman with information too personal for a stranger to know.

I inch my way over, taking an inconspicuous seat at a table beside her. Just as I am about to speak, an older woman approaches. She embraces the woman, who immediately begins to cry. I overhear the woman explain how she remembers making her kids breakfast and complaining to her husband about having to take his shirts to the cleaners and complaining to him about not spending enough alone time together. Complaining . . . And then, "I love you." She said it without thinking.

Her husband tells me, *"She was always nervous about saying I love you to me. Was afraid I wouldn't say it back. Even when I would tell her how much I love her, she would often hold back, nodding and smiling, not fully letting me know how much she cared. For some reason that morning, she glanced at the coffee-stained calendar on our kitchen wall, saw the date—September 11—and then, just said it. I love you. No holding back."*

At this point, I am in a state of shock, unsure of what to do, not wanting to ask Satori for advice because I know he'll say, "Give what you get. Information is received in order to pass it on." I try to talk myself out of it, tell myself it's late and I'm tired and I can leave her a note, anything but confronting her and telling her what I've received.

I hate being a chickenshit. I hate not going forward. I hate holding myself back out of fear of what she might say, how she may react, whether or not she'll get angry.

At this point, the woman is a wreck, hysterically crying. I can't go up to her. I explain this to her husband. He must understand one has to be ready to receive information from the spirit world. I can't hammer it over her head. "She's not into this 'spirit talk' stuff, is she?"

I see a flash of the film *The Sixth Sense,* then I see this woman walking out.

So why are you here if she's not ready to receive this? I silently ask him.

"Just hanging out. Letting her feel me around her. Laughing at her denial of my presence. Attempting to have her know I am okay, truly, okay. I wasn't. But now I am."

He explains how, at the moment of impact, there was no pain. None. Not a stick of pain or anguish, not in the physical sense. The pain came from the death of his life that would no longer be with the woman he loved. Thousands of people in pain at the same time, mourning the loss of their life, as they once knew it. Not wanting to be where they now were, and not being able to change that fact. He describes the horror of opening his eyes, and being dead, of seeing the people he loves, and them not seeing him.

I know the only way to truly validate what I am receiving is to give the information to a person who can validate it, which is this woman, who is not ready to receive it, which means I must sit with it, trust it, and know there is a higher reason for this encounter.

"There is a higher reason, isn't there?" I ask him.

He doesn't answer. I must come up with the reason myself. I decide that it means to never leave a person I love without telling them I love them.

I look up and see the woman gathering her things, walking away. She leaves only one item under her chaise. A newspaper. Once she is out of view, I pick up the paper, and on the front page is a memorial to those who died on September 11.

Many months would pass before another spirit who "died" on September 11 would come through and as with the first, catch me completely off guard.

I am in my cousin's bedroom in Freehold, New Jersey, staring at a dusty champagne glass covered with wax, wondering why parents leave their kids' bedrooms exactly as they were. Satori pops in and tells me I have a reading with a lady named Julie Uman, who'll be calling in five minutes. I quickly get myself ready by focusing my thoughts outside myself and opening my mind to connect with the spirits. The phone rings, and Julie asks, "Is he proud of me?"

I bring through her husband, who tells me his name is Jonathan and shows me a celebration instead of a funeral. He thanks his wife for that. "He loved hearing people forget all his flaws and focus only on what's great about him," she laughs.

As I'm channeling Jonathan, I'm staring at the wallpaper which has pictures of old airplanes with dates underneath. I feel like Russell Crowe in the film *A Beautiful Mind,* when he tries to decode numbers for the CIA by noticing the ones that illuminate more brightly than others. One plane illuminates for me. The date underneath is 1921.

I know spirits look around, asking, *"What can I make Lysa focus on to show her what I want to say? The wallpaper, I'll make Lysa notice it."* A picture is worth a thousand words.

"I want you to erase the 2 and move the 1 in its place," Jonathan tells me.

I move around the numbers. Immediately—I know.

"Jonathan tells me he was in the Trade Center above the hundredth floor."

"Yes," Julie whispers. "One hundred and fifth, North Tower."

I continue channeling, bringing through personal details. It feels like couples therapy, with lots of healing and honesty going on. Then, right before we end, Jonathan says to me: *"Let her know I got the message, the one she sent before I . . ."*

"Yes, my e-mail. I pressed send the exact minute the first plane hit—8:45 A.M. In the subject line I wrote: ILY—I LOVE YOU . . . I'm glad he got it."

Later, Julie confirms how the week before September 11, she felt so sick she took a pregnancy test and even told Jonathan something bad was going to happen. She figured it had to do with his job, which he assured her was secure.

"Monday, September 10th, was Jonathan's first day at work after us being on vacation," Julie recalls. "He got home around eight and was standing in the kitchen eating leftovers I'd prepared, and for some reason, I couldn't stop staring at him. He was wearing this French blue shirt and was tan and I thought, He is so handsome. He was eating these chicken wings we both love and I was like, God, he is just so beautiful. I couldn't stop staring.

"A voice in my head said, 'Tell him . . . Tell him how handsome he is.'

"I didn't.

"At 8:45 the next morning, I sent the e-mail, and the sick feeling I'd had mysteriously disappeared. I went about my day, cleaning the house, thinking about how nice it'll be having a cozy dinner with Jonathan and the kids. A few minutes later, Jonathan's dad calls me and says, 'Turn on the TV!' I turn it on, see the World Trade Center, and right away I know . . . Jonathan is dead.

"In that moment, I switched gears. It was this thing in my head that said, 'Jonathan's dying . . . Oh, my son can't see this! "Come on honey, let's go see what's on PBS. Oh look, it's *Sesame Street*. Okay, Mommy will be right back." '

"I go into the kitchen.

"Turn on the TV.

"Jonathan's dying.

"What the fuck!"

Julie tells me she went into this mode of, "How can I honor Jonathan? How can I best celebrate his life?" She has had hard days, torturous, angry, frustrated, sad, overwhelmed, pissed-off days. But when she connected with him, when she really felt Jonathan was talking through me, his personality and everything he is coming through, it began to heal her.

Although she still misses him very much, she now feels more at peace.

"From the moment Jonathan died, I thought the least I could do was raise him two happy, healthy great kids, and I'd be damned if I let fucking Osama bin Laden take that away!"

am in the kitchen preparing a salad when a guy shows up, dressed quite neatly. He's peering over my shoulder, observing my cucumber-cutting technique. I feel he wants to give advice but he remains silent, which is obviously not easy for him to do.

Who are you here for? I silently ask him.

"Ron Gilligan."

Are you Ron?

"Yes."

Hi, Ron.

"Hello."

You always early, Ron?

"I am."

That's good. My dad is always early. He gets to the airport three hours before a flight.

Ron is a charming guy. He's extremely private and funny; a family man. He tells me he wants to protect his wife from all the *"vultures out to exploit her story."* I ask him what he means, and just as he's about to answer, the phone rings.

"She's late, my wife. Two minutes late. She should have rung you earlier."

"Ron arrived early," I tell Liz Gilligan, his wife.

"That's just like Ron. How is he?" she asks.

"He wants to take over the reading. He's got it all mapped out, knows exactly what to cover. If I do as he tells me, we'll be fine. He wants to get going. Not waste any time."

"That's definitely him," she laughs.

"Are you prepared?" Ron whispers.

For what?

"Say you are."

I am. . . . For what?

It's too late—I'm already with him, seeing what he went through, stepping into the last moments of his life. "I keep seeing big pieces of . . . whether it's cement or . . . He makes me feel like . . . um, I don't know if I . . . He wants me to describe things that are quite graphic," I tell her.

"That's okay, I'd rather know."

"I'm being crushed, specifically my arm, detached. His soul is out fast. You must know his soul is out fast. There is hysteria and panic, but he uses humor to get people to lighten up."

"He would do that, yes."

"I am furious at the ineffectiveness of others! I was yelling for people to get a grip, to stop screaming, as though screaming would help. Bloody hysteria. Some gave up, surrendered, but not me. I would never surrender! I fought till the end, tell her I fought to survive!"

"That's right. He would fight. He never gives up on anything," Liz laughs.

Ron tells me he's furious he "died." Horrified his daughter was the first to find out. His anger isn't explosive, it's contained, bottled up; it makes his cheeks red. That's how he felt before he crossed over. He didn't want to go, desperately did not want to leave his wife and kids. He did not have a choice, and that angers him more than anything.

"He died on September 11th," I tell Liz after Ron shows me the Trade Center.

"Yes, he did," Liz confirms.

On September 11, their daughter Ashley, who was in her last year of high school, had been late for class. She ran into her homeroom and saw the entire class watching the disaster on TV. "The plane just hit the first tower, the one where Ron worked," Liz recalls after her reading. "I was home washing breakfast dishes when she called me, hysterically crying.

"I ran into the den, put on the TV and saw the plane sticking out of the building. To say I felt kicked in the stomach is an understatement. A mixture of shock, disbelief, and powerlessness came over me. I frantically called Ron's cell phone, his office phone; I paged him but received nothing.

"I could see the plane hit beneath Ron's floor, 103, and was hopeful he might actually make it out. But when the North Tower fell, I knew I'd never see Ron again.

"The rest of the day was a blur. My friends later told me I said, 'Ron will be home soon and I'm sure he'll be starving, he usually is.'

"I wanted answers, regardless of how painful they might be to hear. I knew in my heart Ron had suffered and his confirming exactly what occurred helps me deal with that. I'd rather know than wonder. I now feel acceptance and relief. Your talking about his love of privacy and his humor, that's absolutely Ron. While he was funny and outgoing, he was extremely private and would guard that voraciously."

Prior to September 11, Liz had been studying for her masters in social work and had just completed a post-traumatic stress disorder course and was about to begin a class called crisis intervention on, of all days, September 11.

"I felt strangely prepared for his crossing," Liz tells me, and then relays a dream she had. "On Saturday, September 8, 2001, I woke up from having a terrible dream Ron had died. How or why wasn't clear. His sisters and brothers were crying, asking repeatedly why this had to happen. They were saying, 'If only you'd stayed in the U.K.,' because we'd moved back to the States not long before. The next morning, I told Ron about the dream and he laughed it off and said, 'Nothing's going to happen to me.'"

I thought about how Julie had felt ill a week before September 11, and even asked Jonathan about losing his job. She took a pregnancy test, but was unable to shake off her feeling of impending doom.

And now . . . Liz's dream.

At first, Liz was hard on herself; she thought if only she'd listened to her dream, probed it more deeply, she might have saved her husband's life. "Let me tell you something," I tell her. "If your instincts told you without a doubt Ron would die if he went to work that day, you would've handcuffed him to a chair and forced him to stay home.

"If you had known differently, you would have done differently.

"If you had known for sure, you'd never have let him go.

"But you didn't.

"You don't.

"None of us do."

As a psychic, I can tell you many details about what will happen, and still, that won't prevent every disaster from happening. It won't keep everyone from dying.

Getting people to follow even the simplest advice isn't easy, so just imagine giving them warnings that interrupt their plans, their schedules, their habitual patterns of living.

Some would listen. Many would not.

Most of us don't believe something until after it occurs. Until we can look back and say, "Now I know why I was feeling so sad."

We are not meant to jump from base to base, making sure our other foot never touches the ground. We are not meant to prevent, or even foresee, every traumatic occurrence in life.

Later, Julie tells me her husband's bank statement showed he took out money from the ATM fifteen minutes before the first plane hit.

A split second changes our life . . .

I thought about those who canceled their flights or were fired from their jobs and because of that, lived. We can learn to deal with what happened, with what is, but not with what shouldn't have happened or wouldn't have happened if only . . . We cannot rewind time.

We can choose what to take with us, and what to leave behind. What to remember and what to forget. We can decide to focus on how our loved one lived, or on how they died.

Both Julie and Liz confessed to feeling guilty for feeling good, especially at grief support meetings where people were in unbearable pain. Julie and Liz certainly had their share of torturous days, but if they felt happy when others felt bad, that's when the guilt kicked in. It stopped when they learned that remembrance and celebration, not prolonged grief and suffering, signify how much you love someone, how much they mean to you.

Healing takes time. Sometimes you feel healed and then—there it is again, the pain. It comes and goes, sometimes going more than coming, sometimes coming more than it goes.

Liz's pain came back each time she visited Ground Zero. "I went a week after it happened. . . . I'll never forget it. We were driven by the police and given masks to wear. There was ash and smoke everywhere, like a movie set or a nuclear war would seem. I remember the smell—a mixture of burning oil and dust, and even though people were working around the site, there was an eerie silence. Seeing what was left of the WTC was indescribable, and knowing Ron was buried among the wreckage was heartbreaking. I hated what had become a spectacle. Tourists lining up to take photos while people posed making bunny ear gestures. I wanted to scream my fucking head off at them. I went one more time . . . and then never went back again."

On December 27, 2001, Satori and I go to Ground Zero.

While I am staring at the displays of cards, flowers, photos, personal items, handwritten notes and drawings . . . with tourists elbowing me, nudging me to hurry so they can have a look, I see a woman crying, clutching a photo of a girl.

"I'm here," the girl whispers, *"Don't cry, Mom. I'm here."*

The woman tapes the girl's photo next to a child's drawing of a happy family signed by Willis, age 5, for his dad, "the bravest man in the world."

As the woman turns to leave, her elbow brushes mine. We lock eyes for a split second and I am back to seven years old, standing at the edge of the water beside a mother who's just called God a bastard for taking away her son.

I step away from the crowd, my feet frozen; a gust of wind chills my ears.

As I turn to leave something tells me to look back, so I do, and I see it—exactly the way I'd pictured it to be. It's so beautiful it makes me smile.

Among the crowd of spectators and grieving family members and friends, I see spirits. Fixing photos, reading letters, touching shoulders, whispering. Some want to come back. Some are glad to "be gone." And one does the funniest thing I have ever seen.

In front of the display, there is a large pile of money—twenties, tens, fives, and singles. Nothing holds the money down, and no one touches a cent. The strong winds don't blow it away. I noticed this earlier and thought, How odd. How does the money stay like that?

Now, I know.

I see him—the banker—guarding the funds.

I laugh to myself, thinking, If anyone tries stealing a dollar, this banker spirit will find a way to get the money back. He worked in finance. He's still working in finance.

8

Touring with the Dead

AD·VEN·TURE

Noun

An exciting or extraordinary event or series of events

An undertaking involving uncertainty and risk

A risky or speculative financial undertaking

Verb

To risk saying something that other people may
disagree with or find offensive

To dare to go somewhere new or engage in something dangerous

It is three in the morning when Satori suggests we do it.

I don't remember saying yes, but he tells me I did.

The next morning, a map of the United States is sprawled across the kitchen table, and Satori is asking me to point out the places I'd like to go. "For what?" I ask.

"Your tour," he replies.

"I don't want to just go to big cities," I tell him. "I want to visit places authors rarely go."

My theory was, if it has a bookstore, it has people who read.

My dad, the accountant, adds up the numbers and tells us that leaving town for fifty-six days, driving twelve thousand miles to do free events in thirty-four cities, paying for our own hotels, gas, and food, plus paying our fixed expenses at home, wasn't the wisest business decision. "The cost of traveling alone will put you heavily in debt."

It's advice any normal person would follow, but I remind him, "Dad, I talk to dead people for a living, that right there takes me out of the running for normalcy."

Satori comes up with the idea of asking hotels to donate rooms. He says that since we have a nonprofit organization and are doing free events that serve the community, they'd be happy to oblige. He says if I write the letters, he'll do the follow-up calls.

I think about what a great team we are. When we got married on January 3, 1995, we made a pact to spend every night together. We said unless it was absolutely urgent, we'd never be apart, and eight years later, we've kept our deal.

For the past year, we've been living on faith and action alone. Funding our business without a loan; booking all our own channeling events, media appearances, and private sessions. And now it was up to me to convey our passion to a bunch of hotel managers.

I write to the Marriott, Radisson, Embassy Suites.

Five days later, we've got rooms donated for 90 percent of our tour.

Much of our planning is done by instinct and by asking common-sense questions like, What do we need for the tour? Posters, brochures, books, flyers, CDs, a headset and cordless microphone, speakers, maps, batteries, clothing, dog food, computer, cell phone, tape recorder, video camera . . .

We're burning CDs, pressing on labels, printing flyers and brochures.

Three weeks before we're set to leave, we realize we won't be able to fly as originally planned. We've got too much stuff, and plus, our dog insists on joining us.

We opt to drive, which would be perfect if we hadn't already booked our events based on flying. Now, we have to drive from Los Angeles past Ohio, Indiana, and Missouri to get to Massachusetts, then drive back to Ohio, Indiana, and Missouri, then to Alabama, North Carolina, and so on, until we make our way through Georgia and Florida before driving home.

"It'll be fun," Satori assures me. "An adventure!"

"Remind me of that when I'm tired, hungry and I have to pee, but we're in the middle of nowhere so you stop on the side of the freeway where some trucker whistles as I drop my pants."

*M*onths of planning, scheduling, booking, promoting, printing, publicizing is about to be put to the test. We decide we aren't going to get distracted by whether a lot of people show up at events or very few, or by whether the posters are displayed in the front of the store, or not at all. First and foremost, we are going to have fun.

Some people tell me I'm just lucky. But it's not luck, I tell them. Doing what I love is a decision I made. Many years ago I promised myself that no matter what, even if it meant having no money, no security—and by the way, Satori and I kept a bank statement that said zero—I made the decision to do what I love because the alternative stank.

I worked as a waitress all through college and I used to have breakdowns in the bathroom of California Pizza Kitchen, where I'd be like, "What am I doing with my life!" I'd serve the pizza thinking, I don't want to serve you pizza! I don't want to do this anymore!

It had nothing to do with the pizza.

It had to do with this voice inside of me, this monkey on my back urging me not to settle. I wanted out of waitressing because the thought of playing small felt excruciatingly painful.

I knew if I were to inspire others I first needed to inspire myself, so I created a list of things I would no longer tolerate, like listening to negativity, or focusing on what could go wrong instead of right, or letting fear stop me from doing what I love.

Oprah could have allowed the abuse she'd endured to stop her from reaching millions. The Rolling Stones or U2 could have kept playing music in their garage. MTV could have remained an idea in the mind of its founder. It didn't because he had the guts to gamble on something he had absolutely no proof would work.

These are my thoughts while I'm driving across country.

Actually, Satori is doing all the driving and Siobhan, our dog, is doing all the snoring, and I am the entertainment. My lineup includes singing off-key, telling silly jokes, and pondering the big questions of life, such as, "Honey, how does the moon stay up in the sky?" which I ask Satori at four A.M.

In between entertaining, I peer into cars beside us. In a black van with tinted windows and a bumper sticker that reads, "Your kid may be an honor student but you're still an idiot," a bald guy eats a burrito and doesn't bother wiping the grease from his stubby chin. He catches me looking at him. I laugh and point to the chunk of tomato wedged between his front teeth.

He picks it out, swallows it and smiles.

I smile back.

A moment of connection.

I think about how every place is saturated with memories of what occurred there.

Every person's life leaves an imprint in this world.

I think of this as I doze off. The next time I open my eyes, we're there.

We arrive in Peabody, Massachusetts, an hour before our first event.

It's snowing. It's cold. It's late. We're tired. We carry our stuff into the store, and immediately our mood changes. The place is packed. The people are warm. The event is extraordinary.

We go on to Braintree, Massachusetts, then Salem, New Hampshire, and Westport, Connecticut. An event a night for the first few weeks.

In Glastonbury, Connecticut, I do a reading for a young woman and there is a moment where I say to myself, "Please don't be her parents," because the woman is so young and I don't want her parents to be dead. "Someone tried to convince them not to take their car," I tell her. "Yes," she says. "My parents' friends suggested taking one car, but they refused."

I hear the name "*Lauren*" in my right ear and I tell her.

"Lauren is my name," she says.

I mentally ask Lauren's mom how many people were in the car with them.

"*There were four,*" she tells me.

Family members?

"*Friends.*"

You all die?

"*We all die.*"

I'm right in the middle of telling this to Lauren when a store employee cuts in and says, "I'm sorry to interrupt, but you'll need to wrap up. It's getting late."

What is she talking about? It's the afternoon and this woman's parents were killed and I'm channeling them and I need to wrap things up? I ignore her and try to continue.

I can't. And right there in front of everyone, I start crying. I feel so sad this woman lost her mom and dad. I want to tell her they're just on vacation, they're not really dead.

"We're not," her mother tells me.

Lauren was once able to see you and touch you and hold you, and now, she cannot.

"It doesn't matter. She knows we're here."

It's not the same thing.

"Do you believe in heaven?"

As a state of mind, I do.

"And hell?"

Hell is Lauren's pain.

"She needs to write; tell her this."

I tell Lauren what her mother has said. She smiles and she hugs me, and I cry and she cries, and she says she'll keep in touch, and I tell her to please do.

Months later, Lauren sends me a thank-you note along with a website for her newly published book of poetry about the emotional journey she experienced after the sudden death of her parents. In the front of the book, a caption describes that on Friday, June 4, 1999, a tragic automobile accident took the lives of Lauren's parents along with four of their dearest friends. A man driving a Mercedes-Benz, going approximately seventy-five to eighty miles per hour, crashed into them.

'm emotionally drained and starving after our Glastonbury event. It's late, and the only place open is Dennys, which we're about to enter until we spot a twenty-four-hour diner across the street. As we're leaving the parking lot, we hear sirens and not one, but two, police cars pull us over.

"Did you know you were driving without your headlights on?" an officer asks Satori.

I'm thinking, If he knew, he would've had them on. But I keep my mouth shut. Play nice. It works. The officers let us off without a ticket.

As a thank-you, I sign two copies of my book and run to catch them before they drive away. No sooner does my foot hit the pavement than both officers leap from their vehicles, doors ajar, hands on their guns, one of them shouting, "Get back in the vehicle, ma'am!"

"I'm unarmed," I shout. "A good book is my only weapon!"

They laugh and accept my gift.

Two days later, I receive this e-mail: "Hi Lysa, My husband came home from work this morning with your book. He and his fellow officer had pulled you over in Rocky Hill. I must tell you, I read it in one day! I found it so captivating and life changing. I really can view people and relationships in such a different way now. My husband is going to read it next and then my mom already has dibs on it! Thank you."

The response I received from this simple gesture shows me that when you least expect it, people acknowledge you for being kind. I often put money in parking meters before they expire. Once, just as a meter maid was about to give a ticket, I slipped a quarter in, and as I was walking away, a guy ran up to me and thanked me for saving him from getting a ticket.

"No problem," I told him. "Just do the same for someone else."

knew that by doing an East Coast tour, the likelihood of encountering people who lost loved ones on September 11 would be quite high, but after doing events in New York, New Jersey, Philadelphia, Maryland, channeling those who died from suicide, murder, illness, car accidents, botched surgery and old age, not one person who crossed over on September 11 comes through. At least, not in the bookstore. They come through after the event, over the phone.

A woman asks, "Can I contact my friend's husband?"

"I know about my boy," the friend's husband tells me. *"I saw my son before he arrived. I was on my way out and shortly after, he was born."*

"Yes," the friend says. "His son was born after he died. He didn't know it was a boy."

"Now he does."

This was so incredible; to have a father cross over and meet his unborn son—giving him a quick high five like a guy who passes his buddy in the hallway at school.

A woman asks for her husband. I see the World Trade Center. She confirms this is true. I go through the entire reading not realizing it's the very same guy who met his unborn son.

A week after that, this guy comes through again, this time for his sister.

By now I recognize him, "Hello, how're ya doing?" Even though his sister has a different last name, I know the guy.

Every few days I start channeling and see it, the World Trade Center, the planes . . . and after the ninth reading, I start feeling afraid because all the people coming through are husbands who died on September 11. Why only husbands?

Is it because Satori is the person I cannot fathom living without? What are you trying to tell me that I may not want to know? I'm serious, I feel sick inside.

"It's to remind you to appreciate every moment you have with Satori and never take him, or anyone you love, for granted," a spirit tells me.

Before the tour, I remember sitting in Satori's office surrounded by his karate medals, organizing them as a surprise for when he came home. This eerie vibe came over me, followed by the thought, What if he dies? What if I never see him again?

I immediately stomp it out. "Don't be ridiculous. He'll be home."

The moment I think this, the phone rings. It's Satori calling to say he loves me and he'll be home soon, and he just had the most unsettling thought. "I was getting ready to leave and thought, What if I die and don't get to see you again?"

I nearly drop the phone. "I cannot believe you just said that. Don't even go there."

He laughs and says not to worry. "Nothing's going to happen to me, Lysa."

The same thing Liz Gilligan's husband told her three days before he died.

We hang up, and I remind myself—This moment is all we have.

am riding up the escalator at Barnes & Noble in Paramus, New Jersey, when it see it.

I feel like a rock star.

There are two hundred people leaning against walls, sitting on couches, on chairs, on the floor, standing in the back. I wish my parents were here to see this. Men, women, children, teens, moms, dads, grandparents, people of all races, all ages, are here to see me.

I don't want to rush. I want to soak it in, to be here fully.

"You overdo everything," I tell a guy with jet-black hair, three nose rings, and a beautiful smile. "Whether it's eating, drinking, smoking, gambling, shopping, drugging, cluttering, especially cluttering, your house is a mess. I want to come over and clean it."

"Go right ahead," he laughs, along with the rest of the audience.

"Do you want to change now?" I ask him.

"You mean right now?"

I nod.

"Sure, why not?" he says arrogantly. "Where do I start?"

"The beginning is always a good place, or, *before* the beginning,"

"Huh?"

I say this to interrupt his pattern, to knock him out of his comfort zone. It allows me to speak to the honest part of his soul, not to the guarded mask he normally wears.

"I'm familiar with addictions," I tell him. "I know the insanity of eating pizza out of the garbage. I know the discomfort of trying to fill that bottomless pit."

I tell the guy he's getting a big payoff staying screwed up. He receives attention, just as I did when I was bulimic. He lives at home. His parents pay for everything. They send him to rehabs and therapists. They kick him out of the house then let him back in. His life is one big project that everyone, except him, is working on.

I tell him there is a positive intent behind his destructive behaviors.

By having problems, using drugs, alcohol, food, and clutter, he gets to feel significant.

"As long as you see yourself as a screwup, you'll continue acting like one because we always remain congruent with the identity we hold for ourselves," I tell him. "If you see yourself as a procrastinator, you'll procrastinate. Why? Because that's what procrastinators do—they procrastinate."

I think about how I stopped going to OA meetings because I didn't want to continue having the identity of a recovering bulimic. When I left OA, it had been eight years since I'd thrown up. Now it's been over eighteen. When do I get to no longer be a recovering bulimic? How long do I have to go without throwing up to be recovered, not recovering?

According to OA, you're always recovering. Never recovered.

I disagree.

I refuse to live in fear of going back to my old behaviors. Food is now something to nourish me, nothing more. I know everyone can be free from addictions if they find something more powerful with which to replace them.

This guy's entire existence is based on filling himself up so he'll never feel empty, but no matter how many addictions he engages in, it's never enough. Same as, no matter how many doughnuts or gallons of ice cream I used to consume, I still felt hungry because I was using food to fill something it was not meant to fill—My soul.

I don't believe our intention is to ever harm ourselves. Even when a person commits suicide, they do it because they think dying will be less painful than living, until they discover there is no death and they have to deal with the issues they thought dying would resolve.

We don't have to die to feel dead. A young girl in the audience feels dead, although I know she will never admit it.

A spirit does.

Cautiously, I say to her, "I see you hurting yourself. You can stop cutting yourself now."

The girl lets out a painful howling so loud that it startles everyone. The store manager rushes over to see what's wrong. Nothing is wrong. What's happening is good. Her emotional release of shame needs to come out. People begin crying, identifying with her pain. Her secret is revealed. Now she can begin to heal.

The very thing we don't want to face is exactly what we must.

The guy has to face the pain he uses his addictions to avoid. The young woman has to face the rage she turns against herself. I promise each that no matter how hard they cry, how many pillows they slam; if he can handle downing twenty-four beers and she can handle a razor blade tearing through her skin, they can both handle whatever emotions came up when they began to deal with their painful past.

The only purpose for bringing up the past is to heal it, face it and move on. Period.

If it was horrifying enough when it occurred, you don't need to rehash it a million times.

Your past is healed when it no longer rules you.

There is more than enough for everyone in this world—enough success, enough love, enough opportunity to achieve whatever we desire. But if we continue to believe in lack, then lack will be our reality. If we believe in abundance, then abundance is what we will find.

Madonna isn't the most sensational singer, but she believed she could do whatever it took to become a superstar. It wasn't easier for her. She had rejections, negative feedback from record executives. She could've easily believed them instead of herself. She chose the latter and it made all the difference in the world.

Life is not rejection free, just ask Stephen King, who put a nail on his wall after the thumbtack became too small to hold the over two hundred rejection letters he'd received from book publishers.

"You may encounter more obstacles or challenges than someone else, but it doesn't mean you are committed to a life of misery. That's not anyone's karma or destiny," I tell the crowd.

"No one comes here to live a shitty life."

*S*o far, everything is going smoothly: no hitches, no problems until an hour before our event in Huntington, New York, Satori tells me the store manager said I'm not allowed to do readings. "It's Barnes and Noble's policy not to allow psychic readings in the store," the manager repeats when we get there. Satori points out that we've done readings at all their other stores and haven't had problems. The woman doesn't budge.

I come up with a plan for how to sneak in some readings because I don't want the audience to feel disappointed. I start off by telling the crowd, "I'm not allowed to do readings tonight, that's what I was told by management."

A loud sigh of disappointment ripples through the crowd.

"*But*, if I were allowed to do readings," I continue, "like for example, if you sir, yes, you in the back row, if your father were coming through, hypothetically of course, he might say something like, 'You didn't fix the boat and sell the house like you promised. I wish you didn't see me dying. I hated being helpless, connected to tubes, having to shit in a pan. It was awful.'"

The man looks shocked. I've definitely struck a chord.

"That's what I would say if I *were* doing a reading, which of course, I'm not. But if I were, I'd ask you, 'Does that makes sense?'" He nods, wiping his tears.

Even if it meant having a manager angry with me, it was a lot better than pissing off the spirits. You don't want to do that. They just won't go away.

In Holmel, New Jersey, I am washing my hands before an event and a guy comes up to me and says, *"In the corner, the blue shirt. You gotta talk to her, talk to her, she's really upset; she doesn't look upset because she doesn't cry in public, but she's gonna cry."*

For a second I forget the guy is dead because I tell him, "Will you be quiet already! You're giving me a headache."

He follows me out, muttering, *"Blue shirt, first row, corner, gotta talk to her, gotta talk."*

I begin the event and the guy's not around. Then I start reading from my book and I hear him whispering, *"Blue shirt, in the corner, she's gonna cry, look at her face, she's gonna—"*

I snap the book shut and turn to the woman in the corner wearing the blue shirt, and say, "This guy is coming through. He's giving me a headache. He's been talking for about a half hour about how I gotta speak to you, speak to you. He followed me into the bathroom and I don't mean to insult him but—he is very obsessive."

The woman cracks up and tells the crowd he was diagnosed with obsessive-compulsive disorder shortly before he died. His habit was to ask her things a million times, and never let up.

Readings are definitely filled with laughter, which surprisingly, isn't from the people who've had the easiest time. It is from those who endured the most painful losses—the ones who came home to find a note from their kid about why they ended their life, or received a phone call from the police asking to come identify their mother's body.

The laughter, the joy, the love, is what spirits remember the most.

Satori videotapes every reading at every single event and what occurs during these encounters is nothing less than awe-inspiring testaments to the continuation of life.

The spirits are as human and as real as the people who come to my events. They are as funny and poignant as when they were in a body. Yet not all are greeted warmly by the people for whom they come through.

"He makes you line up his shirts—in perfect little rows—and then he beats you," I tell a woman with short blonde hair and nervous eyes in Avon, Indiana.

The woman nods, twitching slightly—an unconscious response from years of abuse.

"He's nasty, this man. If you look at my body right now, I can't move. I'm rigid. Tense. He makes me nervous, like if you go to the left today, it's fine, but tomorrow it won't be. The rules change but he doesn't tell you they've changed, he only punishes you when you make a mistake. You're always on guard, never knowing the right thing to do."

The man tenses my neck, clenches my jaw and rolls my hands into tightly wound fists. It feels as if he puts a rubber band around my head to show how his mind felt on a regular basis.

I am not channeling this man.

I am becoming him.

Even though I allow this to happen, it feels torturous. I imagine how it felt living in his body with so much anger and so many ways of inflicting pain on others. Must've been pure hell.

I think about how we are all born optimistic and we learn to be pessimistic, fearful, and angry as a way of protecting ourselves, sometimes with good reason, like in this woman's case.

"Are you responsible for creating this problem?" I ask her.

"He said I was."

"Did you force him to beat you?"

"He said I did."

"I don't care what he said. What do you say?"

She looks around, as if the man is hiding in the wings waiting to hurt her again. "He still taunts me, tells me I'm worthless, no good to no man."

"Is he really the best person to listen to? Is this the guy you'd go to for advice?"

She laughs . . . then forces herself to stop. Obviously, laughing wasn't okay with him.

"If laughing became a habit, it would really piss him off, you being all happy and shit."

"Yeah, that would make him angry." She smiles, savoring the thought.

"His anger was not because of you. He didn't know how to deal with his problems and took his frustration out on you. He can't do that anymore. After tonight, he can't project his angry voice in your head because he knows I've got connections. I know people."

She laughs, but this time doesn't look around nervously. She doesn't seem to care if he's around. He's not. I mentally told the man to leave, said not to come back unless he wants to apologize for his abusive deeds.

A few days later, I receive a letter from her.

He hasn't been around since.

*P*icture this:

Driving to Mississippi.

Running low on fuel.

Praying to the Mobil Gods to make a gas station magically appear.

There's less than an hour before my next event begins and we can't step on the gas because we have no gas. Then, magically, like in one of those Westerns where the man crawls through the desert desperately in search of water and right before he's about to pass out, sees a well. We see a rickety old gas station that saves the day.

We get to Barnes & Noble on time. I'm looking forward to seeing my posters in the window and rows of people excitedly anticipating an inspiring event. Instead, there is nothing. No chairs. No posters. No people.

The manager tells us, "Folks in this area aren't into psychics. They're rather religious and I didn't want to promote for fear of scaring the regulars away."

"Then why did you ask me to come to your store?"

She shrugs, hasn't got an answer. "Forget it," I tell Satori. "Let's just go."

Satori assures me we'll get people. We've done it before, shown up at bookstores that forgot we were coming. We'd quickly Xerox flyers and hand them out, filling the place. I didn't feel like doing it today.

A woman starts asking Satori about what I do, and next thing I know, Jerry Brooks, the cameraman from WJTV-CBS in Jackson, arrives to film my nonexistent event. That's when I remember I'm supposed to be on the news. Satori asks if I can give the woman a short reading. Jerry asks if he can film it. I ask myself why don't I ever let myself take a break.

Myself doesn't answer because a horrible headache begins pounding away. It's not my headache. It belongs to a blonde. I know this because I see her—this woman's sister—standing beside me, and I hear it—the argument—a fight on the night she died.

"Tell me about my sister," the woman asks.

"I'm drinking, and not the occasional cocktail, I'm drinking, heavily."

I tell her this. "Yes, very heavy drinker," she confirms.

"We're fighting, my husband and I. I felt badly. Said things I shouldn't have. I don't remember much. One of the hazards of battling booze."

"She makes me feel on edge. Nervous. She wants me to pick up a cigarette even though I don't smoke. Does that make sense for her?"

"All of it makes sense. The other night I dreamed she was sitting on the lawn chair smoking a cigarette."

"She was trying to get a grip, calm her nerves. She just got married. Says, *'I just had the wedding.'* It's not like she was crying for help. She kept things hidden. Not about her drinking, but about her relationship, or rather, how she felt in relation to her relationship."

"I had no idea what was going on with her. She got married three weeks before. . . ."

"She doesn't feel enormous regret. She had a hard time being here and is upset about what she did, but isn't saying 'I want to come back.' She's just upset about the way she left."

BOOM! I hear a gunshot. I feel an implosion through my brain—a bullet to the head.

"Your sister shot herself."

"Yes," she says quietly, looking down. "She did."

Jerry tells me we need to go. The news van is waiting. I apologize for cutting the reading short, give the woman a hug and say good-bye.

News reporter Jeff Rent and producer Richard Garner are waiting to take Satori and me to some remote location. Thirty minutes later, we arrive at a house taken straight out of a horror film, complete with broken windows, chipped paint, a caved-in porch, and a creaking front door.

Dianna, an ex-Marine, arrives and leads us into the house of horrors.

At first I cannot breathe, the stench is so bad. There are mounds of dust covering counters, old newspapers, a crate of moldy fruit, cartons of expired milk, a sheet with a stain resembling dried blood, and a clump of dark brown matter that definitely looks like shit.

"Is that shit?" I ask Satori.

He walks over, takes a closer look. "Looks like shit to me. Is that shit, Dianna?"

She comes over to inspect it. "Yep. Armadillo shit."

Perfect. Surrounded by the shit of armadillos.

Chopped-up body parts flash in front of my face.

"This place was a hospital. When patients died, their limbs were buried on the property." The cameraman captures my words, my nauseated look, my need to run outside before I hurl on the dilapidated floor. On the lawn, Dianna confirms the house was used as a hospital in the late 1800s. "They buried limbs there," she says pointing to the heel of my boot disappearing into the mushy soil. Automatically, I jump back.

"With limb pits, the topsoil never quite hardens," she adds.

I'm not listening. I'm busy watching a little boy running toward me. He looks like the kid from the Oscar Mayer hot dog commercial. He's different in only one respect—He's dead.

The boy cries, *"Go in the house! You must grab a peek at what's in the freezer!"*

We go back in the house and I immediately hold my breath. The heat from the sun has made the armadillo shit smell extra fresh. I follow the boy toward a six-foot freezer with a glowing orange light to signify it's on. Satori films me getting ready to lift the lid.

One. Two. Three. It's too heavy. Dianna helps me. We barely get it open before the most putrid smell overtakes my senses. I look inside and cannot believe what I see: Rotten, thawed plastic bags of "food" swarming with maggots and other bugs.

"Why in the hell would anyone keep a freezer with rotten, maggot-laden food?" I ask Richard before noticing something that should not be in there. "What the fuck is that?"

I point to some dull-colored meat with ridges like a brain, and bones, big bones, the kind of bones humans have. It's wrapped in clear plastic and covered with maggots.

"It's probably deer meat," he says.

"I've seen deer meat and that's not it," I tell him.

I am sickened. I hold my nose to take a closer look. I think I see a human bone.

"I think the guy next door told me he keeps deer meat in the freezer."

"Right . . ." I tell him. "So did Jeffrey Dahmer."

*T*ouring gives me a lot of time to think about why people keep rotten, unidentifiable meat in their freezer and whether I'll ever fully understand how I do what I do. Driving through Hickory, North Carolina, I see a mailman and think about how some psychic mediums speak of this work as though it's no big deal, "Oh I'm only the messenger," they say.

Well, yeah you're only the messenger, but to minimize the importance of the messenger is like saying the mailman is unimportant in the delivery of mail. The letters and packages are what get you excited but they don't miraculously show up at your door. They need a means of getting there, just as spirits need a means of getting through to you. That's where mediums come in, as a sort of FedEx for the spirit world.

I think about how I don't want people to walk away from my events saying, "Wow, look what Lysa can do." I want them to feel, "Wow, look what I can do."

I want them to see the strength and possibility inside themselves and to gain insight into channeling spirits, to understand the nourishment their souls receive when they connect with the people they love.

In Fayetteville, Arkansas, I do an exercise to show how I hear spirits. I ask the audience to say silently to themselves, inside their head, "Boy, do **I** look hot tonight!" Then turn to the person sitting next to them and in their sexiest voice, say out loud, "Boy, do **you** look hot tonight!"

It's funny because there are these two guys sitting beside each other, not doing the exercise, and I whisper, "Come on, just do it, tell him he looks hot tonight. Give the guy a compliment."

One guy quickly turns to the other and says, "Man—I like your shoes."

There is this incredible burst of laughter and I tell the crowd this is exactly how I hear spirits. Just like when someone is speaking to you, as opposed to you thinking something inside your mind.

Next, I hold up my book and tell the audience to look at it. Then,

I hide the book and tell them to keep their eyes open and continue seeing the book as if I were still holding it. They can only do this for a couple of seconds because the image fades, and they have to think about the book to conjure it up again. I tell them this is how I see spirits. The images are shown to me, but it takes my focus to capture and relay, within seconds, what I see.

To train your ability to comprehend, process and relay what you see, have a friend place three to five objects on a table and cover them with a dark cloth without your knowing what they are.

Have them take the cloth away for thirty seconds while you look at the objects and hold the image in your mind before they put the cloth back. Then, recite what you saw. As you improve, you can add more objects and uncover them for shorter periods of time to train your mental speed and ability to process and relay information, which is useful both in the material world and in channeling spirits.

*S*atori has many roles. He is my husband, lover, best friend, coach, tour manager, booking agent, bodyguard, laughing buddy, and partner in "crime."

Okay, so what we did wasn't a crime, but it certainly made my heart pound.

Satori tells me, "Wait until I whistle then run as fast as you can into the room."

I wait with Siobhan, our golden retriever, in the stairwell. I hear Satori whistle and run like hell! "Come on Siobhan!" We dash into the room. Slam the door. Victory!

Okay, normally we don't do stuff like this, but we couldn't leave Siobhan in the SUV. Plus, she loves hotels, and snuggling and sleeping late until we open the curtains.

A few days ago, we do something extra gutsy. While driving, we see this amazing castle, and I love castles, so we stop and discover it's a hotel. Satori suggests we ask the manager for a room, which I think is just crazy because the chances of walking in and having them donate a room are highly unlikely.

"You never know unless you ask."

"Why don't we just pay for the room so we don't have to ask," I tell him.

"It's not about the money, Lysa. It's about doing something that scares you."

I do feel scared, unsure of how the manager will react. I normally trust my instincts but when fear enters the picture, it screws everything up, crosses all my psychic wires.

Next thing I know, I'm standing in the manager's office. He's looking at his watch, saying he's got to go, something about his son's bar mitzvah. I speak quickly, and before I'm done, he tells us it's all set. He's giving us a room. "It's my pleasure," he adds. "I'll try and make it to your event tomorrow. I've got to run."

Satori and I look at each other, dumbfounded. . . .

Before he goes, I ask him, "What made you say yes?"

He thinks for a moment, "Something told me to. I've never done this before, donated a room to complete strangers. It felt right. I have a good feeling about you both," he smiles.

This becomes an important lesson in never again telling myself the answer before asking the question. I thought about how many times I didn't ask for something because I told myself the people would only say no.

By not asking, I said no for them.

They might have said yes.

$\mathcal{M}$y eyes dart through the audience.

A time bomb is about to go off. Something is about to erupt. I can feel it.

Lysa, relax. Remember where you are. Barnes & Noble. Orlando, Florida.

Good, now breathe and continue reading.

The moment I do, a man in the back of the room bolts from his chair and begins shouting. "The Lord your God says speaking to spirits is wrong, I say, wrong!"

"That's just great, sir. Now sit down!" a woman snaps.

I don't say a word. I continue reading from my book.

He continues reading from his.

I raise my voice.

He raises his, and I am right back playing "Can ya top that?" with my brother.

Finally, I blurt out, "Sir, if you have something to say, I'm sure you want people to listen, but they're not. They're telling you to be quiet. They're telling you to go home. If you want to be heard, this is not the best way to go about it. Raising your voice isn't going to make them want to listen; although it may force them to, it doesn't mean they'll care about what you have to say."

He keeps talking. He keeps preaching. It makes him feel significant. The event coordinator, Lisa Dore, steps in. "Sir, you need to take your seat."

"I speak the word of God!" the man cries. "I am a servant of the Lord!"

Satori touches the man's Bible.

"Don't you touch my Bible, motherfucker!"

God personified.

He is in a deranged state of madness. I see it in his eyes. He's not listening. He just wants attention. Like a child throwing a tantrum, he'll do whatever it takes to get through and it's working. We're paying attention. We're giving this guy exactly what he wants. So I stop doing it. I start talking to the crowd, ignoring him, not giving him one more second of our time.

It works . . . for a second.

"God is telling me to cast out thou demons!" the man shouts at the top of his lungs. "God is telling me to save his followers! God is telling me to cast out—"

"God is telling you to get out of Barnes and Noble right now!" I shout! I've had enough.

The crowd cheers wildly. The cops finally arrive. They escort him away.

Riding down the escalator, the man continues his sermon. He isn't willing to change his approach so the police change it for him. They slap him with a permanent restraining order that states he can never set foot on the shopping mall premises again.

After the event, the manager warns Satori and me that the man is waiting on the street corner. He says he wants to kick our ass! He told police that Satori touched his Bible and he wants him arrested. Several guests and security guards escort us to our car.

I think about how Gandhi, John F. Kennedy, and Martin Luther King Jr. all had one thing in common besides standing up for what they believe.

They were all shot.

*F*inally, a day off, and what do we do? Go to see three movies with my dad in Fort Lauderdale, Florida. We're nearing the end of our tour and I'm ready for a vacation from the spirits, not because they're a pain, but because channeling is all I've been doing for the past two months—day and night—talking to spirits—before events, during events, after events. In the bathroom, on the beach, in the shower, even at a taco stand where a man's father comes through and says he's proud of what his son has done with the family business.

The next day, I arrive at the beautiful estate of a woman named Katherine, who tells Satori she saw me at a bookstore but won't say which one. Satori goes off with her cat while we sit in her grand living room overlooking the intercoastal. I look toward the window and see a blonde woman turn into an eagle. I know that sounds strange but that's exactly what I see. "I see a blonde woman making herself an eagle," I say.

Katherine smiles. "An eagle flew down in front of my windshield and I knew it was my daughter. I felt like she was trying to tell me she is free and at peace. The eagle often stands for spirit. 'Your body may be gone but your spirit lives on,' that sort of thing."

"Talk about the gun," her daughter interrupts.

I don't want to talk about the gun. I want to talk about the eagle.

"Talk about the gun!"

"She wants me talk about the gun. She used it on herself."

Katherine nods.

"I feel drunk, like I'm going to throw up. I must tell her to stop making me feel this way."

Katherine laughs. "Yes, that's her. She was a very heavy drinker."

"I had an argument with my husband, too much to drink. He told my family he wasn't there, didn't see me do it, but he did."

I tell Katherine this. She tells me, "Her husband told us he was at the store. She's saying he wasn't?"

"Yes . . . Um, who is Amanda?"

"She is," Katherine says, stunned to hear her daughter's name.

I ask Amanda to describe what happened the night she died.

We go to eat with a friend, and yes, I drink a lot. Husband gets angry, wants me to stop, I don't, he gets angrier, I storm into the ladies' room, call my girlfriend crying. He comes after me, apologizes. At home, I'm a total wreck, drunker than I'd been in a while. As a 'fuck you' to him, to myself, I grab the gun he'd taught me how to use, a bullet blasts through my head.

I'm having this moment where I'm hearing what I'm saying and I can't believe I'm saying it. I'm split in two—one part of me speaking and one commenting on my words. I continue channeling Amanda until Katherine finally says, "Today you've told me the exact same things you told my other daughter two weeks ago, and you had no idea we were related."

I've given nearly seventy-five readings in the past two weeks. I have no idea who she means.

"In Mississippi. A cameraman filmed it. It was a short reading at the store."

"The five-minute reading at the store where no one showed up, that was your daughter?" I laugh, absolutely stunned. "For as psychic as I am, I had no clue. Usually if a spirit comes through twice, I'll recognize them. 'Hey Bob, you're back. How's it going?' I guess spirits are like the CIA. Revealing details on a need-to-know basis."

*D*ays before we're about to return home, Satori tells me I have an in-person reading at the hotel. Before the guy arrives, I begin feeling strange. Uncomfortable strange.

I try to relax by breathing deeply. It doesn't work. This nervous, edgy feeling won't go away. I ask Satori, "What would I do if I were sitting face-to-face with a murderer and ended up channeling the person they murdered?"

"Run like hell?" he laughs.

"I'm serious. I have this awful feeling and I don't know why. Can you stay outside the door during my reading?" This is totally uncharacteristic of me, but Satori promises he will.

A knock at the door interrupts our conversation. In walks Sean, a nice-looking man in his fifties. I immediately laugh at myself for worrying so much.

"Yeah . . . Looks are deceiving," a voice whispers.

Stop it . . . shut up, fear . . . go away . . . Satori signals he'll be right outside the door.

Sean takes a seat across from me and INSTANTLY a woman appears . . . Lying on a bathroom floor . . . in a pool of her own blood . . . with a gun in her hand . . . and a bullet in her. . . .

Oh my God. I immediately know why I had been feeling so strange. It had nothing to do with a murder. Two states. Three cities. Three people with three different last names. All connected to one woman—Amanda. The same woman who came through in Mississippi, the same whose mother had a reading with me last week, and now, this man. He must be her husband.

"I want to set the record straight," she tells me.

By the tone of her voice and the feeling in my gut, I'm not so sure I want to hear this.

The same details come through: She shot herself. She was an alcoholic. They'd just gotten married. There was a fight the night she died. She speaks about the arguments they had during the months leading up to her death.

She is in her thirties, just got married, and she comes home from dinner and shoots herself? I like Sean. I really do. He is in so much pain over his wife's death. He can barely speak. His sadness is overwhelming. But something doesn't add up.

Weeks later, Katherine faxes me the coroner's report which states that Amanda's blood alcohol level was at .45 percent.

Between .4 and .5 is comatose.

I look at the date of Amanda's death and realize I did the reading for her sister in Mississippi only twenty-six days after Amanda crossed over, which was twenty-three days after marrying Sean.

I receive a letter from Katherine:

Dear Lysa,

We are all healing better since our readings with you.
We miss Amanda and have a difficult time believing she is gone. We still believe there are parts Amanda's husband is not sharing and this is the reason for his extreme grief, as even the detective had doubts.

You mentioned an argument between Amanda and her husband, which her friend confirms. She said Amanda called her from the restaurant that night, upset about a fight. An argument would certainly not be a reason for her to take her own life. Perhaps these are the normal doubts one has with a suicide.

The most profound lesson I've taken is the knowledge that when we die, our spirit remains alive. It just leaves the body, but the spirit of the person we love is around us. We do not disappear when we cross over, that's nice to know.

Connecting with my daughter cleared up questions I was

left with after her crossing. As a result, I am able to be still with myself. So many little things just don't matter, they really aren't important. I now appreciate more and am captivated by birds— hawks and eagles, and the majestic way they fly. They represent serenity and peace to me.

I now experience a whole new meaning to their flights.

—Katherine

*A*manda taught me that while we want to protect our secrets, spirits want us to reveal the truth. While we worry about being found out, spirits worry about the damage of living with lies. While we want only to remember the good, spirits want to remember it all—the good, bad, ugly and beautiful. *"To remember and learn,"* is the spirits' motto.

With suicide, there is often so much shame, guilt, self-blame, and concern about how a loved one's choice of departure reflects negatively upon us. Weren't we enough to make them want to stay? "It really wasn't an overdose, can we just put it down as an accident?" a mom in Des Moines, Iowa, asks the coroner, worried her church group will find out her daughter lived, and died on vodka and speed.

A son yells for his mother to come up to his room. Says he needs to see her right away.

She walks up the stairs, feels weird in her stomach, maybe something she ate, she thinks. She opens the door. Sees her son in the closet, a rope tied around his neck, a chair beneath his feet. He kicks it out the moment he sees his mother's face—the ultimate fuck you.

"Mom tells people I died in my sleep," he tells me. *"Lying is destroying her, breaking down her spirit. I was drunk, drugged. Angry. Stupid. Selfish. I admit it. I don't want her to forgive me, only herself. It's not her fault. She walks around nervous someone will discover the truth—her son killed himself. What does that say about her?"*

"I failed," his mother tells me.

"What would it mean if you did?"

She is silent. Her rhythmic breathing is heard through the phone.

"It would mean I failed as a mother."

"What else could it mean?"

"I failed as a person."

"What else?"

"I wish I would've been different, treated him better."

"What else?"

"I hate him for what he did. I'm ashamed to say it, but I hate him."

"If you didn't hate him, what would you feel?"

"Hurt he left me. Hurt he didn't give himself another chance."

"If you didn't feel hurt, what would you feel?"

"Sad he felt the need to end his own life."

"What is underneath the sadness?"

She chokes on her words. I tell her to take a moment. There's no rush. Take time to feel. She finally speaks, "Love. I miss him so much. I cry all the time. I wish I could trade places with him, I do."

Suicide renders us powerless. Wondering what we could have done to prevent their death is a question without an answer. We don't know what could've been done. We only know what was or was not. Speculating gives us a false sense of control. At least I can go over what happened and make up different endings so I don't have to feel so bad. But no matter how many endings we make up—it doesn't change the ending that occurred, our loved one is dead.

Spirits who've committed suicide tell me there is a difference between preventing someone from killing themselves (suicide prevention) and helping them find a powerful enough reason to live. Stopping them from dying doesn't change the quality of their life.

A blonde girl in her teens comes to me after one of my events and asks if I can sit with her for a few moments under one of her favorite trees.

The sun beaming down on this girl's beautiful face makes her look like an angel. I smile, and she asks me why I'm smiling, and I tell her, and she takes out a bottle of vitamins and pours what looks like a hundred pills into my hand.

I study one closely as the girl's mother comes out of the store, waving, walking toward us. I look at the girl's face. I know she wants to hide. "These are your mother's Valium," I say. She nods and quickly confesses to stealing her mother's pills, a few each month until she built up her collection. She was going to end her life today, she tells me. She'd even written a note, but then her mom invited her to come to my event and, "You screwed up my whole plan," she says. "Now I know I can't die, but I still don't want to live."

"You don't want to live the way you've been living, but if you found another way to live, then you'd want to live. I'll make you a deal. . . . I'll help you find a powerful enough reason to live, and you make a commitment to yourself that no matter what, killing yourself is not an option. Take it off your list because no matter how you feel or what happens in your life, suicide can't be on your list of ways to get out of the pain. The only way out is through. You must go through your life to get to the other side."

She shakes my hand. We've got a deal.

We lean against this huge tree, which has probably heard more secrets than the walls of the Oval Office. This tree, which has stood strong through life's most devastating storms, is symbolic of the girl, who in an instant, came this close to ending her life before it had truly begun.

When I was a teenager, I'd be eating breakfast and halfway through the meal, start thinking about what I was going to eat for lunch. At lunch, I'd be thinking about what I was going to eat for dinner. That's how exciting my life was, back then.

A few years later, I did a complete turnaround, and instead of wanting to speed things up and get to the next moment, the next meal, I wanted to freeze moments of my life and savor them, relishing the joy. I didn't want the moment to end.

Then, I meet a Zen master who asks me to sit quietly facing a wall.

"And do what?" I ask him.

"Nothing."

"What do you mean? Do nothing. What's the point of doing nothing?"

"Sit . . . and see."

I take the tiny meditation pillow and shove it under my ass. I look at Satori facing the wall, a perfect little Buddha angel, all peaceful and shit.

I convince myself that beneath the Zen master's bleached white garb, beneath talking about consciousness and expanding love, it's all a lie. No one can be so peaceful and still. No one can find enlightenment by staring at a fucking wall!

Lysa, shut up and meditate. . . . See how relaxed you feel. . . . Ohmmmmm. . . . Yes, this feels. . . . Shit, I need to pee. Am I allowed to pee? I don't know and I can't find out because we're not supposed to speak. Let me just focus. Wipe an eraser over the clutter of my mind.

B-r-e-a-t-h-e deeply. Hmmm. Wonderful . . .

What's that smell? It smells in here. Did someone just fart? Did someone just interrupt my perfect Zen moment with a fart no one can escape due to strict instructions not to leave the room? Are we forced to endure the stench of undigested soybeans and brown rice, all in the name of enlightenment?

This is my mental conversation. At a beautiful Zen center amid flowing waterfalls, brilliantly colored flowers, and peaceful souls, my mind simply would not shut up.

Then . . . it did. I became silent, not vacant of thought, but allowing thoughts to drift by, one after the other; I'm hungry. I'm tired. I have to pee. I love Satori. It feels nice here. I love the flowers. I have to pee. I'm bored. This is cool. My knees ache. Ohhhhmmmmm.

The moment I finally felt peaceful, the master hit the gong. Time was up.

When my mind stopped resisting what was taking place in the present, it surrendered and became still. Not silent. Not in this state of nothingness, but this state of simply being with what is going on right now in this moment.

I learned the enlightened state is a fluid cycle of feelings, thoughts, and emotions that are continuously changing, shifting, transforming. The cycle contains what it contains and it's not up to me to judge, alter, or fix it, but simply notice and allow it to move on.

But that's where we get stuck, with the moving on, moving forward part.

How do we allow ourselves to be happy in spite of the pain we've been through? How do we allow ourselves to cry when we have no idea what's wrong? How do we understand that being unhappy, doing what we dislike, staying in situations that no longer serve us, has dire consequences?

After my Zen experience, I go to do my last in-person reading with Stewart Weil, a guy with a strong Jersey accent. I like the guy even after he tells me he's doing this on a dare from his friend Joey P, otherwise known as the Prophet of New Jersey.

"You know what I see, Stewart?"

"Tell me what you see, Lysa. What's in your invisible crystal ball?" He mocks me.

"You speak all enthusiastically. You're smiling, looking all happy, as if you've got your shit together. But you're not happy, Stewart. You're fucking depressed."

"It's because I have no confidence. I'm a loser."

"Okay."

"You agree with me?"

"You want me to argue with you? You want me to say, 'Stewart, you're not a loser. You're a wonderful man,' so you can fight with me, try and convince me you're really a loser?"

"I never say no, that's my problem. Anything anybody wants, Stew's the man. I'm like a fucking 7-Eleven, open twenty-four hours, seven days a week."

I laugh. He cracks me up, his delivery and everything. I can't help but laugh.

"You think my life is funny?"

"No. I think *you* are funny. . . . Why don't you do comedy?"

"Get the fuck outta here."

"Come on, tell me a story. You've probably got lots of funny stories."

"I ain't doin' it."

"You're not going to do it?" I ask, just to be sure.

He runs his fingers through his hair, releasing pent-up frustration on his scalp.

"You said you never say no but you just said no to me. You're cured."

He smiles for about ten seconds and then says, "I still have no confidence."

"How come you're so confident about your lack of confidence?"

"You're confusing me."

"Better to feel confused than depressed . . . Listen, you think you have to be a Mr. 'Nothing's a Problem I'll Run to the Store and Get You Nachos at Four in the Morning' kinda guy. You walk around feeling miserable and I see that 'something's not right' dissatisfied feeling you live with oozing out of your pores."

"I ain't gonna do the, 'I had a fucked-up childhood' routine," he says.

"Just do comedy. That's what you want to do, isn't it? Be a comedian."

"Did Joey tell you that? How the fuck could you know that? How could you know what I want to do? I don't look like a funny guy so you didn't get it from me." He starts pacing the room like in one of those movies where the guy is being interrogated for a crime he knows he's committed. He looks for an escape, but can't get out.

"My dad said I could make a laughing hyena stop laughing, that's how bad I stunk at comedy. My dad's dead and I'm glad and I don't care if I go to hell for saying it. I will never allow that asshole to rest in peace because God knows he never let me. I have good reason to hate my father."

"We all have good reasons, but do your reasons give you what you want? If you walk around angry all the time, you can have the best reason in the world, and you know what you get for that? You get the privilege of living a miserable life. But don't worry, you'll have lots of company. This place is packed with people who have good reason to be pissed off."

He looks at me, his eyes sad like a wounded puppy. I soften. "Look, if you walk around hating your father, you're the one carrying the hatred. It's in your body, poisoning your cells, destroying your passion for life, and if you want to know how to be free of that, I can show you."

"What I want is to be a comedian."

"So what're you doing about it?"

"Working at Starbucks."

We look at each other and burst out laughing.

"Hey, don't knock Starbucks. It's a prestigious job, other than the fact that I hate the customers and the people I work with are idiots, I make good money and plus, discount coffee."

"Oh, well, that right there makes it totally worth it."

He smiles, looking at the floor. His mind is somewhere else. . . .

After a moment, he tells me a story about how when he was nine, his dad gave this big New Year's Eve party and, in front of all the guests, made fun of Stewart, mocking his desire to become a comedian. Instead of being crushed, Stewart gets up and does his comedy act. He's telling jokes and everyone's laughing, having a blast, and when he's done, the crowd cheers and people hug him and his dad shuts everybody up by sending Stew to his room.

"What I remember most about that night," Stewart tells me, "even more than my dad being a dick, is this picture in my head of all the guests laughing and me thinking I'm the one doing it to them, I'm the guy who's making them laugh."

"You're still the guy making people laugh. When you have a passion to do something, it follows you like a stalker, reminding you what you came here to do," I tell him.

"Yeah, but it's hard, comedy. It's so much work. Everyone wants to be famous."

"Fine, so here's the plan: Keep working at Starbucks, throw away your dreams, and in ten years, you'll have yellow teeth and a nice big ulcer and you'll still be wanting to do comedy, only you won't because then you'll give the excuse that now you're too old."

"Is my dad around?" Stewart asks. "I've got a few things I want to say to him."

Stewart spoke, and his father listened. He didn't have a choice actually, because his dad couldn't get a word in without me, and I didn't let him interrupt once. Stewart needed to say what he never allowed himself to, which allowed Stewart to move forward. Now he's on the road doing comedy, filling his mind with pictures of people laughing, all because of him.

*D*riving home from our tour, I think of how everything begins with a decision.

On March 30, 2002, Satori and I made the decision to pack up our SUV and our dog, and head out on a journey to visit places we'd never been. We needed to trust that whether one person or two hundred people showed up, whether we encountered an electrical storm on a night we didn't have a hotel (it happened!), whether a man spewed obscenities in the name of God, whether we were tired or hungry or had no idea if we missed the exit, we'd still have the most incredible time of our life; no matter what happened, we'd still have fun.

As close as Satori and I were before we left home, as we made our way back, we were even closer. As we peed at our last truck stop, or freeway ditch, whichever came first, as Satori sang to Michael Bolton and Siobhan snored in the backseat, I allowed myself to remember: Sitting at our kitchen table, deciding where to go. Calling stores, booking events, printing posters, sending packages, faxing, mailing flyers to clients (thank you for helping!), arriving at our first snowy destination to a warm, loving crowd, driving while almost out of a gas with not a station in sight, seeing the maggots—"Is that deer meat?," driving fifteen hours a day, asking locals, "Where did you say we were?" Smiling, eager faces—"I hope she calls on me. Oh no, what if she calls on me?" Over 492 readings in thirty-four cities in fifty-six days. What in the heck carried us through?

How did we do it?

When can we do it again?

9

WHEN A CHILD IS MURDERED

'm sitting at a friend's kitchen table in Sweden when I meet her.

By the fingertips pressing deeply into her neck, the large hands tightening around her collarbone, and the simple jerking motion that causes her body to hurl through the air and forcefully slam itself into the ground, I know she was murdered.

She tells me her name is Jennifer and describes to me how she died.

"I am practicing karate with the instructor. The smirk on his face disgusts me, as does the smell of his stinking warm breath. How strange it feels so close to death when all I want is to live. I am eighteen years old. A quick snap of the wrist, sharp steady pressure applied to exactly the right spot, will kill me. 'Please, don't do this!' I beg him. 'Listen to me. Just listen. I've got plans for the summer and a job and . . . you're not even listening. Think about what you're about to do. THINK!'

"Before the officer arrives at my house, my mother knows. . . . When she walks in my room that morning and sees the untouched CD she'd left on

my bed the night before . . . she knows something is terribly wrong. She knows this because of a mother's intuition.

"She knows I am dead because I tell her."

When Satori's friend Anna calls and asks if I'd do a reading for a Swedish couple whose daughter was murdered, the first thing I say is "Don't tell me their names, any details, nothing." The less I know the more validations I can bring through.

The following day, we arrive at the countryside home of Jennifer's parents, who introduce themselves as Dagmar and Anders Wallin. In their eyes, I see much pain. I know nothing of how it feels to lose a child.

A family friend, Swedish singer Denise Lopez, arrives to lend support.

This time Jennifer goes into more detail about the night she was murdered.

"I'm tired. Sweaty. He tries to kiss me. I push him away. He pulls me closer. I spit in his face. He slaps me. I run. He catches me, grabs my arm, twists it around, and shoves me into him. He looks at me, then releases. He twirls me around so my back is pressed against his chest. He takes his large hands and wraps them around my neck.

"I try to wriggle free, 'Loosen your hands, you're hurting me,' I tell him. He doesn't.

"I cannot breathe. I cannot scream. I cannot break free . . . and then WHAM! He flips me over his head and slams me into the ground. As the back of my head hits the floor, I remember thinking, I'm going to die. Not a conscious thought, just simply, My life is over. Everything I'd planned for my future is squashed, same as rubbing out a cigarette with the heel of your shoe."

Dagmar confirms everything. Satori translates it just to be sure.

"He wrapped her in a blanket, drove her to the woods and dumped her body under a tree. But the blanket is gone," I tell them. "He gave it to someone as a gift. I know that's sick, but—"

"Yes, he wrapped her in the blanket and took back the blanket to give to his father as a gift," Dagmar explains. "He is a sick man, yes."

"He's very manipulative . . . cocky, reminds me of this murder in Central Park." I explain Robert Chambers strangling Jennifer Levin in 1986. I am astonished by the similarities. Both are named Jennifer, one was seventeen, the other eighteen, both murdered in the summer, both found under a tree, both strangled, both killers claimed it was an accident, both were cocky, good-looking men who later made themselves out to be the victims.

Suddenly, Jennifer shows me her hands. "She is showing me something is wrong with her thumb," I tell them. "Injured. Broken. Jennifer's thumbs are broken."

Her parents shake their heads no. Satori translates what I've said into Swedish.

"She insists her thumbs were broken because she is showing me a snap in the bone."

"No."

"Are you sure? Did you see the autopsy report?"

"Yes, we saw it. Nothing broken. Nothing with the hands."

"You're sure?"

"We're sure."

"Huh. That's strange. She keeps showing me this and a deep scratch on his face."

"No. No scratch on his face," they say.

"You're sure."

"We're sure."

I let it go and move on.

Jennifer describes a conversation she had with her mom ten days before she died.

They are sitting in the car, conversing about boys, school, clothing, nothing heavy, when Dagmar brings up the subject of Swedish law and complains how murderers and rapists get away with only a slap on the wrist. "I've got to do something!" Dagmar exclaims. "I must!"

"Yeah, Mom, right, whatever . . . You think you can change the whole world," Jen laughs.

"You've got to start somewhere. I can't complain and do nothing. I can sow a seed."

"You think you're Superwoman," Jennifer chides, and kisses her Mom on the cheek.

A week later, Jennifer says, "Mom, I've thought about it and I think you should do it."

"Do what?" Dagmar asks, forgetting about their conversation.

"Sow a seed, begin to plant. Say what you think. Make a change. I know you can do it."

"I will. I will do it," Dagmar promises.

"You mean it?"

"I will. I'll start in the fall."

"Promise me, Mom. Don't just talk."

"I promise."

"Good, and I can help you out. I'm gonna have lots of schoolwork, but I can help out."

Dagmar confirms the conversation. She cannot believe Jennifer remembered.

"She won't get off your case until you do something. You know that, don't you?"

"It's too hard now," Dagmar says. "Before it was easy. It wasn't personal like this."

"I'll make her write a book about me, with all my karate trophies and all my friends saying how great I am," Jennifer laughs.

"I'll think about writing and doing something," Dagmar says. "That's all I can promise."

Anders interrupts. "You both come to court tomorrow and see the monster."

I can't believe that two months after Jennifer is murdered, her family has to face her killer in court.

Noon, the following day, Satori and I walk in the courthouse.

There are no guards. No policemen. No metal detectors. No X-ray machines.

The only thing letting me know I am in a courthouse is the sign outside the building.

Jennifer's mom runs toward us. "Her thumbs were broken!" she cries. "Autopsy photos show her thumbs broken. The scratch from Jennifer's nails is on his face. We said no yesterday, but today, we saw it in the photos, in the coroner's report. He told us himself."

Once again, a spirit reveals what their loved ones did not know.

Dagmar leads us into the Ikea-decorated courtroom to join twenty spectators, half from the murderer's side and half to support Jennifer. In Sweden, only three out of five jurors must agree to either convict or to let the murderer walk free.

Jennifer's family and the prosecutors are to my left. The murderer, his defense team, and his bodyguards, sit to my right.

Only the jury faces us.

During questioning and cross-examination, the witnesses sit between the defense table and the prosecution table. They never face the murderer or the family whose child was killed. The lawyers do their questioning and cross-examination while seated. They never make eye contact with the witnesses or use their body language or voice to intimidate anyone on the stand.

I want the killer to know that although he has taken Jennifer's life, he has not gotten rid of her. He cannot kill her spirit. He is not that powerful.

His name is Dimitrios Wennman. But Jennifer prefers I call him The Murderer.

I look at him, with his slicked-back hair and clean-shaven skin. He cocks his head and smirks at me and immediately I want to slap him in the face! Jennifer tells me he's not worth it because thoughts of his deeds will haunt him forever.

Jennifer's mom holds her hands across her heart and mouths "thank you," and I mouth, "you're welcome," and I think about how painful it must be sitting so close to the man who murdered their child.

Yesterday, I was channeling Jennifer and today, I sit near her killer.

His family is behind me. Can they feel Jennifer's presence? Can they feel the pain their son has caused?

The judge slams down his gavel, startling me out of my trance.

Court is now in session.

Let the lies begin.

Satori translates what they're saying from Swedish to English as quickly as he can write.

The energy in the room is borderline comatose; nothing at all like the emotionally heated sensationalistic trials one sees in American courtrooms. Here, everyone is overly pleasant and cordial, with lots of nodding and forced smiles. Several times the judge tells the prosecutor to speak up. She is meeker than a mouse, which scares me because we need an elephant, not a rodent, to bring justice to Jennifer's family.

First on the witness stand is Jennifer's close friend. The murderer's lawyer asks if Jennifer had many boyfriends. The girl says no.

No further questions.

Next witness. Same question.

This friend elaborates, saying, "Jennifer had boyfriends, just average for an eighteen-year-old."

No objections. No outbursts. No further questions.

Wait! I have further questions! Like why is the murderer in a psychiatric ward instead of a jail? Is it because he threatened to commit suicide, then miraculously recovered when offered art therapy and naptime instead of becoming somebody's bitch called Barbara?

Jennifer's father, Anders, gets questioned next.

The defense asks how much he earns and how much he's lost since his daughter's death. The lawyer doesn't call it murder, which angers Jennifer to no end. *"Death is illness, freak accidents, old age—I didn't die! HE MURDERED ME!"* she screams in my ear.

Anders tells the court he cannot think straight. He cannot work. He cannot function.

"You own your own company, is that correct, Mr. Wallin?" the defense lawyer asks.

Anders nods. "Yes, I do."

"You work for yourself then, is that correct?"

"Yes."

"Who decides your salary, Mr. Wallin?"

He is silent. The lawyer is insinuating that because Mr. Wallin works for himself, sets his own wages, he should not be entitled to receive money for loss of work, pain, or suffering.

"Who decides your salary, Mr. Wallin?" the scumbag lawyer repeats.

In a low voice, he responds, "I do."

"No further questions."

Court is adjourned.

Not one mention of Jennifer's brutal murder. Not one graphic depiction of the horrors that took place or the impact left on her family. Did Jenny have boyfriends? Do you set your own salary? These are the crucial elements of today's courtroom dramas.

A few days later, Dagmar addresses the jury: "I am Jennifer's mother. I'm fifty-two years old. My husband and I are here because our daughter, Jennifer, is not coming home. It's not because she's away at camp. She's not away on vacation. She was murdered. And because of that, we have pain that no pills or Band-Aids can heal. Jennifer wanted to be an old lady. She wanted to leave this earth lying in a field of wild-flowers, old and wrinkled, this is what my child told me when she turned sixteen. . . ."

Strong and centered, Dagmar faces the murderer and blasts his name, "Dimitrios! You are a master at lying! Your position in society is between the dirt on the ground and the heel of my shoe. You are not worthy to call a man. You are not worthy to be a father. You call your-self a 'good man' but I say—the devil has got a new face!"

In less than a month, a man in England will receive fifteen years in prison for having sex with his girlfriend after she said no, while the man who murdered and then dumped Jennifer Wallin like trash, receives only ten years, which in Sweden, means he'll be out in six or seven.

On March 19, 2003, I receive a package from Dagmar that reconfirms there is always hope . . . and a way to heal. It is the book she wrote for her daughter called *Älskadé, Jennifer,* which in English simply means *I Love You, Jennifer.* It is complete with photos of Jennifer's karate trophies and letters about what a great person she is from all her very best friends.

n Pacific Palisades, California, while making funny faces in the bathroom of Village Books as part of my pre-seminar ritual, I meet Angela.

I'm about to leave the bathroom when I feel a tug on the end of my sleeve and look down to see a little girl with tussled hair. She's so cute. She climbs on the toilet seat and points to my reflection in the mirror and whispers, *"Who're ya looking at?"*

A rather strange question, but I silently answer, "Myself."

"How do ya know it's you?" She giggles.

I'm thinking, This kid is deep, so I challenge her. "How do you know it's not?"

"I didn't say it's not. Which part is you?" She wraps her tiny fingers around my nose. *"Is this you?"* She touches my lips, *"Is this?"* She taps on my ears. *"Are these you? Think 'bout it, now come on, we have an appointment. My mommy's not here tonight, but her friend is."*

She jumps off the toilet seat and disappears.

Next thing I know, I'm in front of the room and she's sitting on the floor. *"I was murdered,"* she whispers. I tell the crowd what she has told me. *"She says her mommy's friend is here tonight."* The room is silent. No one replies. Then I hear, "Lysa, over here!"

"My friend's daughter was murdered," a woman in the far corner admits.

"She was six years old," I say. She nods. "Her name is Angela."

"Yes," the woman confirms. "Angela's the little girl."

I spend the next few minutes channeling Angela. I'm about to wrap up when this woman raises her hand and says, "I don't understand why this kid is taking up all our time when her own mother didn't show up and there are people here who also want to connect!"

"Excuse me, but this kid had only six years on this earth, give her a little respect!" I tell the woman.

Angela cheers! She's 100 percent spunk. She follows me home, and for weeks, she's talking to me, teaching me how to relax, yelling when I'm at the computer too long, reminding me to go into Satori's office instead of him always having to come into mine. She tells me she's planning a surprise and will see me soon.

Two months later, she's back again.

I'm doing an event at Brentanos in the Beverly Center in Los Angeles and she comes in screaming at the top of her invisible lungs, *"Mommy's here!"*

She points to a woman wearing a funky hat and tells me that's her mother.

"She put my photo in the pouch around her neck," Angela says. Her mom confirms it.

Several weeks later, I'm at Brentanos in Century City speaking about Angela to the crowd. As I say her name, a cell phone rings, and a woman cries out, "Oh my God!" Out from behind the bookshelf walks Angela's mom holding her phone, saying it was turned off. "It rang when you mentioned Angela," she says and I think, "What does this little girl need her mother to know?"

Nine months go by before I finally find out.

Angela's mom comes for a reading, and as she's waiting in my office, I'm in the bathroom clutching the sink, spitting up mucus, feeling terrified of what I've just seen.

Angela shows, in vivid detail, the brutality of what these monsters did to her little body—brutally raping and beating her.

"They can torture my body. My spirit remains whole."

Angela insists I tell her mom every graphic detail. I refuse. She says I must. I fight, I don't understand why. She says I will and asks if I trust her. I do, and so, I say it, all of it, having to stop every few minutes to catch my breath.

It is brutal.

It is disgusting.

It is necessary.

When I am finished, Angela's mom looks at me and says, "Everything you said is correct. I know because I was there, in and out of consciousness. I saw what they did to her."

"No one can touch her spirit. No one can destroy her soul. She is not what they killed."

It becomes clear why, the first time we met, Angela asked me how I knew I was looking at myself in the mirror.

None of it—not my nose, my ears, my cheeks, my lips—is truly me. If Angela was her body and her body was destroyed, then she would be destroyed, but she's not. If she were, I wouldn't be able to speak to her. She wouldn't be able to come through.

"Mommy thinks I died because she spoke up about what she believed," Angela tells me.

Her mother believed in an extremely good cause, but certain people wanted her to shut up. They threatened to kill Angela if she didn't stop. She never thought they were serious. She didn't believe they would follow through.

When Angela died, her mother went into hiding. She shut down and made a decision to never speak out again because speaking out = pain. Silence = safety.

She spent thirteen years in hiding. She spent thirteen years without a voice, and you know what I mean by a voice—truly speaking her mind and being who she really is.

I tell her that speaking up doesn't cause bad things to happen. There isn't a direct correlation, even though she'd formed one. If I hit my head and my head gets a bump, there is a direct correlation between my hitting my head and the bump. The hitting caused the bump.

Her speaking out did not cause her daughter's murder. She could speak out again and nothing bad would happen. Although there are no guarantees because every time we speak what we believe, we risk retaliation due to intolerance. But not speaking up is much worse because, by remaining silent, we feel dead.

Satori works with her to switch her associations so that remaining silent will equal pain and speaking out will equal freedom.

Nearly a year passes before I receive a phone call that completely blows me away. Angela's mom calls to say she's headed to New York to be one of the lead speakers at a convention of Parents of Murdered Children and . . .

For the first time in fourteen years . . .

She does not feel afraid.

10

LIVING WITH UNCERTAINTY

*I*magine:

You.

Alone in your bedroom at night.

Candles lit.

Cozying up with a good book.

Right in the middle of an exciting chapter, you hear footsteps. You quickly jump out of bed. The steps get louder. Closer. Your heart is pounding. You can hardly breathe. The bedroom door flings open. A stranger walks into your bedroom. Points a shotgun at your head. Your heart stops. This can't be happening. Oh my God!

Imagine:

You.

Alone in your bedroom at night.

Candles lit.

Cozying up with a good book.

Right in the middle of an exciting chapter, you hear footsteps. You clutch the covers. Your mouth becomes dry. You can hardly breathe. You quickly jump out of bed. The steps get closer. Your heart beats louder. The bedroom door opens. The love of your life is at the door!

Hearing footsteps in the house is scary only when you're not expecting company.

How do we live through a tragic event and not remain terrified forever? How do we deal with the uncertainty of not knowing what's going to happen, when it's going to happen, or even if it's going to happen? How do we get over the fear of living in a world where so much uncertainty exists?

Yesterday, I heard a message from my dad telling me he's going in for surgery. I hear him explain how doctors say he needs a pacemaker and they need to remove a cancerous tumor in his ankle. Tears stream down my face as I think of him dying. I never want him to go.

"He can die when he's ninety-eight!" I shout at the spirits. "You can't have him until then!"

I lay on my pillow. Crying softly, careful to not wake Satori.

I mentally watch old movies of my dad and me—going to Jones Beach, seeing three movies in a row, talking for hours.

I think about the first time I saw him cry. We were sitting on the steps of the St. James Church in New York City and he was telling me how much he loves me and how divorcing my mom and moving out of the house was the single most painful experience of his life.

My dad assures me he'll be fine.

"I'm not done," he says. "I'm not leaving anytime soon."

Facing our mortality—the fact that one day we will not exist in the way we now do—is something our mind cannot fully comprehend. No matter how much we think about death and what happens when we die, we will never fully grasp it. Yet . . .

How do we learn how to say good-bye to one form of life and hello to the next?

When someone we love dies, our life becomes this tunnel and all we can focus on is the person we love who is no longer here. Nothing else matters.

How harsh the world feels in contrast to our pain. Noise is louder, people feel harsher, the hustle and bustle of daily life rubs like sandpaper against our wound.

Pondering the crossing of my parents, of anyone I love, causes this overwhelming ache of sadness in my gut. My first instinct is to wipe it out, to think happy thoughts, and not go there, not feel.

The spirits have taught me better.

"Whatever you resist—persists."

"Whatever you avoid—follows you."

"Whatever you fear—controls you."

Worrying doesn't change anything.

Worrying is a distraction we use when we feel out of control. It's a diversion while we're waiting for the police officer to let us know if they found our child. If we sit by the phone worrying, at least our mind is occupied.

If worrying changed the outcome, I'd say, worry all the time. But it doesn't. It just makes us feel sick inside. Instead of worrying, we need to focus on what we can control—our thoughts, our actions, the direction of our mind.

Letting go scares us.

What would happen if I let myself go and allowed myself to feel? What do I fear would happen if I stopped resisting?

When I think of resisting, I think of my friend Tom Degree, who died of AIDS many years ago. Once he took me to a white-water-rafting site and asked me, "What do you see?"

"People in rafts, screaming," I laughed.

"Watch the water and the rocks. Look closely."

I squinted my eyes, searching for clues to his inquisition.

I shrugged. I saw nothing but water and rocks.

"Does the water go into the rocks or around them?"

I looked closely, noticing how the water cascaded around the sides of the rocks.

"The water knows exactly where to go," he said. "It doesn't tense up and say, 'I hope I don't hit the rocks.' It relaxes and goes around the rocks, not just once, but every time."

Back then, I found this story a bit trite. Years later, I thought about it again, about the people screaming in rafts, as if screaming would help their boat not crash into the rocks, and the story taught me an important lesson.

Screaming was totally ineffective yet people continued doing it.

They needed to feel certain about something, so screaming is what they chose. I believe the way to live with uncertainty is by focusing on what we can control. Our thoughts. Our focus. What we tell ourselves: "I will get through this. I can get through this. I am getting through this. I am through this."

We assume we'll receive another day in our body.

We don't know for sure, and that scares us.

We need assurance because we don't trust. We don't see the life we're meant to be living so maybe a psychic will, or if we do see it, it looks nothing like the life we're currently in.

We need to believe life is not just a series of random incidents and unrelated events.

We need to believe there is a light, not just at the end of the tunnel, but at frequent intervals along the way.

The only way we can live with uncertainty is by knowing that life is uncertain.

An hour from now I may not be here in the way I now am. Neither may you. You are here now. So am I. This moment is all we have.

*S*atori comes rushing into the house, "Honey, Tony Robbins is doing Competitive Edge in New York. We have to go!"

"I don't want to go," I say, raining on his parade.

"I want to go, and you know I won't go without you, so you have to go."

I know he won't let this slide.

"Maybe we can stay with my grandmother," I say, as he kisses my entire face.

My grandmother lives in Forest Hills, Queens, in the apartment my mother was raised, which meant we'd be sleeping on the same bed my mother slept on. It crunches when you lie on it, like Styrofoam. That's how old it is.

"I go to the toilet at night. I'll wake you," my grandma informs me.

Grandma's place is out, but my dad's pal offers to let us use his apartment for two days.

"What about the other five days?" I ask Satori.

"We'll get a hotel."

Tony's event isn't until the following week, so Satori and I decide to attend a seminar called the Forum, which is an updated version of the EST seminar I took when I was thirteen.

Some people attend seminars to be fixed, some to be reminded of what they know, some to bitch and complain about their life, some to pick up men or women. We attend to have fun—lots of it. After the seminar, we're hanging out with some of the people we met and I ask this lady, whose name I don't even know, about good hotels in the area. Next thing I know, I've got the keys to her apartment.

She tells us she's going out of town and if we remember to feed her cat and take in the mail and leave the place neat, it's ours for the week. I'm thinking, It can't get any more woo-woo than this!

The next day, Satori meets my grandma, Sylvia, my mom's mother, who once chased a mugger five blocks to get back her purse, and that's when she was eighty-two.

Now she's eighty-four and spunkier than ever. She's never at home. "Grandma, where do you go at ten o'clock at night? I call, you don't answer."

"What, do you want me to sit around like an old person?" she laughs.

At lunch, she tells us about how my grandfather came to her in a dream, which she says wasn't a dream; he was there, he was real, she remembers it clear as day.

"I'm sound asleep when something wakes me. I sit up and there's your grandfather at the end of my bed. 'Murray, what are you doing here?' I ask him, and that's when it occurs to me, he's here to come get me. It's my time to die. I yell, 'I'm not going anywhere! Go on, get!' I kick him as hard as I can, and then I wake up."

Before we leave, my grandmother whispers, "You did good. The way he adores you, holds you around. You take care of each other, and grow your hair long. It looks better long. Put those streaks in again. Will you do that for me? The blonde streaks."

"Yes, Grandma," I tell her.

Several months later, I receive a frantic call from my uncle Bob.

"We arrived to pick her up for Passover dinner, but no one answered," Bob tells me. "The apartment manager let us in—"

"Was she at the corner of the bed, in the front?"

"Yes. The medic said she must've fallen getting out."

She didn't fall. She tried to kick Grandpa out, but this time, she didn't have a say.

I hang up and dial my mom's cell phone. I'm hoping she doesn't answer. I'm not ready to tell her that her own mother just died.

On the fourth ring, she picks up. "Where are you, Mom?"

"Driving. What's up, hon?"

"How far are you from home?"

"Lysa, what's going on?"

"Can you pull over?"

I wait in silence, thinking about how I should word it. I've never told someone news like this. I don't want it to come out harshly or bluntly, or . . . "Mom, Uncle Bob called. It's about Grandma. . . ."

That's all it takes for my mom to know.

At her funeral, I keep looking at the casket, thinking, My grandma's body is in there.

When I was a kid, I remember standing beside my grandpa's casket and, when no one was looking, putting my hand against his face. It felt like rubber. "Why did they make Grandpa feel like rubber?" I asked my mom.

"It's just his body," is all she said.

At the time, I didn't realize there was anything more.

A spur-of-the-moment trip to New York to attend a seminar led to Satori meeting my grandma for the first time, and to me seeing her for the last. . . .

Being willing to step outside my comfort zone and trust Satori about going to New York taught me that anytime we have an opportunity to do something with someone we love, we must take it, go for it, and not allow worry to hold us back.

Sometimes, we're led somewhere for a bigger reason than we may know.

I think of my mom's friend, Gary Levine, a dentist who wanted to be an actor.

At age forty-five, he closed his practice, enrolled in acting class, and auditioned for a play. When he got the lead, he told my mom, "I feel like a kid again. I can't sleep, I'm so excited about waking up. My parents think I've gone crazy. My friends think I'm a schmuck."

"What do you think?" my mom asks.

"I think I'm going to be a star!"

Four months later, doctors tell Gary he has cancer.

"I closed my practice because I knew if I didn't do it now, I'd never do it. I crammed everything I've wanted to do into four months of absolute bliss, and I can honestly say that when my time is up, I will die a happy man."

A month later, Gary died. Smiling.

11

BEING UNSTOPPABLE

What stops you? Do people's negative comments stop you? Does fear of looking stupid or fear of what people think stop you?

If I allowed people's negative comments to stop me, I'd never leave the house because if there's one thing people love giving, it's their opinion.

My friend once told a group of his colleagues, all doctors, about the work I do, and several of them laughed in my face. One guy, a proctologist, challenged me to give him a reading on the spot, to which, I replied, "Not before you give your friend here an exam."

We are all influenced by what other people think.

"No!" you may say. "I think for myself! I make my own decisions! I decide my life!"

Although we'd like to believe we choose our own clothing, music, jobs, home, car, what we're attracted to, and what turns us off. We don't, not always.

Everyone is telling us what they think we should do, wear, eat, what movies to see, friends to have, vacations to take, jobs to apply for, people we should date or marry, how we should feel. We receive so much input, it's a wonder we can even hear ourselves.

To top it off, spirits tell me they're sending us thoughts, ideas, things to take action on.

"Just because you get an idea, why do you automatically think it's yours?" a spirit asks. *"I thought the same until I died and started sending people ideas. People are going along and suddenly—an idea hits them! They can't contain themselves. They talk about it so much then forget to take action, until one day, they see their idea in a store window and scream, 'Somebody stole my idea!' Nobody stole your idea. We drop the same idea on many people, and if you don't act on it, someone else will."*

The spirits say our destiny is what we've always wanted. Since I was a kid, I loved writing and helping people. But loving something isn't enough, they say. It must be backed by action, which must be backed by the belief that you will succeed doing what you love.

"Your life can be used for something extraordinary if you let it."

Years ago, I used to start a project, stop in the middle, and start another. Start, stop, start, stop, until I had a trail of unfinished projects behind me. The spirits explain how everyone has supporters in the spirit world, these guides who are assigned to assist us in making our dreams come true, but every time we start something and quit, we're screwing up our true destiny.

Just imagine all your guides have been asleep because you haven't taken any risks for a while. They're just chilling until one day you get this idea. Your guides go nuts, shouting to the others, "Get up! Get up! She's got an idea! She's going to take action! We have to get to work!"

Say your idea is to write a book. You begin writing, and it's flowing and you're jamming and your guides are assisting, sending you the right words exactly when you need them, while others are working their butts off trying to orchestrate "chance" meetings to have a friend happen to know a good agent who happens to want to represent you.

Then, you go to the library and you're standing there looking at all the books and you tell yourself, "Look at this place! There are millions of books, how is anyone going to find mine? It's too hard. It's not worth it, all that rejection and pain and critical reviews. Forget this."

You quit. You throw your book in a drawer and immediately resume your old, safe life.

All your guides are like, "Oh man, there she goes again! Quitting what she loves. Okay, you know the drill, it's back to sleep until she has the next brilliant idea."

We'd love every person to achieve and fulfill their destiny, but not everyone will, and it isn't because they're meant to fail. It's because they don't do whatever it takes to succeed. They sell out, give up, and stop listening to their soul. They cower in the face of challenge instead of becoming unstoppable and forging ahead.

I'm not big on cowering. I tried it. It sucks. I'm not big on quitting, ignoring my vision, or allowing others to silence my voice, which can sometimes be a challenge.

Case in point: Hollywood producers.

After hearing me on the radio and seeing me on TV, Hollywood producers came knocking, and it seemed everyone had the next big idea for what would make a hit psychic show. Everyone, except the psychic they wanted to hire for her exceptional psychic skills.

"What I do is create great TV," a producer with a ponytail down to his ass tells me. "Picture this: You're facing three closed doors, the studio audience is on the edge of their seats, they're waiting for you to tell them, get this: Who's behind door number one!"

I'm thinking, Unless it's Tom Cruise, I don't really give a fuck.

Oh, wait! I know what's behind door number one—my ass as I leave your office.

Next stop, Dick Clark Productions. There we meet Al Shapiro, a producer for more than twenty years who tells me Peters Hurkos once gave him a reading that totally blew him away.

We meet with USA Productions and VH1.

VH1 executives Kim Rozenfeld, Lisa Lee, and Liz Vesanovic sit around the conference table, waiting to hear our show ideas, but I can't concentrate until I get something off my chest. This wasn't the kind of atmosphere where I could just blurt out, "By the way, did any of you feel like puking at eight this morning, and did a friend call to say she may be pregnant?"

But that's what happened, so I needed to say it.

Liz flips out, "That's totally weird. I felt nauseous this morning and was going to call in sick. A friend of mine called and said she might be pregnant."

"Well, tell her she is," I laugh.

"Anything else we should know?" Lisa Lee asks me.

"There's a show you guys are developing, *Late Night with Zak* I think it's called, and, I don't mean to be rude, I know it's not on the air yet, but it'll be canceled after two months."

That night, Liz calls to say her friend took a home pregnancy test and is pregnant.

Late Night with Zak gets on the air, and is canceled exactly two months later.

"I could save the networks a lot of money," I joke with Satori. "Predicting the fate of their television shows."

I love the impact a TV show can have reaching millions of people, but I wasn't willing to compromise my vision just to get on TV.

Paramount Pictures Television (yes, the company that fired me when I was a temp) does a deal with a production company for a new prime-time series in which a spirit medium, tarot reader, runes reader, and psychic all do a reading for the same guest. When a ten-page contract offering me the job of spirit medium for the pilot show arrives in the mail, I feel excited . . . for about five seconds.

Although Sylvia Browne claims psychics cannot do readings on themselves, I was reading myself loud and clear, and what myself was telling me was that this show would never air.

I tell one of the producers, "Deb, I don't see the show getting on the air. I don't see it working the way it is."

She laughs, "Lysa, you're a wonderful psychic. The show is getting enormous support with Kelsey Grammer's company and Paramount behind it. I am certain it will air."

My head is spinning. I am confused. How do I know which one of us is correct? Can't she be right? Why is my belief it won't work stronger than her belief it will? I need to know for sure. I need a sign, something to help me make this decision.

In the legal jargon, I find it. The contract states I can't work on any other television projects for one year while they decide whether or not to air the sample episode. If they air it, I am contractually bound for seven years, whether or not another episode ever airs. All they have to do is pay me $500 a week to prevent me from working on any other show.

This is like breaking up with your significant other, then paying them $500 a week not to have another relationship. You don't want to be with them. You just want them to be there in case, someday, you do. In the meantime, they must remain alone.

Two years have passed, and the show has never aired.

'm in the kitchen when I hear these words, *"You are meant to do something bigger. You are meant to do something more,"* which are followed by, *"He speaks to the living. She speaks to the dead . . . and they just happen to be married . . . to each other."*

I write it down and then change it to: She's a Radical Psychic Medium. He's a Kick-Ass Life Coach. And they just happen to be madly in love and married . . . to each other.

I don't know what this means, but I tell Satori I'm onto something and to put on his brainstorming gear because I'm ready to throw around ideas.

"Let's do a show called *Breakthrough*," I tell him.

"What's the show about? Who's it for? What going to happen?"

I look at him and shrug. I have no idea. I just start speaking, as if I know what I'm talking about, *"Breakthrough* is a show that reminds us how, in a second, our life changes. Just like that. There it is. Now it's gone. Someone you love dies. Walks out the door. Leaves you forever. Your dreams feel distant, impossible. You think about the person who's gone, and you desperately want them back. You get close to success, then stop yourself. You know what you want, but don't know how to get it. You act one way and feel another. You don't want to waste your life, but feel stuck and trapped. You're in desperate need of a BREAK-THROUGH!"

"Yeah, baby, that's it," he says, grabbing me around my waist.

In that moment, a show was born.

We're totally revved about the show, which from the start, Satori and I see on MTV.

"There are lots of networks," our agent, Dina, tells us. "If not MTV, someplace else."

"Dina, we want MTV."

Months pass and still no meeting with MTV. "John Miller is the president of original programming, he's a busy guy. You just can't call up and say you want a meeting," Dina tells us.

Why not? If it's meant to be, he'll respond. If it's not, we'll try again.

At three in the morning, after searching every production site on the Internet, I find his e-mail address and send him a note introducing myself, telling him what our show is about, and explaining how I'd like to meet with him as soon as possible.

Ten o'clock the next morning, I receive a reply: "I'd love to meet. My assistant will call to set up. Peace, J."

When I read it, part of me felt like, Oh shit, this was too easy. People will hate me. It's not okay to shine. The quick thought raced through my mind, in one ear and out the other, leaving me feeling a bit ill at ease.

I look at the Nelson Mandela quote taken from his 1994 inaugural speech, sitting on my bookshelf. I dust it off and read it again. "Our deepest fear is not that we are inadequate. Our deepest fear is that we are powerful beyond measure. It is our light, not our darkness, that most frightens us."

Satori and I meet with John Miller and executive Jessica Samet to pitch our show. They like the idea but need something more. Satori and I work on it for five more months, learning, studying, talking to people, asking questions and absorbing answers about how to create a television show.

I do phone readings for John and Jessica, which gives them first-hand experience of what I do. I edit a reel of Satori's work to show them his untraditional approach to therapy and how quickly people make changes.

Two days before we're set to fly to Sweden for our annual vacation, we walk into the MTV offices, ready to put our hard work on the line.

From the second we press play on the video demo we put together, they're smiling, laughing, genuinely touched. We leave feeling happy. The decision is now in their hands.

Vertitude reminds me, *"You don't get any points in life for watching the game, thinking about playing the game, or giving excuses for why you didn't. You may not always win the game, but if you play full out, you never lose."*

12

Money and Spirituality

Money doesn't get rid of our problems.

It just gives us a bigger house in which to deal with them.

If you're a broke angry bastard, and you win the lottery, chances are you'll still be an angry bastard. You'll just wear nicer clothes.

Money doesn't change people, although some people get money, and change.

People steal when they don't have money, and people steal when they do have money, which proves money is not the issue. What we believe money represents is.

"You shouldn't charge for your sessions," a woman once said. "You're spiritual."

Okay great, so I will give my heart and soul. I will connect myself with the spirits of your loved ones. I will assist you in every way I can. I will travel around the country and do free events at bookstores. No, wait, I can't travel because I won't have money for a car, and you can't call me for a session because I won't be able to afford a phone or a place to live. I must suffer in poverty to serve you. That's not being spiritual. It's being stupid.

If you want to fly to see your sick mother in Nebraska, you're going to need money. If you want to pay your sick child's hospital bills, you're going to need money. The more you have, the more you have to give to others, the more you can create in this world.

"There is nothing spiritual about being broke," the spirits tell me. *"There is nothing spiritual about spending your time worrying about how you're going to pay the bills. Beautiful things exist in this world. It's not our place to judge people for having them. They are available to all who are willing to work hard by doing what they love and never quitting. Tough times are temporary. Quitting is forever."*

I think about this and realize that if I want to live in a beautiful house on the water, I won't apologize to people when I move in. I'd rather invite them to come and enjoy the view.

Vertitude tells me, *"High-level spirituality is, I will be an example of what is possible. The more I have . . . the more I have to give."*

Just like Oprah uses her wealth wisely by giving to charitable foundations, I want to open a school for psychic and mediumship development. I'd love it to be in an old castle where people can come to study and learn how to strengthen their psychic, mediumistic, and intuitive ability.

If I want to be an example of what is possible, it certainly won't happen if I tell people, "You can have enormous success, but I cannot."

How silly is that?

Ena Twigg, the British medium, did a session with a man whose entire existence was driven by purely material values. At the end of the session, when he revealed his real name, it was the name of one of the richest men in the world.

He said, "Mrs. Twigg, I'd give anything to have what you've got. I have everything money can buy, but I haven't got a thing of value."

"The fault is with you," Ena replied. "Money is a tool that can be used, but if you are going to sit like King Midas and look at gold, breathe gold, and think gold, well, that is all you will have. But there's a big hungry world out there. Go out and use your money for others, and you'll find your values."

You can't hoard money, or love, or material possessions, and expect to feel wonderful. You can't keep every penny locked in a safe and expect to feel abundant. This man had all the money in the world and still felt poor. He didn't experience himself as being rich and didn't use his wealth to make others feel rich. He denied enjoying what he'd worked so hard to create.

Inside, he felt bankrupt.

"It's who you become in the process of achieving wealth that matters," Satori reminds me. "Sure, having fancy cars, a big house, and a profitable business you built on your own is wonderful, but it won't necessarily make you feel successful."

Many people believe if they just lost weight, got a boyfriend or girlfriend, landed a record or movie deal, or achieved whatever they think they're lacking, they'd feel like a success. But they don't because their success is defined by material means rather than by who they become in the process of achieving wealth. Sometimes people keep themselves from having success and money because of the negative association they have around rich people.

"What gets you up in the morning?" I ask Peter Sung, a twenty-five-year-old aspiring artist.

"I've got to pee."

"You have to pee? That's what gets you up?"

"Yep, that's how exciting my life is," he says.

"You're an incredible artist, you know. You could get out of bed to paint and pee."

"Don't tell me to make it a business. I won't be a sellout."

"I didn't know you were so selfish, keeping your art all to yourself."

"I haven't suffered enough. People pay more for suffering artists."

I laugh.

"Suffering is noble. It creates depth people can relate to. I want to be successful, I do. It's just that I smoke pot and sleep till noon and I think it's getting in the way of my drive."

"What would happen if you already filled your suffering quota? What would be left in the space you used to fill with suffering?"

"I don't know."

"If you did know, what would it be?"

"I don't know, nothing, an empty slate, a blank canvas."

"A blank canvas is good. You start with a blank canvas before you paint."

"I'll give my paintings away, then I won't be selfish," he says.

"No, then you'll be broke. I'm not saying you can't donate stuff; of course, that's fine. But you deserve to make a good living by selling your art to people who can afford it."

"Rich people? Hell no. Rich people disgust me."

"Who, specifically?"

"All of them. I like who I am. I'm cool with me, I mean, yeah, I could give up the weed and drinking and the occasional hit of Ecstasy, but I don't want to become like my buddy Bruce, who sold his first painting for a hundred grand and became a dick."

"His not giving you money to buy weed made him a dick?"

"Guy's got a hundred grand and he can't fork over fifty; that's bull-shit."

"Maybe he woke up. Changed his life. Didn't want to support you in destroying yours."

"Yeah, fine. I got it. You're right."

"Insight is worthless if you don't do anything with it. If you don't go out and use what you know, who cares how much you know?"

"I'll prove you wrong. I'll sell my paintings."

"I don't want you to prove me wrong. I want you to prove you right. This has nothing to do with me. It has to do with your beliefs about what it means to be wealthy, what it means to be successful. It means changing your belief that suffering is noble."

"What if no one digs my work? No one wants to cough up the cash."

"Come on, you've got at least a billion potential buyers, so don't tell me you can't find at least sixty who will buy your work."

After a year of submitting his work to over 643 art galleries around the globe, Peter sold his first painting on December 12, 2002, for $28,000, of which not a cent went to buying pot.

13

How to Trust and Be True to Yourself

When I die, I really hope I'm not ignored.

It would suck to be talking to the people I love while they're denying my existence.

Spirits feel the same.

They understand if we don't recognize them immediately. They know it takes time to learn *how* they communicate and come through. They have patience for that.

Our denial is what hurts them.

Until we acknowledge that spirits do speak to us, we cannot learn *how* they speak. It's like saying you want to learn how to ride a bicycle but don't believe bicycles exist. How can you learn to ride something you don't believe is real?

Kids acknowledge stuff more easily because they don't have as many filters as adults. They trust themselves to say what they feel. "Grandpa likes the flowers you left by his grave. Grandma says to get me a new puppy."

Kids don't question spirits. They question adults.

"Mommy, why does Daddy's best friend stay overnight when Daddy is out of town?"

"Honey, go wash your face."

"Why?"

"It's time for dinner."

"Why?"

"You have to eat."

"Why?"

"Because I said so!"

Kids trust themselves completely, before adults come along and mess with their thinking.

Steven, a twenty-two-year-old client, trusted himself until a voice told him he was no good. No matter how many people said he was wonderful, this voice overruled them all.

"The voice tells me to hurt myself," Steven mumbles, looking down at his shoes.

"And you listen?"

He holds out his arm to show the gashes etched deeply in his skin. He points to a fresh one. "Steak knife," he says.

"Whose voice is it, Steven?"

"Mine."

"It's not yours. You weren't born with a voice telling you to cut yourself. What does it say? What does the voice tell you?"

He doesn't answer.

"Steven, it's your father's voice, not yours," I reply softly.

"If he's here, I don't want to fucking talk to him. I have nothing to say to that man."

"What you said was quite beautiful." I smile.

He laughs. "You're fucked up, you know that? It's cool. I like people who are fucked up."

Though Steven's father had control when he was child, when he could lock Steven in a closet or give him a beating, he no longer had control. Only Steven didn't realize this yet. He thought his father was instructing him to carve his skin.

"My dad is under my skin. I have to cut deep enough to get him out," Steven tells me.

"I'm surprised you didn't take off an arm."

His whole face lights up. He looks beautiful, and I tell him so.

You see, once he discovered the voice was not his own, he kicked it out and replaced it with a new voice that made him feel good. He learned to trust himself and no longer be ruled by the dictates of a man he vehemently despised.

He gave himself permission to be free.

I remember the first time I gave myself permission to be free.

I was walking with my mom in New York City.

It was cold. Butt-freezing cold, and we were on Fifth Avenue in the heart of upscale Manhattan.

Christmas shoppers were passing us, with bags from Gucci and FAO Schwarz.

Holiday fervor was in the air. Then suddenly, out of nowhere, in the middle of the crowd, I shouted, "MOVE ASIDE!" and went charging down the block, doing three cartwheels in a row.

I don't know what came over me. It was an urge. An impulse I had to fulfill. I didn't run through a series of questions: What will people think if I do cartwheels in the middle of Manhattan? What if I fall over and embarrass myself? What if I rip my pants?

I went straight from thought to action, no stopping in between.

That's acceptable when you're eleven.

When you're an adult, you're taught to think before you act. Actually, not only think, but obsess, worry, give yourself an ulcer, yell, go over an issue a zillion times to make sure you don't screw up, don't give the okay on that project because it may turn out to be a flop, or say yes and marry that person, only to find out you've made a mistake.

If you act and screw up, oh no, adults are not allowed to screw up. We can only obsess to the point of exhaustion.

I believe thinking before you act is useful when it comes to running in traffic or doing something harmful to yourself or others, but racking your brain with all the things that could possibly go wrong, before taking positive action, is a waste of your precious time and energy.

I know. I've done it many times. I've worried about speaking up and getting a backlash of anger from those receiving my words. I've fretted over screwing up a relationship with someone I love. I've questioned myself until my head pounded and my heart ached, and the only voice I heard was my own screaming for me to shut up!

To trust yourself, you must realize how much you already trust yourself.

You trust yourself to know when you have to go to the bathroom.

You trust yourself to know whether or not you like a movie.

You trust your heart to beat.

You trust the sun will rise tomorrow.

You trust politicians to deliver what they promise. (Maybe not.)

You can trust yourself to trust yourself.

How?

By listening to your gut. By trusting yourself to trust yourself.

Over the years, I'd hear my mom say she was soul searching, looking to find herself, and I'd be thinking, Why would you be searching for something that's already inside of you?

Was there another self I didn't know about? A self that only adults had access to?

To find out, I looked in the mirror and introduced myself to myself.

"Nice to meet you, Lysa," I said.

"Nice to meet you, too," I replied.

"So what do you like to do for fun?" I asked.

"I like movies, acting, dancing, music, writing, reading, being goofy," I said.

"Me, too!" I replied, excited that me and myself had so much in common.

You may think this is silly, but it's something I now do at least once a year. I introduce myself to myself, and Satori and I introduce ourselves to each other. We do it to keep things fresh so we never take each other for granted, so we constantly see each other with brand-new eyes.

I believe that who we are at our core, our essence, our spirit, remains the same. We grow and learn, yes, but most of our life is spent returning to ourselves, to the original us who arrived with all our dreams, possibilities, and curiosity intact.

Look in the mirror and introduce yourself to yourself and ask, "What makes you feel excited? What makes you feel sad? What do you love talking about? What bores you to tears?"

I did this process most intensely when I was recovering from bulimia, when I didn't know who I'd be without binging and throwing up. I wrote one thing a day I liked, just for me, not because my mom liked it, or because it would impress my dad, or anyone told me it was cool. I wrote things I liked purely because I liked them.

This is how I began to construct an authentic life.

*O*ur human needs are certainty, variety, significance, connection and love, growth, and the need to contribute beyond ourselves.

The question is not *if* we will fill these needs, the question is, "How will we fill them?"

Being a reporter taught me how far people will go to be seen and heard; to get significance, connection and love; to get variety and certainty.

After September 11, Osama bin Laden couldn't have paid someone to get that kind of publicity: *Larry King Live, Time, People, Newsweek, USA Today, CNN, Los Angeles Times, New York Times,* every major newspaper around the globe featured the face of a guy who led his followers to destroy thousands of innocent lives.

"Giving criminals enormous media exposure sends the message: If you commit a crime, people will take notice of you. The more horrific the crime, the bigger the book deal. The media rewards negative actions by giving criminals the celebrity they desire."

Does it mean the only way to get significance is to become a criminal? Of course not. It means we need to start rewarding acts of kindness, love, and bravery, just as much, if not more, than "rewarding" acts of violence and crime.

We do everything for a reason, and a purpose, that serves us. Gang members choose to be in a gang because it fills their needs, albeit, in a way that does not help them to contribute and grow. They feel *certain* they can count on their buddies. They get *variety* because, at any moment, someone could get shot. They *connect* with their gang family and kill for each other as their way of showing their *love.* They feel *significant* being part of something not everyone can join.

People keep doing what they're doing as long as what they're doing works for them. If criminals get out of jail and go back to stealing, then stealing works for them. They haven't discovered a powerful enough alternative with which to replace it, and jails aren't teaching them how.

If we don't take the time to help people, we don't have the right to complain about their behavior. We see the consequences of this neglect in this world, where kids come to school packing a 9mm with their peanut butter and jelly sandwich, and adults know how to make a lasagna, but not how to make themselves feel happy. We seek and search and work so hard to find love, only to fear it will be snatched away.

To be lonely in a world with 6 billion people is like eating a six-course meal and feeling famished at the end.

I've come to the realization we are afraid of only two things:

We're afraid of not getting what we want. Whether it's a relationship we want; success in our career; a body that looks a certain way; our dreams fulfilled; closeness with our family; esteem for ourselves; the chance to shine, to be in our element, to do what we envision. We're afraid we won't get it, and if we do get it . . .

We're afraid of losing what we have. We get the relationship, then feel terrified of it ending or the person dying. We achieve success and are scared it'll disappear. We get our body in top shape and fear ballooning up again. We're afraid of losing what we have. . . .

It's not about never feeling fear. It's about whether or not you live in it.

To trust and be true to yourself in a world that challenges every decision you make, and to no longer be ruled by the fear of not getting what you want, or losing what you have, is to know the meaning of happiness and inner peace. You do it by doing it. By having trust in the eternal not the material. Being aware that what you take along with you when you "die" is what you need to focus on while you're here.

14

Stories That Move Us

Risking and doing things you never thought you could do is exhilarating.

Playing it safe and tiptoeing through life is exhausting.

Keeping all your gifts trapped inside tires the crap out of you.

It takes the same amount of effort to create something extraordinary as it takes to create something ordinary. Except with extraordinary, you have to think with another part of your brain. You have to tap into a mental, emotional, and spiritual muscle that may have lain dormant.

At least once a week, I let myself fantasize, taking off the barriers and limitations of the material world to experience the ultimate version of my life. I let myself go beyond where I'd normally go. I let go of the limiting doubts and worries. I let go of my story.

We all have a story. A story about how we can't make it in the world, about how depressed we are, how difficult it is to find someone to love. A story of how happy we feel, how lucky we are, how easily we attract loving relationships, and what fantastic parents we have.

Our stories either move us forward or make us feel like shit.

"You're a writer," I tell a young woman in Fort Lauderdale, Florida.

"Everyone always told me to be a writer," she laughs. "I always wrote everything great."

Screams of torture—a young girl running across a field, crying hysterically, alone.

"Um, uh, I was just shown what you've been through," I say, carefully.

The girl gasps. Her hand covers her mouth. She begins to cry. A friend holds her.

"Let me put it this way, you have a lot of stories to tell and you might as well make millions of dollars off the hell you've been through." (She laughs.) "I'm not kidding. You can either have your past be a wound or you can use it to move yourself, and many other people, forward in life. Once you start using it, your life will transform because your pain is not just your pain. It's millions of other people's pain. Millions of other people who just want to know who they are is much more than what happens to them. So can we expect to come see you here at Barnes and Noble in a couple of years?"

"Yes," she says, nodding and laughing. "You can, the name's Jennifer Rouse; remember it."

Here was a young woman, told she was a great writer by many, while given the message she was garbage by the man who violated and abused her. For a long time, she took on the identity of a bruised and battered girl, not of an author or contributor.

That night, among seventy strangers, she made the decision to break her silence and allow her story to be heard.

When a sixteen-year-old gang member shoots Melanie's thirty-year-old husband as part of his gang initiation quota, she calls me, hysterical, "They found him in the gutter, like a dog."

Melanie had enough stories to fill volumes, stories that were valid, stories filled with pain. She had every right to grieve over the sudden death of her husband. She had every right to feel cheated from the life she'd been planning with him.

A year after his death, people kept telling Melanie it was time to get on with her life.

According to whom? Whose time schedule were they going by?

"People say 'It's time to move on' when they're uncomfortable dealing with your pain," I tell her. "When they don't know what else to say, when they desperately want you to feel better."

You don't move on.

You move forward.

You don't leave behind the people who've crossed over. You take them with you. You take what happened with you and you learn how to live with it.

Grief isn't the plague. It isn't something to get rid of, or cure.

Grief says, "I miss you. I love you. I want to be with you, and you're gone and I'm alone and I don't know what to do."

People want to get rid of their sadness, be done with their grief, now, yesterday.

They call me, "It's been a year since he died and I'm still crying every day," or "I can't stop picturing the pain she endured," or "I'm suffering because they suffered. If I let go of the suffering, who will I be?"

"You don't have to be in pain for us to know you care. It is quite the opposite. We enjoy you enjoying life. As you grow, we grow. Your pain brings us pain. Your sorrow makes us sad. We don't want you to suffer because suffering is not a measurement of love. Honoring us by living happily is."

I once cried for thirty-six hours straight. I didn't know it was humanly possible to cry for thirty-six hours, until I did. My mom took me to California Pizza Kitchen and I was crying in the pasta; mixing the fettuccine with my tears. I'd broken off a relationship, which brought up this tornado of emotions from every loss I'd ever endured. No matter how hard I cried, no matter how badly I wanted the tears to stop, I didn't stop them. I couldn't have if I'd tried. My mom didn't tell me to stop them. She just stayed with me, for as long as I cried, until I was done.

At midnight, they stopped. The tears were finished. They'd completed their work.

I didn't have all these rules that told me I couldn't cry in public or in the middle of eating lunch with my mother. If a little boy can cry in public because he didn't get the new Spider-Man toy, I could cry too. Tears do stop on their own. They don't need us to stop them.

Your heart will heal when it's ready, as long as you don't keep telling yourself things that make you feel badly. As long as you don't keep yourself suffering because you think suffering keeps you loyal to the one you love.

Our emotions are not problems we must immediately fix. When a person goes to a psychiatrist and says, "I'm feeling sad and lonely." The doctor says, "Oh here, take this pill."

Since when did emotions become wrong? Who made it not okay to go through sadness, grief, fear, apprehension? Sometimes we feel sad. Sometimes we want to stay home and have someone take care of us. Sometimes we don't want to talk with anyone or answer the phone or take a shower or care about what normally consumes our mental time and energy.

When we try to stop whatever emotions we're feeling, we cut off our potential to have a powerfully healing experience.

"The only way out is through."

Melanie's pain subsided after she connected with her husband and created a compelling future to live into, one that no longer included the love of her life, but took his memory and his spirit along for the ride.

She quit her grief group because they kept telling her how much worse her pain would get. They confirmed her worst fears about living with a hole in her heart. She started a new group that focused on finding ways to be happy, and to live through a tragedy and become stronger.

When Melanie took away her role as wife, lover, business partner, best friend—when she stripped away all these roles—what was left?

She had to create a new identity, and calling herself a widow was out of the question. "It sounds too depressing," she told me, and decided to call herself a woman of strength.

Giving up her story meant she would no longer use what happened as an excuse to hide and remain in pain over an event she could not change. She would make up a new story about how best to honor her husband's life.

It's not about denying or sugarcoating your painful story with positive thinking. It's about being honest with yourself regarding what you're using your story for, why you're hanging on to it.

Every year, inspiring movies come out based on the true stories of people who've found a way to triumph in the face of tragedy, love in spite of loss, have faith in the face of fear.

Everyone has a story the world needs to hear.

The question is, Are you are telling the same stories to remain connected to a painful past, or are you telling them to inspire yourself and others to move forward? Do your stories make you feel better, or worse, about yourself and life?

When a woman's father comes through telling me a story of what he did to her, I tell him I will not repeat that information in front of the crowd. He tells me to say this: *"Summer 1983, Aunt Rachel's house. The pink-and-blue checker dress."*

I mention the pink-and-blue checker dress. The woman bursts into tears.

What have I done?

After the event, I sit with the woman as she shares her story. "He bought me the pink-and-blue dress cause my prepubescent nipples showed through. After Daddy died, I tell Mom what he did and she gets real mad, saying I should be ashamed for lying about Daddy. For thirty-eight years now, I've been angry. I'm so tired of damning him for my failed marriages, for everything gone sour in my life. When he said that about the dress and what he'd done on me at Aunt Rachel's, I silently said to him, 'I forgive you. I still hate you, but I forgive you for being ignorant and mean.' I said it for me, not him. I did it for me."

"Just like that?" I ask her.

She thinks for a moment . . . a smile spreads slowly across her face. "Yeah, just like that."

The next evening, I speak with a woman who was raped, and I tell her, "The identity of someone who is damaged goods, unwanted garbage, is the one you hold for yourself. How about the identity of a survivor? How about the identity of a woman who teaches others how to kick some butt? How about the identity of a woman who doesn't allow a scumbag to take away her passion for life? Are you going to let a man you vehemently despise control your life any longer? Are you going to give so much of your power away?"

We are so much more than what happens to us.

"You don't understand," a woman tells me. "I don't want to be hurt or abandoned again!"

Great, so just never fall in love, leave your house, speak your mind, stand up for what you believe, go for what you really want, or love anyone, ever again, and you'll still be miserable because you can't be happy playing it safe. You can't feel joyous pushing away love.

The very act of being alive opens you up to every possible outcome, good and bad.

Whatever you tell yourself, your whole life becomes about gathering evidence to back it up. If you tell yourself you're unlovable, your life becomes about: "She didn't accept my date, that proves I'm unlovable." Or, "I told you the guy wouldn't call. Just goes to prove I'm unlovable."

You can also gather evidence of how lovable you are.

It's about deciding what you want to gather evidence about.

When it's over, how will you look back on your life? What will you remember?

atori comes into my office. He says he feels sad and frustrated. He doesn't know why.

He is a transformational therapist, kick-ass coach, and peak-performance master.

He's not allowed to feel sad or frustrated; he thinks this is true.

I look at his face. I know that face. I love that face. It scrunches when he cries.

"After all the studying I've done, seminars I've attended, books I've read, masters I've trained with, what do I have to show for it?" he asks. "I want people to love listening to my music, feel inspired reading my book. I want a team of coaches who empower people to move forward. I want to . . ."

"You want to be loved."

"Yes." He smiles. "I want to be loved."

"If you put your music, your book, your passions, if you put everything out there, you might not be loved. To remain safe, you keep your music half finished, your book half done, your ideas and passions on hold, because then you have control. You get to keep your fantasy of making it someday safely tucked away in your mind where it remains unscathed by the harsh critique of others.

"If you put your work out there, some angry book reviewer or overworked music executive could give their negative opinion of your work. By holding yourself back, you're protecting yourself from potential disappointment and the loss of love and approval."

"I don't feel passionate about my music. I don't want to do anything, but I don't want to not want to do anything, that's the problem," he tells me.

"Having a strong passion to do music and not doing it feels torturous, doesn't it? What you did is lessen the torture by diminishing your desire to do anything at all. You think diminishing your passion makes it easier for you not to do it, but it doesn't. It bothers you.

Instead of putting in time and effort then failing, you're cutting right to the failure."

"That's what I'm saying, I should be over this by now. With all I know, I shouldn't be feeling this way. I know better."

"What you're saying is you should be perfect by now. You should never feel anything but happy, passionate, fearless, peaceful, excited, and totally successful."

"Exactly." He laughs.

"I should be able to fly."

"It's not the same thing. Humans can't fly."

"Humans can't maintain ideal emotions twenty-four hours a day, seven days a week, no matter what happens in their life. Not even Tony Robbins. We're not meant to *only* feel happy, peppy, and gay. We're also not meant to feel like shit most of the time. You think feeling frustrated, or not feeling like doing anything, means something is wrong. Yes, it means something needs to be looked at, but that's a good thing. Your frustration with singing comes when your voice doesn't sound the way you'd like it to sound. Frustration means you're not there yet and you don't know how to get there, or *if* you'll ever get there, which challenges you."

I think of Kelly Clarkson from *American Idol,* who came out to Los Angeles to make it as a singer, met with a producer who shopped around her demo. Nothing worked out. She moved back home until her friend urged her to audition for the show, which she won, and her album shot to number one. Kelly had a vision of what she wanted, and being a cocktail waitress at Hyena's Comedy Club in Burleson, Texas, where she'd worked, certainly wasn't it.

How many stories have we heard of artists who were just about to quit, throw in the towel, and then something happened to propel their lives forward. Thousands. It's the boulder dropping in front of your car to test whether you'll figure out a way around it, turn back and go home, or stay where you are and bitch about it. It's a test to discover what you have inside.

"This is your journey, honey, and it's all about the journey. It's about knowing that everything we do, we do for a reason and a purpose, and it serves us.

"Remaining safe has served you—until now."

Talking with Satori brought up my fear about putting myself out there on a bigger scale. To remain behind the veil of comfort, shielded from critics who may glance over my work and give their thorough opinion based on not knowing me at all, came with the territory. But not putting myself out there had far worse consequences. It meant ignoring the very person I wanted to become.

Life isn't about making sure you cover all the bases. Life is about doing whatever it takes to prepare ourselves for success, then surrendering to what we cannot control. Nothing in life is stagnant.

It's up to us whether we move forward, or hold ourselves back.

Which will you choose?

15

CHALLENGING BELIEFS

If you put on a pair of glasses and then add another pair on top of the first, and another on top of that, you have several filters through which to view the world. The more filters you have, the harder it becomes to see. The less clearly you see, the more distorted the world looks.

When I took off my glasses, I began to see.

When I took the cotton out of my ears, I began to hear.

When I threw away my suit of armor, I began to feel.

We don't see, hear, and feel until we are ready.

Sometimes we think we're ready when we're not.

The way you know you're ready is when your thoughts and actions change.

Those who remain ignorant to what is obvious, stuck in their limiting beliefs, have the hardest time seeing because they have an investment in keeping things as they are, rather than exploring the possibility of what is or what could be.

We don't need to understand something in order to use it.

I don't have a clue how electricity works, but I use it daily. I benefit from knowing how to tap into it by putting an electrical plug into a socket. Similarly, you may not understand how I see, feel, and hear spirits, but you can benefit from my bringing through messages from your loved ones and by showing you how to connect with them yourself.

Traveling by plane was once thought impossible. Being able to speak to people around the world using a funny-looking gadget called a telephone was absurd, and speaking on it without a cord attached, ridiculous.

Today, we take these things for granted. They're part of our everyday lives.

If I can press a keyboard and have a person in Tokyo receive my letter via e-mail or fax, why is it so hard to comprehend that we can speak to the spirits of those we love?

Technology didn't create itself. People created it by tapping into their visions and translating them into material form.

We didn't create electricity, we just found a way to harness and use it. Electricity, like spirits, was always present. But it wasn't until Benjamin Franklin fastened an iron spike to a kite and flew the kite during a thunderstorm that he discovered a spark jumped when lightning struck.

In 1792, Italian scientist Alessandro Volta showed that electricity could be made to travel from one place to another by wire, which led him to invent the first electric battery.

One after another, scientists studied how best to use and manipulate electricity so it could be applied to enhance and improve everyday life. They no longer questioned, "Is electricity real? Does electricity exist?" like many people do regarding psychic mediums. Once scientists had adequate enough proof, they stopped questioning if and started asking how it could be used.

Just as the telescope and microscope reveal what the naked eye alone cannot see, and radar, X-ray, radio, and television capture vibrations beyond our visual and auditory range, psychic mediums attune themselves to the vibrations and frequencies of spirits.

I am able to pick up information at an extremely high level because I train my ability.

Many people ask me if everyone can do what I do at the level I do it. Can everyone play basketball like Michael Jordan, or golf like Tiger Woods? Would everyone want to?

I have no desire to play basketball or golf, and not everyone desires to be a psychic or talk to other people's dead relatives.

I do believe everyone can speak to their own loved ones, but to think we can all talk to the spirits of people we've never met, channel for other people, is like saying we can all sing like Mariah Carey or design clothing like Calvin Klein.

Imagine if everyone had exactly the same interests, exactly the same level of talent. Imagine if everyone was a rock star, but no one owned a grocery store, or fixed cars, or painted, or wrote books, or created software. We are diverse because we are meant to be.

Some people excel at a higher level because it is their destiny to do so. They're born prepared, like Mozart or Beethoven, with their gift already in place. Whether they realize their gift early on, or many years later, does not matter; the foundation of their ability remains solid. It doesn't mean they are better people, it just means they started at a higher level, and went up from there.

The key to success is always setting your standard beyond what you believe you can achieve. This leaves you hungry to grow and learn, and helps you avoid becoming lazy or complacent.

We can each excel in our own way depending on the point from which we begin. For an alcoholic who drank every day for ten years, a single day of sobriety is a huge accomplishment.

There are standards for nearly everything in this world—from the expiration dates on milk cartons, to the years of schooling you need to become a surgeon, to the test you must pass to drive a car—yet, for some reason, anyone can claim they're a psychic medium. Anyone can open a shop, throw in a couple of crystal balls, and voila! You're good to go!

Sports achievement is measured by a player's ability to score points.

Psychic mediumistic ability is measured by the clarity, accuracy, and detailed nature of what comes through.

Here's an actual excerpt from a female psychic medium giving a reading on TV:

> "Is there a J person around you? A male . . ." the psychic medium asks.
>
> "No, there's a female J," the woman replies.
>
> "Is there a JO . . . ?"
>
> "No."
>
> "Is there a JA or JE?"
>
> "There is a JA."
>
> "Is it a James or a Jan?" the psychic medium asks.
>
> "No, it's Jason."
>
> "Jason isn't your son, is he?"
>
> "No," the woman replies.
>
> "I didn't think so. You said earlier you're going to Disney World with your son."
>
> "Yes."
>
> "Please make sure when your son goes on the rides, he's strapped in extremely well so he doesn't stand up," the psychic suggests.
>
> "Well, he's only 7 months old, so I don't see that being a problem," the woman laughs.

I think John Edward is great.

I think this woman sucks.

Satori walked out of the room. He couldn't watch this lady crucify my profession.

Sometimes our beliefs about certain professions come from a few people who screw it up. A couple of seedy lawyers make all lawyers scum. A few Miss Cleos tarnish the view of psychic mediums. It happened in April 2003 when the show *Secrets of Psychics Revealed* aired. The show led viewers to believe they were about to see real psychics exposed, except there weren't any real psychics, there were actors posing as psychics doing these ploys to give viewers the impression that psychics and mediums cheat.

I was truly upset.

Follow me anytime. On the road. Go undercover. You won't find any tricks. You won't find any fraudulent deeds.

Check things out for yourself instead of allowing TV to become your informant and newspapers your guide.

British biologist and social philosopher Herbert Spencer once said, "There is a principle which is a bar against all information, which is proof against all arguments, which cannot fail to keep a man in everlasting ignorance; that principle is contempt, prior to investigation."

Too many people make judgments prior to investigation. We make split second decisions about who we think people are based on how they look, how they speak, who their friends are, what their level of education is, or what others have told us about them.

To shut out possibility—to stop asking, seeking, and discovering for ourselves—is to stop the evolution of our soul. The moment we say, "This is the way life is and how it will always be," we die. Not a physical death, but a death to what is truly possible.

The great adventurers and scientists of our time, upon making a new discovery, never claimed, "This is it." This may be it for right now, but not forever. There is no time in history when scientists accurately claimed, "There is nothing further for us to explore."

They kept their minds open . . . always seeking to know and discover more.

On the flip side—THIS IS IT.

Right now. In this moment. Your entire life is contained.

This means, in every moment, this is your life. If you're angry, screaming at your loved one, it's your life. You could die and go out on that note. You never know.

If this moment is my entire life, how do I want to spend it? Do I want to explore possibilities, or remain stuck in my comfort zone? Do I want to move forward, or hold myself back?

Change is the disintegration of what you know.

People fear change because they fear the loss of what they know, of what is familiar and comfortable. Things always change—your body changes, your health changes, what you want to do with your life changes, your relationships change.

Change is inevitable. Growth and progress are not.

You can go through life and change your clothing, your friends, and your job, but do these changes mean you're progressing as a human being?

If you go to college and get good grades, get straight As, that's nice; but it's not progress. You're doing what's expected of you, getting good grades is one of those things you're expected to get in school.

If you start off getting Cs and progress to As, that's fantastic actually; but it's not outside the realm of the expected, meaning, we go to school and are graded for our work. This is within the confines of receiving an education.

Doing *beyond* what is expected of you means doing what otherwise would not have occurred if not for you. Starting a club, making changes in the system, doing more than asked. When you do something outside the established curriculum, you progress and impact people at a far higher level than if you do what you're supposed to, what is expected of you, within the established parameters of society.

We've all met people who complain, and do nothing to change what they're complaining about, even though they swear they've tried everything. A miserable person who walks around feeling betrayed, upset by the unfairness of it all, intolerant of others, is going to impact every person with whom they come in contact.

You are not an island.

Your presence makes a difference in this world.

The question is: What kind of difference do you want to make?

Do you want to uplift people, or constantly piss them off? Do you want to inspire others, or put them down? Do you want to stand for possibility, or be the poster child for apathy? Do you want to judge harshly, or praise people?

If you don't believe your presence makes a difference, skip through the aisles of a grocery store, singing, "I feel pretty, oh so pretty . . ." You'll see how quickly you make a difference. "Oh, I could never do something like that. I'm not that kind of person," you say.

"What kind? The happy kind?"

The way to be the happy kind is by doing what happy people do. Look for people who have the telltale signs of happiness—smiling, being nice, loving, laughing.

Ask them how they do it. What do they believe about life to be happy? What do they believe about themselves? What do they believe about going through challenges and struggles?

You may think they have it easier than you, that they haven't been through the kind of tragedy you have. I'm telling you, they have. Some of the happiest people I know have been through the worst tragedies: losing their entire family in a fire, seeing their spouse die at the hand of another, losing their child to illness. They don't have an easier life. They've just attached different meanings to the tragedies they've endured than have those who are miserable.

They've told themselves whatever they go through makes them stronger, and living a happy life does more to honor a loved one than anything else.

We'd love life to fit into a neat little compartment. We want a place to put all our stuff, which is why we use labels to describe people and things.

John is a lawyer. Samantha is a doctor. Gary Condit is a . . .

Well, you get the picture.

We put our labels in folders and then name them. **Men Folder:** My last three boyfriends cheated on me, which means all men will cheat on me. **Women Folder:** My mom was beautiful and controlling, which means all beautiful women are controlling. **Painful Experiences Folder:** Everyone I love leaves me, or dies, which means I can never let myself get close because I will be abandoned.

Whatever you believe becomes real for you.

The more limiting your beliefs, the more limiting your reality; the more you expand your view of yourself and others, the more others will expand to fit your view.

When someone tells me they've been depressed for twenty years, I tell them it's impossible to feel anything nonstop for twenty days, much less twenty years.

We don't remain in one emotional state. Nothing in life is that constant.

Remember, we are either moving forward, or holding ourselves back.

Stagnation does not exist.

In this world of dynamic, ever-changing energy, everything is alive, vibrating, pulsating.

Life is movement. Death is movement. Time is movement. Nothing stops. Nothing stays the same. Contrary to the saying, "Nothing lasts forever," love does, even though love's form does not.

It's like growing. Most kids don't feel when they're growing. The changes are happening on such an intricate level, they don't notice them until after they've occurred. My friend grew five inches in two months. His bones ached from the pressure, which made him notice his growth more than I noticed mine. Both of us were growing, but his experience was more pronounced.

When we don't see the changes occurring, we may deny they're taking place.

Just because you don't see something doesn't mean it's not there.

I've never seen oxygen, but I know it exists. I've never seen air, or radio waves, or microwaves, but I know they exist. I've never seen a thought, but I have them. I've never seen a feeling, only the expression of one. Direct experience is the most powerful way to solidify a belief that something exists.

Direct experience is what turned a cranky New Jersey waitress, who rolled her eyes when she saw my book, into a woman whose tears drenched my veggie burger.

"Whaddya want on your burger?" the waitress asks.

"Lots of lettuce."

I see a fireman.

"Tomato."

World Trade Center.

"Avocado."

Frank.

When she comes back with our food, I tell her, "I apologize if this imposes on your belief system, but . . . did you have a husband named Frank who was a fireman?"

She nearly drops the food.

"He died in the World Trade Center," I say, and she bursts into tears.

That is direct experience.

A lady calls me three times and asks, "Are you sure I won't go to hell?"

She thinks she'll go to hell if she has a reading, because she was taught that's what happened to people who contacted spirits. So I ask her, "Do you pray to Jesus?"

"Most certainly. Every day."

"Does Jesus answer you?"

"Why yes. He's good like that, always gets back to me."

"You actually hear Jesus speaking to you?"

"I do."

"Did Jesus die?"

"He did. For our sins."

"You already talk to dead people," I laugh.

She is silent, and then . . . "Well, I guess I do!"

Renowned British medium Ena Twigg once answered a critic by telling him, "You are closing your mind to the teaching of Jesus, and to the disciples. Jesus chose these disciples for their innate psychic gifts, their healing powers, for the works they were yet to do. The New Testament is crammed full of psychic phenomena."

We can believe in angels and guides, have the experience of their being around us, yet have no actual proof of their existence. We believe in Jesus, although we've never met him personally. We believe in God, although our concept of God may differ.

Sometimes we find progress threatening because we think it reflects poorly on us.

How can someone do what I cannot? How can they see, hear, and feel what I do not?

People do stuff all the time I have no clue how to do. They make amazing discoveries and do extraordinary work.

Mark Walker is a three-year-old kid who started playing basketball when he was in diapers. Now, he can sink eighteen straight shots in an eight-foot hoop! The kid's only three and he's already famous for his two-handed over-the-head shot. It goes in every time!

No one knows what cannot be done.

Read that a few times.

No one knows what cannot be done.

It means that you cannot prove something is not possible. You can only prove it is.

Since there's always the *possibility*, you can never close the door and say with absolute conviction that something is impossible.

People have defied the odds by doing seemingly impossible feats.

For over a century, athletes had been trying to run a four-minute mile.

"Impossible!" scientists said. "The human body cannot do it!" That is, until a determined fellow named Roger Bannister ran a mile in four minutes flat. Journalists around the world witnessed his amazing feat, and six months later, over thirty-four people ran a four-minute mile. This was all because one man raised the bar for what could be achieved.

Those who seem to know **everything** understand **nothing**.

Those who remain curious and open to probing life's unanswered questions will have an extraordinary life indeed.

16

The Training of a
Psychic Medium

The person we love is alive.
Snap your fingers.
They took their last breath.
Snap again.
A car hits your child.
Snap again.
Your father shot himself in the head.
Again.
Your wife didn't wake up after surgery.
Again.
The paramedics got there too late.
Again.
He shouldn't have been playing with that gun.

Seventeen people are crammed in my living room. Twelve, I have never met before. Three, I have done readings with over the phone. Plus, my mom, my agent, Dina, and Satori.

There are seven men and ten women, and all, except one lady, profess to have no psychic ability whatsoever.

"We'll see about that," I tell the group.

Psychic training is not about getting something "right." It's not about comparing yourself to your neighbor, or holding back for fear of being "wrong." It's about relaying exactly, specifically, and *only* what you hear, see, feel, taste, smell, and experience.

It is fast, and easy to overlook if you are not paying attention.

This is not about trying to convince people you are right and they are wrong. It's not about proving yourself for the sake of gaining approval. This work is not a game used to impress people at parties, not a magic trick, or dog-and-pony show.

It's about being detached from the opinions of others to remain clear enough to receive messages and relay them. It is a service: a gift for those who desire to know everything is possible; that love cannot be destroyed, and neither can those with whom we share it.

When I started doing this work, I wanted it to be practical. I didn't want to have to meditate for an hour to get ready, or have all these complex rules about what kind of mood I had to be in for spirits to come through. I wanted to understand the work, use it to the highest level, and teach those who were interested in doing it on their own.

I started keeping a notebook of what I noticed when channeling spirits, jotting the distinctions between my own voice and a spirit's voice, noticing the common thread of what was different when I was clear, and when I felt muddled. I wrote down how, specifically, I taught myself to get out of my own way and recognize spirit messages and my own psychic voice. After several months, I decided to record my findings on a CD, *Building a Bridge to the Other Side,* so people could learn how much they knew that they didn't know they knew, which was great because it meant this stuff could be taught. Maybe not everyone can speak to the spirits, but we can all develop our intuition and learn to trust ourselves.

People told me one of the best aspects of the CD is the part about learning the identity of their spirit guides, which I fully believe people need to do on their own. I help them to recognize their guides, but don't tell them who their guides are.

Whatever you think your spirit guides' names are, that's what they are, and you don't need to waste $700 for someone to tell you their names because it won't make a bit of difference in your life. Trusting yourself makes a difference, trusting what you receive.

We all get impressions, instantly, immediately.

Just walk into a bank, a store, your office, you'll get impressions about the people around you, about what they do for a living, how they're feeling, what's on their mind.

But it's not always obvious. Sometimes people look opposite of the role they play, like the guy who has rings in his eyebrows and his nose, and is a corporate lawyer. At work, the rings come out, and his custom-tailored Armani suit goes on.

It's about looking beyond what you see and knowing things aren't always as they appear.

At one of my seminars, there is a guy standing in the back wearing a suit and tie, looking totally uptight. He's with a woman who's smiling and enjoying herself, while he's giving me dirty looks.

I say something funny and he laughs. I look at him and he immediately frowns. He doesn't want to give me the benefit of knowing he is enjoying himself, so I silently ask the spirit world to tell me something about him. "Please, one thing, anything. Humor me."

The guy is wearing boxer shorts jamming on an electric guitar.

No way! I look again.

Yep, there he is, a combination of Tom Cruise in *Risky Business* and Jimi Hendrix in concert. At this point, I am reading from my book, but I keep looking up and see this guy jamming. It is distracting, so I finally say, "Excuse me, sir, but every time I look at you, you're wearing boxer shorts, jamming on an electric guitar; does this make any sense?"

The woman next to him cracks up and says, "This is my husband, and when he returns from work, he goes to our basement and plays electric guitar in his boxer shorts, in his underwear."

The guy looks stunned, totally blown away. All he keeps asking me is how I could possibly have known what I just told him. He's shaking his head, mouthing, "No fuckin' way."

"I know this because it's in you. I am shown what's inside of you. I can also tell you that you're making wads of money, you hate your job, and you're mean to your wife. (She's nodding.) I think you need to quit your job, move to Seattle, and start a band," I say, jokingly.

A year later, he quits his job. He and his wife move to Seattle, where he forms a band with a bunch of old farts who enjoy playing music and don't give a rat's ass about being famous.

The best part is, he's happy now. He no longer walks around swearing, blaming his wife for his misery. His wife thanked me for bringing her husband back because as long as he was stressed out, working ninety hours a week as an investment banker, his dreams of playing music dwindling away, he wasn't much fun to be around.

Now, he's fun.

In order to channel spirits, I had to first know myself inside and out. How else would I be able to tell the difference between my voice and a spirit's voice? I needed to know what my voice would say. I needed to know my moods, my likes and dislikes, my habits, my fears. How else would I know whether my moods were mine or a spirits?

I see a flash of a little girl drowning in a pool.

I hear a voice crying out, "Rob . . . Rob . . . Help me, Rob!"

I feel the pain of a little boy frantically trying to fish his sister from the pool. . . .

The little girl is beside me . . . and I know . . . she is dead.

When I Am Channeling Spirits:

1. *My hands become ice cold, clammy, and often drip with sweat.*
2. *Images flash before me, a series of scenes in a movie or snapshots in an album.*
3. *I have other people's memories, and know details about people I have never met.*
4. *I hear (most often in my right ear) whispers, cries, shouts, laughter, speaking, singing.*
5. *Feelings come over me: nervousness, happiness, excitement, fear, anger, peace, agitation.*
6. *Smells are present: stinky, musky, woodsy, cookies, flesh, smoke, cigarettes, alcohol, mold.*
7. *I feel pains: choking, falling, aching, burning, broken bones, a bullet through my head.*

None of it is scary. All of it is real.

Psychic training is about getting out of your own way.

It's about being honest with yourself, knowing if you sneak a box of cookies before bed, it's not a midnight snack. You're trying to fill up some part of you and using cookies to quiet what's going on. If you keep stuffing your signals, you're not going to hear them, and they won't go away. They'll get louder. Stronger.

Recognizing and understanding messages takes practice, especially if you have spent much of your life ignoring your instincts and gut feelings.

Spirit messages show up in a myriad of ways. Sometimes the lights flicker, and it's a spirit. Sometimes it just means you need a new bulb. Ask for another sign. Trust what you receive. The lights may flash again, or something else may happen that ordinarily does not.

"I never listen to rock stations, but I couldn't stop listening today," a lady writes me. "You came on the air. I called in. You brought through my boyfriend. It changed my life."

Many times, we are led to a place for reasons unbeknown to us, like when I went to the storage space thinking I was going to buy a dog crate, but instead, I met the love of my life.

A man is visiting some friends in Florida. He is depressed and wants to be left alone. His friends refuse to let him sit and cry, so they take him out to dinner and stop off for a cappuccino at Borders, where I happen to be speaking that night.

The man sits in the back of the room, his body stiff and tense, his eyes on the verge of tears. He does not say a word until I finish. Then, he takes me aside and asks if he can have a reading with me. I bring through his entire family.

He thought he was going out for dinner, but what he got was so much more.

Each time you follow your gut feeling, you strengthen your psychic ability and reinforce that inner knowing. A gut feeling is when you feel pulled to do something that doesn't have inherent negative consequences, like getting a dog crate for my pup. It's about noticing the difference in your body between having a compulsive urge, say, to clean your house when you've got work to do, and having a gut feeling to call a friend because your instincts tell you she's not feeling okay.

You can practice feeling the difference doing a simple exercise where you ask yourself questions to which you know the answer is yes. For me, I would ask, "Is your name Lysa?" Yes. "Are you a woman?" Yes. "Is your mom's name Linda?" Yes. "Do you love Satori?" Yes. Then, throw in a question to which the answer is no, but answer yes anyhow and see how it feels. "Are you a pineapple?" Yes. "Is your hair blue?" Yes.

When I answer yes to things that are truly yes, my body feels calm, balanced, and congruent. When I answer yes but the answer is truly no, I feel a slight jolt in my gut.

Now ask yourself questions to which the true answer is no. "Is the date 1957?" No. "Are you from Alaska?" No. "Do you have ten kids?" No. "Are you a fish?" No.

When I answer no, it resonates differently in my gut than when I say yes. Notice how it feels when you answer no when the answer really is no. Then answer no when the answer is yes. Does your body feel different? How?

The purpose of this is to notice how your body unconsciously reacts to questions of which you already know the answer.

Now, take this into spirit communication. Hearing from a spirit happens outside you, even though you process what you see, feel, hear, smell, and taste inside. The same as when you say, "An idea just hit me!" or "I thought of what I'd love to do tonight." The latter you thought up inside your mind, and the former just came to you, from the outside.

When someone says to you, "I couldn't make it because I got stuck in traffic," notice immediately if you feel, "Yes, they are telling the truth," or "No, they are lying." If you've already practiced how a truthful yes and no feel, you'll be able to determine, instantly, whether or not a person is telling the truth. Although they may vehemently stand by their words, always trust what you get.

*S*pirits aren't badgering me, asking questions, sending messages, telling intricate details about every person I pass on the street.

Spirits don't bombard me.

I don't have them tapping on my shoulder at the movies, or asking me for a favor when I'm in bed. They do stop by unexpectedly, but I can tune them in, or tune them out.

It's the same as when you're talking in a noisy restaurant, you automatically tune out the conversations around you and focus on the person you're with (I hope!).

Some spirits speak so loudly I cannot help but hear them. The other night, I went to a gospel concert at the House of Blues, and Patty LaBelle came onstage and I immediately felt her mom around me, telling me about how Patty made sure her mom looked pretty while she was bedridden, dying. Patty made sure she never felt neglected, or looked unkempt, right down to her, mother's lipstick; she was fixing up her momma till the end.

When a singer named Ann came onstage, I saw flashes of a woman being beaten, which meant it was either her, or her mom. It became too much to handle. I told the spirit to go, and he did. It wasn't the right time. He'll come around again.

e're going to do a little experiment, I tell the group sitting in my living room.

Immediately, I see their smiles fade. Fear enters the picture. What's she going to have us do? What if I think I'm right, and find out I'm wrong?

"I'm going to pass around this candleholder, and I want you to hold it for ten seconds before passing it to the next person," I tell the group. "As you're holding it, be aware of words you hear, images you see, and the feelings you receive about whether I bought this, or someone gave it to me. If someone did, who is this person, how do they look, what do they do for a living? Notice any particulars, whatever comes to you, write them on your pad immediately, without hesitation, but no matter what, do not speak."

I am blown away by the results!

Three people see the color pink associated with the candleholder. I take out a small box. Inside is the last candle Charley burned in this candleholder, which was his.

The candle is pink.

One man saw a musician. Charley wanted to be a professional pianist.

Two women felt an ache in their head exactly where Charley's head hit the pavement.

Four people heard either the name John or saw the letter J.

"Jonathan, Charley's father, gave me this candleholder, which Charley used all the time."

I feel so proud of everyone, so excited.

Next, I take them through an exercise where you sit in front of a person you've never met, and, without saying a word, you write everything you see, feel, and hear regarding that person.

Everything, from whether they sleep in the nude to what color their bathroom is. The key is: the person you're getting impressions from cannot smile, offer encouragement, make hints, nothing. They have to remain silent.

This is an exercise in self-trust.

After five minutes, I tell them to switch so the person being read now does the reading. When I say stop, they share with each other what they got.

I tell the group, "If your partner tells you they got that you are divorced, and the truth is you've never been married, say that. This is not about protecting people's feelings. It's to teach you how to give out exactly what you get without holding back, without making last-minute changes. It's about the practice of stating your words and impressions with conviction."

In my workshops and channeling seminars, I never put people on the spot, never pressure them to share, or even speak. They're allowed to sit, listen, observe, and learn.

When I first announce this exercise, two women don't want to do it. They feel afraid.

I ask them if they're willing to be afraid together, and they say yes.

Later, when I ask who wants to share their experience, these women raise their hands.

"I saw her being divorced," the first woman says.

"I am divorced, thank goodness," the second woman laughs.

"What, specifically, did you see or hear to know that?"

"I saw a wedding ring. I saw her taking the ring off and heard the word divorce."

"I saw a little girl with long blonde hair horseback riding," the second woman says.

"I have horses, and my little girl has long blonde hair," the first woman confirms, taking from her wallet a photo of her little girl with long blonde hair standing beside a horse.

These women, who were terrified of doing the exercise, lost their fear once they were told they didn't *have* to do it. Now, they had a choice, and by choosing to do it, look what they got.

One of the participants raises his hand. I know what's coming. I see it on his face. "I got it wrong. I said he was married. He's gay. I said he lives in a big house. He lives in a tiny apartment."

"So how'd you get it wrong?" I ask him.

He looks confused. Doesn't know what I mean. I explain. "To get something wrong means one of two things, either you got it wrong because you just didn't tune in **or** you were in your head rather than tapping into your partner's life. Meaning, once you get out of your head, you will get the information you need. You need to throw your thoughts outward, not inward, project your mind outside yourself to see what is going on in the spirit world and/or in the person you're reading. It takes time. It takes practice. But mostly, it takes giving your-self a break. Picking yourself up and doing it over again . . . How many times?"

"Until you get it right," the group says, in unison.

"How many times is that?"

"As many as it takes," they shout.

I do the same exercise at other workshops, and each time, people claiming to have no psychic ability bring through intricate details they could not have guessed about their partners.

Later in the evening, we do a cool exercise where two people sit back to back and one person draws a picture then mentally sends it to the person behind them, who receives and draws what they see. You can do this sending emotions, memories, or thoughts to your partner, which helps strengthen your intuition, visual abilities, and trust in what you see.

"What if I don't want to pick up someone's emotions?" Sandy, another participant, asks.

"You can use psychic self-defense," I tell her.

No, it's not a new kind of martial art.

Psychic self-defense is a way of protecting yourself from the mental crap others dump on you, and I'll tell you, there are some people who just love sharing the crap. They latch onto you, "Let me tell you what a horrible day I had!" They emotionally throw up all over you, then say, "I feel so much better now," and you're just covered with all their crap.

When we spew negativity, we pollute our environment. I'm not saying we should keep our feelings hidden, but we need to notice the difference between dumping, and simply sharing. Dumping makes you feel better, and the person you're dumping on feel worse. Sharing makes you *both* feel better.

Whenever I go into a large crowd, I do this mental self-defense thingy that takes seconds. I visualize a cyclone of gold-lavender light rushing around my body, and I ask the universe not to allow the intense emotions of others near me. I keep the warm fuzzy feelings in, and keep the crap out.

It's the most woo-woo thing I do, but it works.

I created it in Ikea, the do-it-yourself home-decorating store where Satori likes to go because he's from Sweden, and so is the store. We'd usually go on weekends, when it's busiest, and I'd notice myself transform from this huggy-kissy wife to total bitch woman.

Was Ikea responsible for my shifting moods?

No. It wasn't the store. It was the people rushing to pick out a new sofa before their two-year-old woke from his nap, or the woman obsessing over whether to buy the blue, or yellow, sheets.

I felt like Mel Gibson in the film *What Women Want,* where he hears everything women are thinking. I'd be walking along, happy and calm, when all of the sudden a kid would zoom around the corner in his super-duper Ikea furniture cart, and I'd spin out of control, picking up his frenetic energy. One time that happened, I created a cyclone of brilliant light circling my body, moving dynamically around me, and I said, "I only allow the happy energies to enter. All others stay out!" And they did. I felt instant calm.

If people drain you, it's because you allow them to drain you.

You are not a sink.

If I didn't know how to remain centered, how to protect and replenish my body, mind, and soul, how to practice psychic self-defense, you'd have to wipe me off the floor, 'cause I'd have the life sucked out of me after a typical week like this:

A woman raises her hand and asks about her sister. My hands go around my neck. "I feel like I'm choking." She nods. Tears well up. "She was choked by the umbilical cord."

Next, I am shivering, sweating, freezing, sweating. My mouth is dry. "It feels like I am going through some kind of detox," I tell two young women in the front row.

"Our mom was a drug addict," the younger one replies. "I watched her go through detox."

Then, I am at Bookstar in Studio City when I lose my hearing. "I am deaf in my left ear."

An older lady says, "My hearing aid in my left ear went out, battery died a moment ago."

Suddenly, involuntarily, my hand clutches my neck. I am suspended in air.

"He hung himself," I say to a woman.

She gasps, covering her mouth, fighting back the tears. Failing miserably.

Imagine how insane I'd feel if I didn't shield myself from absorbing the energy of others. I'd go home with other people's sorrows, ailments, thoughts, feelings.

Strong emotions leave a residue.

Murder sites contain residues of anger, fear, and hatred, which is why I can know murder took place years after it occurred. A piece of your clothing, a ring you wear, items you hold sacred, all contain traces of you, your life, what you've gone through, where you've been.

If we can fit data onto a microchip, why would anyone doubt that memories and emotions, actions and reactions, can remain in a ring, in your clothing, in your home?

Psychic self-defense is not about defending yourself against some force, but, rather, about maintaining your center no matter who or what is attempting to influence you.

You know how it feels standing next to someone who emanates positive energy? You find yourself moving closer. You also know when you feel the need to back away because something just feels off.

We all have our personal space, the space where, if someone comes too close, we automatically move away. The way to test your personal space is to stand next to someone you don't know and see how close they can get before this silent buzzer goes off, telling you to back off.

You can shift someone's energy, or the energy in an entire room, but not by walking in and announcing, "Okay, listen up, the energy really sucks in here!"

Just as an undercover cop doesn't walk into a drug deal and announce, "Hello, my name is Detective Charles Baker. Please go ahead and finish your drug deal so I can arrest you."

You need to go undercover, and change yourself in order to change the situation. You change your thoughts, attitudes, beliefs about what's happening, from negative to positive, then send those thoughts, beliefs, and attitudes to the people who are freaking out around you.

You can't just think, I'm happy. I'm happy. I adore this schmuck holding up the line because the cashier won't refund his three dollars for the half-eaten can of beans he bought.

This happened to me at the grocery store, and I just looked at the guy, wondering what was going on in his life to make him feel the need to spend five full minutes arguing over a three dollars can of beans.

I finally hand him three dollars.

He won't take it, says it's the principle, not the cash.

I felt like saying, "Fuck principle mister. Just take the money."

Self-help author Wayne Dwyer tells a story of being on a subway in New York where these kids were screaming and running, causing a ruckus, while their father sat silently, doing nothing to calm his kids. Wayne finally exploded, "Could you please control your children!"

The guy looks up, his eyes red with tears, and he says, "I apologize. Their mother just died. We've come from the funeral. I thought they could let off a bit of steam by running. . . ."

What an eye-opener.

What a reminder to look beyond how people are behaving and become curious about what's triggering them to behave this way.

Maybe they're in a bad mood because their mom is in the hospital, and she doesn't have medical insurance. Maybe their kid just entered rehab, and they feel like a failure as a parent. Maybe someone close to them just died.

It takes getting out of yourself long enough to be there for another, which is easy to do when people are being nice, and difficult to do when people are being jerks.

Could you get out of yourself long enough to listen to what people are failing to say? Could you get out of yourself long enough to listen, period?

To demonstrate how we need to fine-tune our listening, I play a game called Telephone with the group. "In this simple game, the person is centimeters from your ear, uttering one simple word or phrase that you will whisper to the person next to you, and so on, until it comes back to the original person, hopefully being the word they said. You cannot repeat the word, or sentence. Say it once, clearly, quickly. Hear it. Pass it on."

I whisper, "Peter likes peppers," to Satori, who passes it on until it travels through eighteen sets of ears, and comes back to me as, "Paper has fun."

Each time we do it, the words come back different. "Blond streaks" comes back as "blend and won." "Live with passion" comes back as "give facts."

"Okay, those of you who were in your head worrying, instead of listening, need to shift your focus outside yourself to hear what the person is saying, instead of listening to your mental chatter. Turn down the volume of your mind, and turn up the volume of your ears."

We do it one last time. I whisper something so simple they have to get it right—my name—and I am thrilled when it comes back as Lysa.

This game has nothing to do with hearing. It has to do with listening.

Someone can hear our words yet not listen to a word we've said.

If you want to connect with your loved ones, it's extremely important to listen so you can understand the different ways they communicate. You must train yourself to:

SEE: The pictures, flashes of images and scenes that play out like a movie, coming and going in a matter of seconds. You may see them in front of you, with your eyes closed, or open. The chair you're sitting on exists even when your eyes are closed. If I told you to keep your eyes open, and picture a rose, even though the actual rose is not there, your mind can formulate the remembered image. *Trust what you see.*

HEAR: I hear on the right side, outside my head. Sometimes I have two voices speaking at the same time and I need to turn down the volume of my own voice inside my head and turn up the volume of the voice outside my mind. *Trust what you hear.*

FEEL: I feel pain in my head, nausea in my gut, tightness in my throat. I've started coughing during sessions, sneezing, or getting the munchies when a grandmother came through telling her teenage granddaughter she knew about her smoking pot. Spirits cannot take over your body without your permission, nor can they hang around indefinitely, like an unwelcome guest. If you ask them to leave, they must. You are in charge—always, always. *Trust what you feel.*

SMELL AND TASTE: You may smell their cologne, a cigar or cigarette, or some other scent, good or bad, associated with them. You might taste a specific food they loved, or alcohol on your tongue, or a dessert concoction. *Trust what you smell and taste.*

Ultimately, a spirit's goal is to convey enough specific, irrefutable information to show you they are here, and to have you understand they did not disappear into some black hole of nonexistence. Open your eyes to the messages given to you daily.

Be aware of cold spots in the house, the lights flickering, or their song coming on the radio just as you think of them. Spirits turn appliances and electronics on and off, and mess with computers, clocks, and telephones. Be aware of feeling as if someone is playing with your hair, or like there are spider webs around your face.

Notice sudden changes in your pet's behavior. Animals often sense spirits, and, yes, pets do come through.

During my tour, I heard a dog making an extremely weird barking sound. I told the crowd, "A dog is coming through with a very strange bark. It is . . . Okay, the dog wants me to imitate his bark. So for the first time in public, I am going to bark."

I make a peculiar sound into the microphone, and a lady starts shouting the name of her dog, who barked exactly as I did. I would have put this at the top of my unique animal spirit experiences list if it weren't for Sammy, the reincarnated dog.

I am doing a reading for a mom and her two kids, describing their beloved dog, Sammy, who had a unique spot that dogs of his breed didn't normally have, when Sammy suddenly shows himself coming back in the body of another dog with exactly the same unique spot. I have no proof what I am being shown will actually occur, but I tell them anyhow.

"Sammy will find you. You will know it's him," I say, feeling ridiculous.

Several months later, they call for another reading. This time, I can't seem to connect with Sammy. "Sammy! Where are you?" I silently shout, but receive nothing.

Until this moment, I have always made contact with the exact animal, or person, someone requests, so this can mean only one thing: Sammy has been reincarnated.

The kids shout into the phone, "Sammy is not there because he's with us!"

The mother tells me she received e-mail from a dog adoption site, and was scrolling through photos when she saw a puppy with the same unique spot Sammy had. The lady at the adoption place said they'd never seen this kind of spot on this particular breed.

"His personality, everything, is the same as Sammy's," she tells me.

Communicating with the people, and the pets, you love is what keeps life meaningful.

Training myself as a psychic medium is really about training myself as a human being. It's about becoming aware of what is around and within me, conscious of the subtlety, and mystery, of life and appreciative for every moment I am alive.

17

The Courage to Love Again . . . and Again . . . and Again

"I LOVE YOU," Satori whispers less than six hours after we meet.

I pull back, suspicious of his intention.

"I just love what I know about you so far, how I feel being with you," he says, pulling me close. I look at him and smile. "You're still not coming up to my apartment," I laugh.

Three days later, he moves in.

A week later, he asks me to be his wife.

Four months later, we are married in front of a thousand people we have never met, at a place called Agape. Reverend Michael Beckwith, begins the ceremony with, "Look at that rock on your finger! Whoa! This boy's gettin' some loving tonight!"

Eight years later, we are even more passionately, madly, deeply in love.

A few weeks before I met Satori, I was going on dates, wondering, "Are you the one? How about you?" Each time I got involved, I asked myself, "How long will it last? Will I leave this relationship? Will I marry the guy?"

When I met Satori, it wasn't like, "It's nice to meet you," it was like, "It's nice to see you again. How've you been since our last life together?"

I don't normally get into past-lives stuff, but Satori and I are definitely aligned in every aspect—from the activities we love, to our favorite movies and books, to our values, to what we find funny or stupid, to what makes us angry, and what we love deeply. If there is such a thing as a twin soul—one who matches perfectly with you—we are definitely it for each other.

Early on, Satori and I decided what's most important in a relationship. Specifically, what we MUST have and what we MUST NOT have to make our relationship work.

Musts and Must Nots are non-negotiable aspects of a relationship that, if not kept up or if broken completely, can end a relationship. Having five of each is more than enough. Too many rules make a relationship rigid, but no rules at all make a relationship fall apart.

Our Musts: We must both be monogamous. We must demonstrate our love for each other consistently. We must appreciate and take care of ourselves. We must support each other in achieving our highest goals. We must constantly re-create our extraordinary relationship by having fun, being playful, loving, nurturing, and finding new ways to help each other grow.

Our Must Nots: We must not verbally or physically abuse each other. We must not lie or deceive each other. We must not threaten to leave the relationship. We must not cheat or compromise the integrity of the relationship. We must not toxify our mind and body.

Coming up with Musts and Must Nots formed our foundation. It laid out the rules of the game, which are essential to know before you get involved. Imagine if I told you to play basketball but left out what you had to do to win the game. You'd be guessing, jumping through hoops, trying to figure out what needs to happen for you to score.

Knowing and discussing the rules helped Satori and me know if we were right for each other. We talked about our values, our beliefs, and the vision we had for our lives.

Years ago, I was dating a guy named Scott from New Jersey. We were outside shoveling snow, and I was wondering why I left Los Angeles for this. Scott takes me in his arms and tells me his dream of marrying me, and us living by his parents' house right down the block, and having five kids before the age of thirty-four. . . .

It was nice knowing Scott.

Our visions weren't the least bit aligned.

It's best to find out up front, not after five months of dating, and definitely not on your wedding night. You don't want to be in bed, after having great sex, and turn to your new spouse and hear, "Honey, I have a surprise. We're moving to Alaska!" And you hate the cold.

After five dates, Satori and I did this thing where he wrote his vision for his future, and I wrote mine, and we couldn't look at each other's until we were both done.

I wanted so much to peek at his paper to make sure I wrote nearly the same thing he did. I didn't want to see us living in a castle in Malibu while his dream was traveling the globe with no permanent home.

Sometimes, people tell you what they think you want to hear.

A man says he's interested in getting married, but really, he just wants to get laid. A woman says she's over her ex-boyfriend, but secretly she wants to make him jealous by dating you.

The way you can see through people's bullshit is by pressing mute on their words, and paying attention to their actions. People will show you everything you need to know.

You just need to trust what you see.

An extraordinary relationship is a union between two people who are willing to tell the truth, even if it means no longer being together once the truth is revealed.

The best question to ask a potential partner is, "Are you interested in having an extraordinary relationship?" If they say yes, then ask,

"Okay, are you interested in having an extraordinary relationship with me?" If they say yes, then ask, "How would an extraordinary relationship look to you? What are your Musts and what are your Must Nots?"

What keeps people stuck is when they don't want to lose what they have, even though what they have is not giving them what they want.

You can have an extraordinary relationship only if you're willing to show up extraordinary in a relationship.

Many people cling to relationships in the name of love, but it's not love that keeps us bound to a painful relationship. It's fear.

A woman says to me, "He'll kill me if I leave!"

I tell her, "You're dead if you stay."

Leaving him felt more painful than staying, until one day, the coin flipped, and staying became more painful than leaving. On that day, she left.

I prayed that day would come for my dad, who'd been married to Eileen for twenty-four years.

"I took a vow," my dad says to me. "I don't want to go through another divorce."

"Did your vow include being abused, belittled, and disrespected till death do you part?"

He laughs.

I don't.

"You're reinforcing her behavior by tolerating it. If you stay, you give up your right to complain because I don't want to hear about something you're not willing to change."

I wondered what my dad believed about himself in order to stay. Together, we retraced his steps, from the first day they met.

"The night I saw Eileen in a bar, I was so smitten, I walked out. I'm in my car, looking at myself in the vanity mirror, saying, 'Come on, Lenny, don't be a putz,'" my dad laughs. "Maybe I should've stayed in the car."

Although my dad was an accountant, and a self-made success in business, Eileen insisted on controlling the money.

"You love your children more than me!" she'd scream, jealous of the closeness we shared. When it came to his kids, nothing was too much for my dad. I often told him, "Dad, if I looked up Extraordinary Father in the dictionary, your photo would be there."

Although family and friends were aware of their relationship, my dad never complained. I felt he might be feeling ashamed, you know, of being so strong in other areas while allowing himself to fold in this one. Finally I confronted him.

That day, we sat for five hours in a yogurt shop in Port Washington, with him spilling his guts about the pain he'd allowed himself to endure.

This was the beginning of truly knowing my father.

He said he was staying for Michael, my half brother. He didn't yet realize that by staying, Michael was learning that closeness was impossible to achieve over a long period of time, that you must always say yes to maintain a facade of peace, and you must sacrifice who you are to stay married.

My dad slept in his den for most of his twenty-four-year marriage because Eileen said he snored, and refused to allow him in their bed.

That was beyond sacrifice.

It wasn't until Michael went to college, and Eileen threatened to damage my dad's personal belongings if he went to visit my brother, David, that my dad finally filed for divorce.

It was the happiest day of my life.

The next day, Eileen fell ill.

My dad canceled the divorce proceedings, and came to her rescue.

Three months later, her illness was gone. . . . And the bitch was back.

"Some might say I'm a schmuck to stay with a woman who calls me names, threatens my well-being, and harms my self-esteem," my dad told me, "And yet, I believe people can get better. Call my beliefs silly or overly optimistic, but my belief in the possibility of people kept me with Eileen throughout these emotionally tortuous years."

The final straw came during an argument one night when, Eileen threatened to hurt herself and claim my dad did it.

Despite her subsequent apologies, he packed up his belongings and left Eileen for good.

I was curious why, for so many years, such an amazing man accepted so much pain. "Dad, you're the greatest. How could you put up with her?" I asked him.

It took a long time for him to stop making excuses for her behavior, and to start looking at what drove him to marry and remain with a woman who was the complete opposite of my mom.

He remembers an incident when he was a boy. "I was living on the East Side of New York in a tenement building. My father was making ten dollars a week supporting four people," my dad tells me. "I came home from the movies one day, feeling excited because I got to see a double feature for only a nickel. 'Yeah, Dad, the man let me stay for two shows. Didn't charge me for it!' I said handing my dad the extra nickel he'd given me to see two films.

" 'Keep it, son,' he tells me.

" 'Wow! I'm rich!'

"My dad looks at me like I'd lost a screw.

" 'We're poor, son.'

"I had no idea what he meant. Me? Lenny Moskowitz, poor? I didn't feel poor."

My dad's father worked thirteen-hour days in a shirt factory, coming home each night covered with grime and sweat. His dream was to open a little hardware store, but my grandmother said, "Absolutely not! Starting your own business is risky." He allowed her ironclad resolve to stop him from pursuing his dream. My dad remembers the day his father told him this, and on that day, my dad made the decision that no woman would ever control him.

After my grandmother died of cancer, and my mom and he divorced, my dad went looking for another mother, and found one in Eileen.

"This is so cliché, Dad. You married your mother," I laugh.

"I divorced her, too," he laughs.

My dad went from living at home, to living in the army, to living with my mom, to living with Eileen, to having Michael live with him, to now, for the first time in his life, living on his own.

Imagine, my dad—the bachelor.

I used to wake him if I called at eleven. Now, he's not home. He's in his sixties, and on Saturday night he calls me and I hear this noise in the background, "Dad, where are you?"

"I'm out dancing," he tells me. "I'm having the time of my life."

He's starting his life again. . . . "It's never too late," he says.

He's always been a wise man. The only difference is, he now knows this.

You see, my dad thought if he got a divorce, it would mean he'd failed.

"No, Dad," I tell him, "You'd fail if you stayed in a miserable relationship."

OVE

We all need it. Crave it. Hold on to it.

We all want it to stay . . . forever.

We all feel devastated when we think it's gone.

I've never seen love leave a room, slam a door, yell, curse, or die.

Love cannot die, although our feelings of love can seemingly disappear.

Love never hurts. The loss of love does.

"I want him to be happy even if it means I'm miserable," says Hallie, over the phone.

"Do you have to be miserable for him to be happy?"

"No one else makes me happy. He's the only one who can do it," she whines.

"How'd he get that job?"

"I hired him."

"That's a lot of pressure on him, being the only man who can make you happy."

"I have friends, hobbies. But I don't want to be with another man."

"If there's only one man who can make you happy, and that man doesn't want to be with you, then basically, you're screwed."

She laughs. "I understand what you're saying, but I could never feel for anyone what I feel for John. I was down and sad before I met him. I started doing things and being happy for the first time in my life. It was all because of him. He lit me up."

"He may have struck the match, but you are the match. He just ignited you. If you put up a wall that no one, except John, is allowed through, you're going to end up alone, and that's not what you want, is it?"

"I want John."

"What if you can't have him?"

"I know I can."

"How do you know?"

"I feel it. We are meant to be together. He's just scared. He needs time."

"How much time?"

"As long as it takes. I'll be waiting."

"He's getting married next week."

"I know. It won't last. I know it in my gut. You tell people to trust their gut."

"It's not your gut telling you to wait for John. It's your fear of never feeling for anyone what you now feel about him."

"I just want him so badly."

"Has wanting him made him come back to you?"

"No."

"Has holding on, making yourself miserable, crying, clutching, being angry at God, made him come back? Has any of it worked?"

"No, but—"

"You think he wants a woman who can't function without him?"

She laughs.

"There was a time in your life before you knew John. You weren't born knowing him."

"I wasn't happy until I met him."

I remain silent.

"I wasn't *as* happy."

Still silent.

"So we had problems and he cheated on me, but he said he was sorry. He didn't mean to. He loves me. He's a good man. What's wrong with me? Why doesn't he want to marry me?"

"Why would you want to marry someone who doesn't want to marry you? If you have to beg somebody to be with you, or threaten to leave if they don't, it kinda ruins that romance thing a bit, don't you think? The person you're supposed to be with wants to be with you. You never have to beg for love.

"It's tiring, all that convincing and trying to make someone see your greatness, see how perfect you are for them. If they don't see your worth, and you stay with them, they're not the one who's blind, you are. If you think of your love as a gift, and he doesn't want that gift, it doesn't mean the gift is no good. It just means he doesn't want it. Someone else will," I tell Hallie.

When some doors close, we try to bash them open. If you've ever thought, If only they loved me, then I'd be happy, you know how it feels not to let a relationship go.

After my session with Hallie, I knew she wasn't ready to let John go.

Having a relationship can be like having a bus parked in your driveway. Imagine the bus is the person with whom you're in a relationship. If that bus isn't taking you where you want to go, get off the bus and tell it to move on, because there's a good-looking bus right behind it. That good-looking bus can't pull into your drive-way as long as the old bus is parked in its place.

If you're in a relationship that's consistently not giving you what you want, not taking you where you want to go, and yet you stay, you can't blame the relationship because you're the one staying.

As long as Hallie focused on John being the only man for her, she couldn't see the men waiting to give her what she wanted. She remained blind, forever idealizing the good times with John, which in reality, weren't so good. She needed to focus on them to remain plugged into him. If she unplugged herself, she would cut off her fantasy of what could be, someday.

It doesn't take long to know whether, or not, someone is good for you.

In college, I dated a French guy I met at the beach. He was gorgeous, suave, and loving, but after three months of dating, I still refused to have sex with him.

I couldn't pinpoint what was wrong. He was a personal trainer, and often went to parties given by his clients, but he would never take me along. My instincts said something was off, though he swore it wasn't. Out of the blue, I asked him, "Are you a male escort?"

In that moment, his comprehension of English conveniently fails him.

"Do women pay you to have sex with them?" I said.

"Oh, no, not just sex. We have dinner first." As if that made a difference.

My instinct not to have sex with him came from listening to my *First Feeling,* which is the first instinct you get with a person that says something is off, or something is wonderful.

First feeling is the gnawing feeling that doesn't go away. You know it's there, you feel it, even if you don't acknowledge it. You might go on a date and some trigger just goes off.

Maybe those twelve bottles of beer at dinner were a sign, but they're so cute, so you ignore the sign, hoping their dimples will make up for the stain they left throwing up on your living room floor. Ten years later, you end the relationship because their excessive drinking got in the way.

It doesn't need to take ten years to know you're with the wrong person.

Think back to your last relationship, and notice what you knew long before you acknowledged it as being a problem. Months, sometimes years later, the problem that arrived at the start turns out to be the underlying reason why the relationship ended.

At the beginning of a relationship, we're willing to overlook so many things. "Oh, isn't it cute the way he leaves a trail of his clothing on the bedroom floor." "I love that she takes two hours to get ready. It means she cares about looking fantastic for me." "It doesn't matter that he hasn't got a job. I love him so much, we could live in a hut."

Yeah, right, until you move into the hut. Then the hut doesn't look so good anymore. And neither does your partner.

It's not about achieving perfection. It's about knowing what you must and must not have in a relationship. It's about aligning your rules and values with each other, and moving forward, or getting out, fast.

What about working things out? What about sticking together through thick and thin?

The deal Satori and I have is, "Whatever comes up, we'll handle it—together."

To do that, you must first be aligned. You must *both* want to work things out, not just one of you dragging the other to therapy. You must both want to be together.

Many people are in relationships they shouldn't be in, like when my dad was with Eileen. They had nothing in common: My dad liked the beach; Eileen couldn't stand the sun. My dad liked exercising; Eileen hated getting off the couch. My dad wanted to take seminars; Eileen wanted to stay the same.

Satori and I have everything in common.

Does it mean we're perfect, that we never argue?

We argue. I get angry. He gets angry. I get irritable. He gets irritable. I misunderstand him. He misunderstands me. Out of a hundred percent, we argue or disagree about 2 to 3 percent of the time, and get along beautifully the rest. Our relationship is easy in that we love each other, and sharing that love is our number one priority, above all else. We work through whatever comes up. We never walk out. And we never, ever, threaten to end the relationship.

Threatening to leave is the most detrimental thing you can do.

If you're going to leave, then leave. If you want them to know what must change for you to stay, then say that. But if you're threatening the relationship to get them to clean up their act, I promise you, even if they do, underneath it, they'll resent you.

No one wants to hear idle threats. It leaves the foundation shaky. It makes a person feel conditionally loved. Threats will destroy your connection.

But you don't need to spend your time convincing someone to see your point of view, or playing hard to get, or doing things to manipulate them so they'll see how valuable you are; that's not what love is about.

Love is about growing, nurturing, and listening. It's about having the willingness to look at yourself from another's point of view, acknowledge the areas in which you need to improve, and work on yourself, rather than waiting for the other person to change and grow.

Relationships become dissatisfying when people feel dissatisfied with themselves. That's when people act bitchy: when they're unhappy with who they are, when their career isn't going as planned, when they don't feel beautiful anymore, when they don't know how to deal with their emotions and they fling their pain at you.

Hallie felt out of control and enormously dissatisfied with herself after John married the other woman. Each month, she called for a fifteen-minute session where I would coach her on what she needed to transform within herself. She'd do it and feel proud, but she'd always end the session with same damn question, "Is John going to leave his wife?"

It got to the point where I felt like picking up the phone, telling her no, and hanging up.

"Are you sure he's not leaving her?"

"I don't see him leaving his wife."

"But seven other psychics all say he's going to leave his wife."

"Why don't you listen to them, and quit calling me!" I laugh.

"I trust you, Lysa!"

"If you trusted me, you would know—He's not going to leave his wife!"

Hallie kept calling wanting a different answer because the one I gave her was not the one she wanted to hear. Her mental stereo kept replaying, "Is he gonna leave his wife? Is he gonna leave his wife?" She desperately needed some new albums.

I've noticed how captivated people get by the possibility of what could be, rather than by what is.

The thrill of the first date is filled with endless possibilities: Will this be the one? Will I get laid? Where will he take me? What shall I wear? What will we talk about?

But no matter how many thrilling dates people go on, after a while, dating gets old; people want to fall in love. You want to *be* in love, not *fall* in love. Falling, anyone can do, that's easy. Being, staying, growing, and making love better and better takes commitment and passion.

If you're looking and not finding, look at the person in the mirror to find the answer to why you haven't found "the one."

Optimism is great, but sometimes it keeps us stuck. Since everything that hasn't happened may still happen, there is always a chance, however remote, that John will divorce his wife and come running back to Hallie. This hope kept her stuck.

I tell her, "The bad thing about optimism is that people always have the potential to change, life always has the potential to turn around, but how long are you willing to wait? If it's truly meant to be, then it'll be. Quit wasting your money on psychics who tell you to sit back and do nothing because John will be coming back soon. If they're so sure, ask them when so you don't have to insult your time here by sitting at home, praying for John's return."

Wanting someone who isn't available is the ultimate in relationship phobia.

You want what you cannot have so it looks as if you really want it. No, if you really wanted a relationship, you'd choose someone who wants to have a relationship with you.

"John used to want me," Hallie cries.

"Now, he doesn't."

"He used to."

"Used to" is in the past; it means before now, it means it's not happening any longer.

I thought about why she made John so important. She made him her savior, her knight in shining armor. If you or I met the guy, we probably wouldn't be gaga to the point of being unable to function. This happens only when we make a person into our drug, into our addiction. We know we've done that when we go through withdrawal. It's different than merely missing someone, or feeling empty when they're gone. It's literal torture.

An emotional addiction takes hold of you, knocking personal

choice out of the equation. You no longer feel in control of your thoughts and feelings. The person you love has taken over the driver's seat of your mind. They aren't the real problem. How you see them, is.

An addiction diminishes you. A passion makes you stronger.

I once dated a dancer named Michael, who clearly didn't care for me as much as I cared for him. My neediness told him, "What you think of me is so important, I will lower my standards just to be with you. What you think of me matters more than what I think of myself." I made him my drug, and after breaking up with him, vowed never to do that again.

It's easy to complain about relationships.

We get lots of sympathy, lots of "Yeah, I know how it is," when we complain. Just go outside and you'll easily find ten people to agree about how difficult relationships are, how true love is scarce, and how the chances of ever finding someone who loves you as much as you love them are next to impossible.

Is it agreement you want, or an extraordinary relationship?

If you want the latter, find people who have the kind of relationship you desire, and ask them what they believe about love, about how to attract someone, about how to keep a relationship dynamic and alive. You may have to look a bit harder because those who have extraordinary relationships are not the ones bitching. The ones bitching are easy to find. You hear them a mile away.

I get many calls from people in their late teens and early twenties who ask me if they'll ever find someone to love, if they'll ever get married. They already feel doomed to a life of loneliness because, thus far, they've been unlucky in love.

Samantha, a fifteen-year-old miserable girl, asks, "Is my destiny to be unhappy?"

"One second, let me check," I tell her. "Yep, it's your destiny to be unhappy, alone, and miserable for the rest of your life. I just checked with the spirits and that's what they said."

She laughs.

I tell her, "Come on, what makes you think you're so special that you were singled out not to have the relationship of your dreams? There is no way you're meant to be miserable, lonely, frustrated. This is not your karma. It's just a limiting belief you used to have."

Some people believe we decide before we are born exactly what we'll experience during our lifetime, that every bad relationship, every horrific experience, was preplanned by us alone.

Since we know what happened only after the fact, it's easy to surmise that what happened was meant to happen, which is silly logic, really.

Someone left you. That's what happened, and then you attach, "I had to go through that. I wrote it in my chart before I was born," to the event so you don't have to feel badly about the way things turned out.

Feeling bad is useful when it propels us to change. Just as burning your hand on a hot stove is a useful reminder not to put your hand there. But don't tell me you wrote being abandoned, needy, lonely, neurotic, filled with self-hatred, and totally broke in your chart, 'cause if you did, you're fired for writing such a shitty chart.

You want to know how someone gets into five abusive relationships?

They make choices based on their beliefs about what they think they deserve. They make choices in this lifetime, not the last, not the next one—this life—right now.

Luckily, we can always choose again.

But not if we keep blaming our parents, or genetics, or bad karma, which may get us off the hook, but living off the hook, filled with excuses about why you don't have what you want, won't bring you a joyful life. It won't make you feel happy. The only thing that makes us happy is learning from the past, doing it differently in the present, and even better in the future.

I'm sure you've heard the saying, "Everything happens for a reason."

What's the reason? We make it up. Why did my dog cry in her crate? So I'd return the crate, take her to puppy school, buy another crate, and meet Satori. How do I know this? It's what happened. Would I have met Satori anyhow? I'll never know.

We have no idea if something was, or was not, meant to be because we have nothing with which to compare it.

Of course, everything happens for a reason, but there isn't an inherent reason contained within the happenings of our life. We make up a reason for why we didn't get the job, or why the relationship didn't work out. We make up a reason to make ourselves feel better, or worse. "I didn't get the job because I'm a schmuck." "I didn't get the job because a better one is coming."

Sometimes people suck at something, like those who audition for *American Idol* and sing completely off-key. After they're cut, they say to the camera, "Everything happens for a reason." Yeah, the reason you didn't get a callback is because you can't sing. There's not some higher, spiritual meaning. Sure, some people who can sing get cut, but we make up reasons all the time about why things happen and why they don't. The key is to make up a reason that propels you to move forward and feel good, which happens when you tell yourself the truth.

We know we're telling ourselves the truth by the freedom it brings inside.

We wake up when we're ready to wake up.

Although I can assist people in waking up sooner, it doesn't mean they will. They do it when they do it, and the fun part is being around when it happens, like I got to see with Hallie.

She calls me up and says, "You know, Lysa, I don't think he's going to leave his wife." It was one of those moments where I felt like saying, "I told you so." Instead, I just said, "You know what, Hallie, I think you're right."

It was so beautiful because in that moment, it felt like, Now . . . we can begin. You see as long as her life was tied up with, "Is he going to leave his wife?" she didn't need to move forward. This mantra kept her safe because the *possibility* of him leaving his wife was nearly as exciting as him actually leaving. It gave her hope.

"I'm still afraid of letting go of the passion I felt with him," she tells me. "He gave me the feeling . . ." She corrects herself, "Okay, that's not true, he triggered the feeling in me."

"That's right. Since he did not give it to you, he cannot take it away. You just need to find other ways to set off those triggers."

Hallie worked with Satori to find new ways to trigger what she thought only John could ignite. She discovered her love of music. Writing songs became her newfound passion. She enjoyed conversations with men that had nothing to do with sex, or falling in love. She took notice of her friends and family. Satori didn't tell her what to do. He merely helped her discover what was already there, what she'd known all along, but had ignored.

In the presence of love, we become more, not less, of who we really are.

Love isn't scary. What people do in the name of love can be.

What we do with our time either heals, or has us continue in pain. Time is just there. How you use your time is up to you. "If it's all up to me, then what's up to God?" a woman asks me.

I believe God is a force, not an entity; a force that guides us if we allow it. It's the whisper that says, "Go to the left," and then we do and we meet the man or woman of our dreams. It's the ache in our gut telling us when we are off track. It's the urge to call an old friend, hear their voice, and reconnect. It's what pulls us through when getting out of bed becomes a chore. It's the spark of inspiration that wakes us early, and has us continue late into the night. And sometimes, God shakes the very foundation of who we are in order to remind us of what is most important in life.

What was most important to Annie Timpone was her husband, Frankie.

I never met Annie until I brought through Frankie on April 9th at Barnes & Noble in Paramus, New Jersey. She later wrote me, describing how hearing from her husband had affected her.

I asked you to connect with my husband. You immediately said he was showing you a shrine I made in honor of him, which I didn't understand because when I heard the word shrine, I thought of a stone. You were trying very hard to get across what you were shown, using your hands, telling me about pictures, mementos of him. Then, you laughed like someone said something in your ear. You told me Frankie was telling you to cut yourself a break.

In that second, I got it! When I finally understood the shrine, you laughed and said Frankie told you to pat yourself on the back, you did a good job, which is exactly something he would do. You captured his personality. Your demeanor changed from serious when you were reading the woman before me, to playful and jokey, which was just like my husband. I felt his energy coming through you. It's hard to describe what I was feeling.

Then, you said something that made my heart almost stop.

You said, "You told your husband it's okay for him to go."

I was shocked because this was one of the last things I said in Frankie's ear. Right before he passed, I whispered, "It's okay for you to let go now. We will be together again. Next time, it will be forever."

Even though he was in a coma, he'd heard every word I said.

I figure losing someone you love is like losing an arm. Every day, you are aware of it missing, but you learn how to live without it. Connecting with Frankie helped to ease my pain, and made me able to live the rest of my life.

—Annie Timpone

*E*veryone has a fear of not being good enough, of not being loved.

The difference between living a happy life, and living a fearful one, is whether you allow your fears to dictate your actions, or lack thereof.

The week before I met Satori, I was tired of listening to relationship advice from people who didn't have relationships, or were in ones that stank. I was tired of abiding by rules laid out in books written by experts working on their fourth divorce.

I asked myself, "When it comes to meeting men, what would I normally never do?"

I thought about it for ten minutes, then asked out seven guys in one week.

Satori was the seventh.

I called him the same day we met. I asked if he wanted to see me that night, even though the books on dating say women shouldn't ask men out, to which I say, "Screw that!" I married the guy. Obviously, calling him worked.

I didn't say chasing. If he'd been an asshole, I wouldn't have called again. Making the first move helped him know I was interested. He thanked me, said it made him feel great.

The faster you're willing to express yourself completely, the faster you'll know whether or not a person is right for you. Satori and I spilled our hearts on the third date, telling every secret we could recall. We were scared, of course, that the other would think, I'm not dealing with a past like that! We both listened, and we both stayed.

Doing things we normally wouldn't do stretches us and has us discover new aspects of our personality. The very act of breaking a habitual pattern jolts our nervous system and causes our brain to form new associations to reinforce our new behavior. The more we do it, the stronger these new associations become.

When I decided my life was about how much I was willing to

stretch myself, not about how many people said yes to a date, I became happy.

The more rigid our rules, the harder it is for us to be happy.

Rules like, "I can't let them know how I feel because it'll turn them off."

Let me tell you something, if someone is turned off by your expression of love, what happens when you express anger, or insecurity, or frustration? How can you build a lasting relationship if the smallest thing pushes them away?

If you believe you've got to play hard to get to keep someone interested, if you play games, act like you're less interested than you really are, or put on a false pretense, your relationship becomes a seesaw. When you pull away, they come close. When they pull away, you come close. The relationship is set up so neither of you have to get close. It's set up to never be together because the moment you put your guard down, they're not interested.

It's all about your energy anyway, which means if you're sitting at home obsessing about a person not calling you, they'll receive your obsessive signals, which will remind them why they stopped calling in the first place. The moment you say, "Screw it. I'm going out and having fun," they'll call, because you've let go and loosened your grip.

You can't pretend to let go.

You must truly let go of needing them to call, which is quite funny, because once you let go, they do call, but by then you don't really care.

How do you let go? *By letting go.* You can visualize them as a balloon on a string attached to your wrist. Cut the string and see them floating off into the distance until you can barely see them any longer. Then, for effect, see the balloon popping. Don't knock this technique. Do it. Just because something is easy doesn't mean it's not useful.

When it comes to obsession, gender doesn't make a difference. I've seen this in male/male, female/female, and male/female relationships, where the tighter the grasp, the more the other needs to escape.

In all the psychic readings I've done, I've never once heard someone say, "I'm looking for a partner whose happiness completely and utterly depends on me. I would love to meet a desperate woman or man; that's my ideal."

None of us cares to admit just how dependent we really are. We love to see ourselves as independent, resourceful, and able to live on our own. The truth is, We need people—a lot.

I'm not just talking about romantic love.

Love for your family, your friends, for yourself.

We want love so much, and yet, love is the one thing we never learn about in school. Sometimes, we don't learn enough about it at home. The majority of us have never been taught how to keep something once we've gotten it. We learn how to go for it, achieve it, but not how to keep, enjoy, and cherish it.

Romantic movies, love stories, always end where the relationship begins.

The guy wakes up after dumping his love the night before, suddenly realizing how important she is. Our hero races through traffic during rush hour, only to discover the love of his life is seconds away from boarding a plane to Peru.

His car runs out of gas, so he steals a bicycle, and you see him cycling, legs aching, panting heavily. Nothing can stop him. He's seen the light! He gets to the airport, tosses the bicycle aside, sprints toward the gate, elbowing an old lady in the ribs, shouting, "I'm sorry!" as he races toward his love. . . .

It's too late! The plane has left. His soul mate is gone.

But wait . . . is it . . . can it be? Yes! His love is sitting in the waiting area. She did not board the plane. She too, saw the light. How wonderful! How grand! They kiss. The passengers nearby cheer! Life is beautiful! The end.

THE END?

I want to see what happens when they get home and she hears the fourteen messages on his machine from the chicks he slept with after she arranged her trip to Peru! I want to know how he deals with her old boyfriend, Chuck, who shows up drunk and threatens to beat him silly.

People take more time planning a vacation to Disney World than planning, and learning, how to be great at love—both receiving love and giving it.

To be great at love, we must find out what our partner needs in order to feel loved, appreciated, valued, respected, which, by the way, you find out by asking, not by assuming.

I could cook dinner every night for Satori, but if I didn't cuddle with him on the couch, he wouldn't feel loved. All the pasta in the world wouldn't be enough to fill what a ten-minute cuddle session would.

Relationships should always expand, not diminish us. Since I married Satori, I've stretched myself enormously. He challenges me, as I do him. We help each other go beyond where we ever thought we could go. We assist each other, giving advice, sometimes taking it, sometimes not. We always have free will.

We all have the power to thoroughly screw up our lives. This means, if you have a reading with me to relieve yourself of the responsibility of taking action, you're in for a rude awakening. If you ask me, "Am I going to speak to Ronald on Friday?"

"You will if you call him," will be my answer.

I *can* say you're going to meet a wonderful person at the store, but if you never leave your house, it's not going to happen. If you do happen to leave the house and you're an emotional wreck, that soul mate of yours is going to run the other way.

So many of us speak about relationships as though they're outside of us, something to possess, not create. People ask me, "Will I ever find love? Will I ever get married? What's going to happen with my relationship? How many children will I have?"

That's completely up to you! I won't be in your bedroom telling you, "Come on! Keep it up! We're trying to create a soccer team here."

I tell you what I see in your relationship, or with your having kids, but what you do with what I tell you is always up to you.

Relationships don't just happen to you. *They include you.*

You play a role in making them happen. You and the other person have a direct part in making your relationship extraordinary, or horrific. YOU CREATE LOVE.

The chemistry, the dynamic attraction you feel between yourself and another is just the foundation, the starting point that gets you interested.

Making a relationship last takes finding out what you can do to make yourself happy and fulfilled, and what you can do for your partner—not just once, not just at the beginning of the relationship when you're trying to impress each other, but throughout its duration.

It's the same as going to the grocery store knowing what you want to buy. It makes the trip easier, doesn't it? Knowing brings clarity. Guessing brings an ulcer.

I remember walking into a New Age bookstore in Los Angeles, and standing there completely astounded at how many books dealt with ways to make us happy, healthy, rich, centered, lovable, loving, energetic, orgasmic, multi-orgasmic, successful, beautiful. The list was endless. I looked around at the jam-packed store, and said to Satori, "If there are so many wonderful self-help books out there, why are so many people unhappy and unfulfilled?"

"They think reading will make everything better instead of taking what they've read, and applying it to their life, not just once, but consistently," he tells me.

Most self-help books and magazines tell us how to be different than we are. If we use this toothpaste, everyone will notice us. If we drink this beer, then pretty girls wearing itsy-bitsy tube tops will swarm around us, laughing at our every word. Wear this outfit, and you'll be cool. Lose the weight, and you'll be popular. Marry someone rich, and you'll be successful. Become rich yourself, and you'll be admired. Become a superstar, and be adored by millions.

We are constantly given the message that we are not enough.

It's the same with relationships. We need to take care of ourselves and learn how to make ourselves feel wonderful *first,* before we look for someone to add to our joy.

If we feel filled with love, then share it with another, and they feel filled with love and share it with us, it's a totally different approach than looking for love to fill you, or fix you, or complete you. You are not broken. You don't need to be fixed. You are not half a person. You don't need someone to make you whole.

It doesn't matter what age you are, as long as you're alive, you can begin again. . . .

A woman came to me when she was forty, and said, "I'd like to go to medical school, but it'll take another two years to get my bachelor's degree, then four years of medical school, then another two years of residency; that's such a long time from now so it's not even worth it."

"How old are you going to be in eight years?" I asked her.

"I'll be 48."

"So either you'll be forty-eight and be a doctor, or be forty-eight still wanting to be a doctor."

Time will pass, and if you tell yourself, "I can't, it's hard, I'm too old, it's too late," you can have that conversation, but it's not a pleasant one and it's not the truth. I can tell you stories of many people who started doing what they love later in life.

My mom went to college in her forties, got her master's degree in her early fifties. She hadn't been to school since she married my dad at eighteen, and she had to work full-time while taking classes.

And guess who my dad's dating now?

My Mom!

I keep telling them it's their destiny to be together again.

Maybe one day they'll listen to their kid.

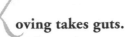**oving takes guts.**

It takes courage to love when you know every relationship has a chance of ending, whether through death, or though someone saying, "It's over."

You cannot enter a relationship without having this possibility present.

We all take love for granted, and even those who swear they don't, sometimes do. It's the nature of habit when you see someone every day, you think they'll be here tomorrow.

After the World Trade Center attack, a father went out desperately searching for his daughter. "My daughter and I had an argument," he told a friend. "She yelled at me. I yelled at her. She stormed out of the apartment. I haven't heard from her since. I'd give anything to hear her yell at me one more time. Anything to hear her shout about how stubborn I am."

I've done sessions for people, where I'm in awe they're still standing.

There is a man named Martin who flies from Michigan to see me. The moment he sits across from me, two little girls show up.

I see a truck.

I see the girls running across the street.

They disappear beneath the massive vehicle.

These are Martin's twin daughters. They'd just turned twelve.

A moment later, his wife comes through showing me she died from cancer.

As I repeat what his wife and daughters show me, Martin is silent, nodding, wiping the tears from his cheeks, quickly, before I can see them.

A boy appears. He shows himself on the side of a cliff. His pals are horsing around, not paying attention to the rock-filled river below, and like a car wreck I can't stop watching, the friend accidentally knocks the boy off the cliff.

I see his head bash against the rocks. I see his lifeless body wash out to sea.

I tell Martin, and he tells me, "That's my son."

I feel sick.

Three children and a wife. How do you live through something like that?

Although it's been many years since his wife's death, Martin hasn't moved any of her clothing. "Everything is exactly as she left it." It is the same with his two little girls, and now, he has to fly back to Michigan to bury his eleven-year-old son.

Martin's question to me was not, "How do I live my dreams?"

His question wasn't even, "How do I live?"

It was, "How do I even *want* to live? How do I begin to care about life again?"

I have clients who are devastated if a business deal falls through, or if someone doesn't call after a date. This man had his wife, two girls, and his son, all die, and he wonders why he should care about living.

I stare at him, speechless. I don't have an answer. No profound words.

The silence is uncomfortable. I tell myself to not fill it with meaningless chatter. I tell myself it's okay to be silent, just to be with this man, in the present moment, which I desperately wish would pass.

Finally, his wife speaks, *"He cannot kill himself. He won't be with us if he does. There are rules. He must face the pain where he is. He must go through it on his own. We will be with him. We will lead the way. There is another life awaiting him. A wife. A child. Tell him this is my promise. He will fall in love again. He needs to know this, and to wait, and see."*

I feel stupid saying these words. His so-called "great life" somewhere in the future doesn't matter because his pain is right now. Words of an idyllic destiny he had no proof would occur were like patching up a third-degree burn with a Band-Aid—it does nothing to heal the wound. His wife urges me to tell him, so I do.

He shrugs, doesn't want to hear it.

There are periods in life when we'll find ourselves challenged. How we deal with these challenges determines how we will go on.

No one confronted with a big situation ever remains the same.

They either become stronger, more compassionate, or become bitter and angry.

Having the courage to love again . . . and again . . . and again . . . Having the courage to keep on when everything inside you wants to stop. Having the courage to say yes when the world is telling you no. It's what love is all about, love for yourself, and for others.

Too many people take no for an answer. Too many people hear a diagnosis of a terminal illness, and obediently lie down and die. They don't fight for the person they love. They listen only to the doctors, and completely ignore themselves.

I know a man whose mother was diagnosed with cancer.

When the doctor told this man his mother had only five months left to live, the man replied, "You'd best not tell her if you know what's good for you! Under no circumstances do you tell my mother she's going to die."

The doctor said it was his professional duty to tell her. He had no choice.

"Well, Doc, I guess mom won't be the only one dead in five months; you catch what I'm saying?" The doctor said he would call the police. He took this man's words as a blatant threat.

The man immediately checked his mother out of the hospital. He brought her home, hired a holistic nurse, bought a stack of Eddie Murphy movies, a couple of James Brown albums, and enough yellow and pink roses to fill the entire room.

A year later, the man visits the doctor. "I want to show you something," he says, and takes out a photo and hands it to the doctor.

"Oh my God . . . This cannot be. . . ." The doctor looks stunned. He turns over the photo and looks at the date. "This was taken yesterday," the doctor replies, flabbergasted at what he sees.

"Seventy-four years old, and not a drop of cancer left in her body," the man replies.

When the doctor tries to give back the photo, the man tells him, "I want you to keep it, as a reminder, Doctor, that you're not God."

A Flower doesn't have a whole conversation about Growing
It just grows

It obeys the laws of its natural state
and just allows itself to shine boldly and beautifully

It doesn't say, "If I'm too colorful or smell too nice,
all the other flowers will be jealous and hate me."

A flower does not stop its growth

It never gets in its own way

When it's given what it needs, a flower grows into exactly
what it is meant to be.

When given what we need - So do we.

18

WELCOME TO YOUR LIFE

It's the last round of your life.

You're coming in for the close.

Ninety seconds left on the clock.

You have one last shot to turn it all around.

Quickly. Think! What can you do to override all those years working in a hideous job with people you despise? How can you let your family know you care, even though you've been distant and unavailable? What can you say to the love of your life about why you left them?

Eighty seconds left to go.

How can you forgive yourself for pursuing your goals and dreams at the expense of your relationships, health, and peace of mind? How can you forgive yourself for quitting on yourself?

Sixty seconds.

How can you apologize for not listening, being fearful, self-absorbed, and angry?

Forty more seconds.

Who inspired you? What do you appreciate most about your life?

If you had another chance to live, what would you do differently this time? To whom do you want to say, "I love you"? Of whom do you feel proud? What do you want to admit?

Twenty seconds left.

Whatever you want to say, **SAY IT NOW**! What have you been holding back? What is the one thing you wished you'd done? Wished you hadn't done?

Ten seconds left.

What was the greatest moment of your life? What stands out most in your mind?

Nine, eight, seven . . .

Tell them you love them, you'll still be around, you're leaving temporarily.

Six, five, four . . .

You wish you'd spent more time, wish you'd paid more attention . . .

Three, two . . .

One . . .

STOP!

You're Still Alive!

There's been a mistake! It's not your time to go.

Since you've been given another chance, how do you want to spend the first day of your life? What do you want to say to yourself? What do you want to say to the people you love?

What are you waiting for?

Your entire life will go by, and you'll have photos, videos, and remnants to prove you participated, that you were here, but will you have been so busy you missed your life?

What are the last thoughts you'd like to have before you die? Your last words . . .

$\mathcal{A}$ fifty-five-year-old woman walked out of a convenience store. A man with a scruffy beard followed her. Little did she know this man made a pact with himself to kill the next woman he laid eyes on.

His hands were shaking as he pressed the revolver to the base of the woman's skull, and whispered, "I'm gonna kill you, bitch. . . ."

After a moment, the woman whispered, "I love you."

His warm breath filled her ear, "You ain't gonna love me after this."

She was going to die. She knew it.

He knew it, too. He was in control of her destiny.

He pressed the barrel to her head, cocked the chamber, closed his eyes, ready to pull—"I love you." When he heard this, he yanked the gun away. "Lady, you crazy?"

She turned to him, calmness in her eyes, and said, "If I am going to die, I want the last words out of my mouth to be, I love you."

The guy took off. Couldn't shoot her after hearing those words.

Honestly, who wants to leave this world bitching? Angry?

Say what you need to say now. Stop putting things on hold.

If you would imagine your entire life being recorded on videotape and I asked you to stop the tape and rewind it to the point at which you were born. Then, I had you watch your life from that moment until today, "What would you be watching?"

Would you be bored out of your mind? "Oh, there she goes again, off to work, hitting the gym, getting Chinese food to go, on the couch, watching TV."

Would you be excited? Horrified? Frightened? Thrilled? Angry? Exhilarated? Proud?

Most of us would see a combination of times when we felt bored, times we felt excited, times we felt pain, and times we were enjoying life. But what would **most** of it be?

Press the record button again. Now you get to **choose** what you're going to watch by how you decide to live from this moment on.

Though you can't choose everything that happens to you, you can choose what you'll focus on and the meaning you'll make out of any situation. You can choose what you're going to keep on your videotape, and what you're going to edit out.

At the end of your life, what kind of movie do you want to be watching?

We all want to live a life that matters. No one wants to die and be greeted by loved ones, only to hear, "What were you thinking? Why did you hold on to so much pain? Why'd you spend so much time worried about not pissing people off instead of stepping up and standing up for what you believe? All right, go to the back of the spirit bus; you've got a lot of reflecting to do."

Our entire life is encapsulated in our memories. Stories we can go back and recapture, one frame at a time, anytime we choose.

Think about it. Remember a time when you allowed yourself to be free. . . . A time when you loved someone deeply . . . when you felt deeply loved . . . when you laughed so hard your stomach ached. Etch in your mind the joyful times so you can access them quickly, whenever you're in need.

Capture your life.

Remember, you don't need to leave your house to take a trip to Hawaii.

You need only to close your eyes.

You don't need to have lots of zeros in your bank account to know you are rich.

Just look at yourself in the mirror.

You don't need to justify your existence, or explain yourself anymore.

Your birth is proof enough that you have a right to be here. You are not a mistake.

Forget the e-mail and the phone call. . . . They can wait a moment.

Why are you running so fast? Where are you going? What's driving you? Pushing you so hard? What do you think would happen if you stopped . . . doing so much . . . and started . . . **BEING YOU**.

How do you do that? Stop and find out.

Take the time to SEE what you did not see before, or maybe what you saw and ignored.

LISTEN . . . not with your ears, but with the part of you that hears what people are saying beneath their words. People say more in their silence than they do with their voice.

We speak to fill the silent pockets of life, the uncomfortable space where air resides. You don't have to do that anymore.

The phone rings.

Satori yells, it's for me. "Tell them to call back, I'm busy now!" I shout. He comes into my office and hands me the phone. "I think you'll want to hear this."

I take the receiver and hear a man's voice. It is Martin. He sounds excited. He is crying. It's been nearly two years since his reading.

"Lysa, I am getting married. My wife is . . . pregnant," he tells me.

The memories come rushing back, his wife coming through and telling him about the woman he would meet and the child they would have.

"It's happening," he says. "I love her . . . is that okay? For me to love her."

"Yes, Martin. It is more than okay. It is what is meant to be."

I get off the phone, thinking how brave this man is, not only to get married, but to have another child after his three children died. There are people who fall in love, have their heart broken, and swear they'll never fall in love again. Yet this man is courageous enough to love again . . . and bring another child into the world, knowing there are no guarantees.

*R*emember who you really are, why you are here, and what's most important to you.

On some level, you already know.

I'm not saying it's not hidden for some people, but if you go underneath all the crap, there is a place where you know what you may have forgotten that you know.

You know when you're in a relationship that stinks, when you're unhappy in your job, when you're acting bitchy, loving, truthful, dishonest, scared. You know what you love and what you hate; the kind of people you prefer to spend time with; what books you like to read and movies you like to see.

You know what really matters to you.

The thing with this knowing stuff is that it leads to responsibility. As long as we lie to ourselves, and say, "If I knew what to do, I would do it, but I don't," then we don't have to do anything.

You are the biggest assignment of your life.

Your life is not just for you, alone. You are meant to share yourself with many people, with the world, because to keep your gifts, stories, and life experiences secret, is to be selfish and rob others of hearing what only you can say, of experiencing what only you came here to do.

Just look at how many violent criminals were captured because John Walsh, the creator of *America's Most Wanted,* decided to work tirelessly after his six-year-old son, Adam, was abducted and murdered.

We all have a story to tell. A voice meant to be heard. The question is, "What do you want to say? What do you want to be remembered for contributing? What word do you want to pop into people's minds when they hear your name?"

Satori once told me the only way to be unhappy is to forget to appreciate what you have.

We are here to help each other to remember.

So please don't allow yourself to get caught up in the rat race of life. Do not push away love. Do not fool yourself into thinking intimacy is what you fear. No one fears intimacy. We fear the loss of it. We don't fear success. We fear what success will mean. No one fears love. We fear losing the people we love.

If you have five seconds, don't waste it by criticizing someone, or by gossiping. Look for the good before the bad. Criticism will never make you feel as good as giving a compliment will.

The clock ticks as your heart beats, reminding you, in this moment you are alive.

I often wonder, when Ronald Goldman was walking to Nicole Brown Simpson's house to return her mother's glasses, if he had any idea it would the last time he walked that path?

As he crossed Montana Avenue, and continued along Bundy, do you think it crossed his mind that he had only three minutes left to live?

In a second, your life changes.

Just like that.

And to spend even a moment of your life filled with hate, instead of love, is to waste it.

It takes courage to face your life.

It takes courage to love again . . . and again . . . and again. . . .

It takes courage to use your voice and your life to contribute to yourself and others.

It takes awareness to remember that . . .

DEATH IS A COMMA, NOT A PERIOD. . . .

19

Honoring Those We Love

My goal in writing this book was to give a voice to the spirits, and the people for whom they came through. Preserving the raw, unedited details of what transpired during a channeling session, how it impacted a person, who they were before their loved one died, and who they became after, is the intention of this section. Many people generously spent hours transcribing their session tapes and writing details of their personal story. I thank them immensely.

To share oneself with fearless abandon, to love without reserve, to rise each time we fall . . . are what makes an ordinary human being, extraordinary.

DAD, I LOVE YOU—
DONNA QUINTER'S STORY

RECORDED TRANSCRIPT OF DONNA'S IN-PERSON READING ON DECEMBER 19, 2001

LYSA: He says you took him to a lot of doctors to figure out what's wrong. There are many treatments.

DONNA: Yes, I took him for different treatments, to see doctors all over the country.

LYSA: I'm being shown here . . . something around the wrists, not bracelets, but . . . two bandages.

DONNA: He was wearing two bandages on his wrists because of bleeding from leukemia.

LYSA: All of a sudden, I'm seeing a pizzeria. He wants to talk about a pizzeria. Does that make sense?

DONNA: (laughing and crying) Yes!

LYSA: Good, because it doesn't to me. It's funny, they never tell me what it means . . . they just tell me to say it and you'll know what it means. I'm just a phone line bringing the order through.

DONNA'S AFTERTHOUGHT: My dad and I had a favorite pizza place in Ocean City, New Jersey. We went there every summer all my life. My mom and I took him in a wheelchair for what would be his last visit. I have a photo of him and I biting into a slice of pizza from that day. I mentally said to my dad if he mentioned the pizzeria, I'd know he came through.

LYSA: He keeps showing me his hand. Something about a wedding ring. He says, "I didn't wear a ring."

DONNA: No, he didn't wear a ring. I don't remember he had one. I never saw it.

LYSA: Well, there is one . . . he has one, a wedding ring he didn't wear.

DONNA: Oh, um, okay.

LYSA: This ring . . . whoever has it . . . they were holding it recently . . . wearing it.

DONNA'S AFTERTHOUGHT: When I played the tape for my mother, she nearly fainted because the day I had the reading, my mom said she found the wedding ring my dad used in their second wedding ceremony. She'd been trying it on, in her mind telling him it was too big for her at the same time my reading was going on, and she didn't even know about it. After hearing the tape, she put the ring on a chain that she now wears around her neck.

LYSA: At the funeral, you put something in his pocket.

DONNA: Yes, at his funeral I put something in his pocket.

LYSA: He knows you did that. They're actually watching as people look in the casket. They're not in their body. They're with you. He wouldn't be able to tell me anything unless he had awareness beyond his body. Who's Charlie?

DONNA: That's his name! Charlie's my dad.

LYSA: He's showing me a pair of pajamas. Someone kept a pair of his pajamas.

DONNA: Um, I don't know.

DONNA'S AFTERTHOUGHT: I later learned my uncle had taken a pair of my dad's fairly new pajamas. I didn't even know Dad owned pajamas because he used to sleep in his boxer shorts all the time.

LYSA: He's showing a photo of Santa and a child, like at Christmas where you take a photo for a card.

DONNA: I don't know.

DONNA'S AFTERTHOUGHT: When Lysa asked me if there was a picture of a child with Santa Claus, nothing stood out in my mind. She was very emphatic about my dad showing her the photo. The morning after my reading, my fiancé walked in holding a photo of my sister's new baby with Santa Claus that he'd just taken out of her Christmas card. (My husband didn't know I had a reading.) The photo was the only one with Santa on it I received this year. The month before my dad died, my sister had her baby, so I took this as a sign Dad is keeping track of us and knew I'd be receiving the photo today, which is why he mentioned it during my reading.

What I Remember Most About My Dad is his dry, kind of sarcastic sense of humor. He was a Civil War buff who had photos of him with every cannon he ever saw. He kept telling me he was building a cannon in the garage, but still needed some parts. He said it was to keep the neighbors off the property, a joke . . . or so I thought.

Sure enough, after his death, I found parts to make a cannon in the garage!

Before he got sick, the most important thing to me was traveling, having a good time, and trying to make it as a part-time actress in New York City. My dad got such a kick whenever I would tell him about some new place I traveled, or some acting job I did. He always made me feel special and important.

On November 11, 2001, my mom called and said I should fly back to Philadelphia as soon as possible. My fiancé and I had just found the house we wanted to buy in Los Angeles, and I quickly took a bunch of photos because I wanted so much for my dad to see the house.

I walked into his hospital room and was shocked to see how much he'd deteriorated. I sat on his bed and showed him the photos of the house. He put on his glasses, and looked carefully at each one. Smiling.

I told him there was a guest room just for him.

The next day, we went back to the hospital, and found him unresponsive, staring. Mom and I were not going to let him die in the hospital, and demanded they release him.

That night, my brother and sisters all came with their children to say good-bye.

To me, it all seemed like a horrible dream. I couldn't believe this frail man was my big, ex-Marine father. I remember holding his hand and telling him if he could understand me to squeeze mine. I thought I felt him trying to squeeze it. Before I went to bed, I told him to think about our good times at the shore, and if he saw a light, he should go to it.

When one of my sisters came to wake me up at 3:30 A.M., I knew this was it. My mom, two sisters, and I stood around his bed and helplessly watched as he cried out for help.

He hadn't been able to speak or move all day but now he was grabbing my mother's hand, pulling her down, clearly calling out, "Help me!" I remember standing there crying, saying, "What can I do, Dad? How can I help?"

He wasn't looking at us, but past us, and was putting up a hell of a fight.

Suddenly, he began gasping for air, and then, just stopped.

My sister cried out, "Dad!" but my mom said, "Don't call him back."

He was gone.

It was the worst moment of my life.

The hardest thing has been walking into the house when I go to visit my mom, and him not being there. I half expect to see him sitting in his favorite chair. It's also hard to see his workbench in the garage with some of his unfinished projects, waiting for his return.

Some people speak about their pain openly. I am much more private in my grief. Although I think of my dad every day, I prefer to talk silently to him, or do things that honor him, like writing this, for example. I am always thinking of ways to preserve his legacy for future generations of the family. I know that is something he would have liked.

Recently, I married Micky Dolenz (yes, from The Monkees!), and as I was walking down the aisle, I felt my dad right by my side.

Dad and me—our last visit to the pizzeria at the shore.

THE LOVE OF MY LIFE—
CHERYL TENNANT'S STORY

RECORDED TRANSCRIPT FROM CHERYL'S PHONE READING ON
OCTOBER 24, 2002

LYSA: I am seeing the name Eric. Does that make sense to you?

CHERYL: My husband's name is Eric.

LYSA: I'm sorry to be graphic here . . .

CHERYL: It's okay. Say whatever you need to say.

LYSA: There's an explosion. Vapors, ash, and fire, come into his face and engulf him. It's a horror film. His body was badly burned. He is running. He shows being at his work.

CHERYL: This is exactly what happened to him.

LYSA: His soul was out quickly. He was out before he crossed.

CHERYL'S AFTERTHOUGHT: I was worried he was suffering and that his soul would be changed forever because of what he had gone through. Hearing this brought a great deal of comfort to me.

LYSA: He's having me take my weddings rings off, but my hands are swollen. He shows you doing this.

CHERYL: Two weeks before my reading, I took off my wedding rings, which was difficult both emotionally and physically because my hands were swollen. I put them on a chain around my neck.

LYSA: You don't have to worry about moving forward 'cause he's coming with you for the ride. You always try to please him, even now, but you've already won his vote. Now you have to honor yourself.

CHERYL'S AFTERTHOUGHT: Eric conveyed he wants me to trust myself and stop worrying so much what other people think, or what I think other people expect me to do, and just do what feels right to me, which was difficult at the time. I needed to know I am making good decisions.

LYSA: He says you have to get a new mantra. He's tired of you saying, "I don't know what to do, where to move, how to redecorate the house, what to do with my life. I don't know."

CHERYL: Yes, "I don't know what to do" has been my mantra.

CHERYL'S AFTERTHOUGHT: After my life had been turned upside down by my husband's death, I was wavering back and forth about where to live, what to do, who I was, who I wanted to be. I was miserable. After my reading, I took a long, hard look at my life, and decided that despite wanting Eric back, I was happy where I lived and with what I was doing with my life. My reading helped me put into perspective what had happened, where I was going, and how to make myself feel happy again.

LYSA: He not only wants you to be happy, he's saying that since he's going to be around you a lot, you'd *better* be happy. He says, *"She knows how upset I'd be if she wasted all this time being miserable."*

CHERYL: That sounds exactly like something he would say. It makes me very happy to hear that.

LYSA: He mentions your dog's neck. He is where the dog will soon be due to the neck thing.

CHERYL'S AFTERTHOUGHT: At the time, I didn't know what this meant, other than he loved the dog and wanted to mention him. However, Lysa said that my husband kept showing her something with the dog's neck. A few weeks after my reading, my dog developed a very serious infection that started in his neck. This infection spread throughout his body, and after a month of being hospitalized, he was put to sleep. I believe my husband was trying to warn me something was going to happen, and at the same time, tell me he'd be there for my dog when he crossed.

LYSA: You literally write to him, not just about him, in your journal. And you've (laughing) got to stop scribbling words out and correcting them. Grammar and spelling are not foremost on his mind, you know.
CHERYL: I do that! I fix the spelling and grammar! Scribbling words out. I write **to him** every night in my journal, and the fact he reads the letters is almost like having a conversation with him every day.

What I Remember Most About Eric is the way I felt around him. Loved. Supported. Cherished. Adored. Honored. He was my husband, best friend, soul mate, and love of my life.

When I was a little girl, I had this reoccurring nightmare about a man running out of a building with his body on fire. I had never seen such a thing in real life, on TV, or in the movies, and had no idea why I was dreaming this, what it meant, or how to stop it.

At 9:40 A.M. on January 14, 2002—my nightmare became real.

Eric was in management at a power plant, and an outside vendor came to help with a job. Something went terribly wrong. There was a huge explosion. He and another person were badly burned. Yet, somehow Eric managed to run two hundred yards, down four flights of stairs, with a burned body, to get to the office to have a coworker call me. He was in pain, and still thinking of me.

I was met at the emergency room by the social worker, head of trauma, and chief resident. They escorted me up to the burn unit, handed me Eric's wedding ring, and asked if we had any children. When I answered "Not yet," they looked at me strangely then turned away.

Over 95 percent of Eric's body had been burned, and he was in grave danger of dying. He was in a drug-induced coma when I entered his room, and I sat in shock, crying, wanting desperately to wake up from this nightmare.

He had left that morning perfectly healthy. He kissed me good-bye, told me he loved me, and said he would see me that evening.

And now . . .

When I held his hand, his heart rate stabilized and his breathing relaxed. I told him how much I love him. How he is the best thing that's ever happened to me. How I would never leave his side. I could almost feel him floating above me, looking down on the whole situation. I knew he could hear me. He knew I was there.

As the day wore on, his kidneys shut down. He began retaining fluid. The doctors said he wouldn't make it through the night and didn't recommend heroic measures to keep him alive.

At about 2:30 A.M., things looked grim. I pulled his family aside and told them Eric wouldn't have wanted to live this way. They said they would support any decision I made.

At 3:20 A.M. I held my husband's hand . . . as he died.

I felt my heart break into a million pieces when I heard the nurse say, "He's gone." I sobbed loudly and fell on top of him. I looked at his face. He was so beautiful. Despite the burns and the bleeding and the bloating, he'd never looked so beautiful.

After Eric's death, I began searching for ways to communicate with him. I talked to him all the time, wrote to him every day, and looked for signs everywhere.

I now know Eric is with me all of the time. He knows what I am doing, watches out for me. He is okay, and it is okay for me to be happy.

It's funny because Eric was not one to believe in communicating with the other side. He was a "here-and-now kind of guy," and probably would have laughed, in a good-natured way, if I said I was going to a psychic. He wouldn't have talked me out of it, he would have just said, "Do whatever you've got to do," but not to include him in the process.

I learned that, just like every relationship is different, everyone grieves the death of someone differently. There is no one right way to do it. What matters is that you trust yourself, listen to yourself, and make decisions not based on what you think other people want, or expect you to do. Trust yourself to know what you need to do. It is a process, and if you trust the process, it will be that much easier to survive.

I know people mean well when they say things to comfort me, but I hope to never again hear: "You're so young, you'll meet someone else." "He's in a better place now." "God needed him." "God has a plan for everything." "At least you didn't have children." "Too bad you weren't pregnant." "It was for the best." "Give it a year or two, and you'll be over it." And the all-time winner: "I know exactly how you feel because my new boyfriend and I just broke up!"

Life is way too short, and you don't always get time to do the things you want, so you have to take every opportunity that comes your way. You have to tell people what you love about them, and live each day without regrets. I am stronger than I thought I was. I can do this, and even though I may not want to do it alone, I will survive. I am not the same person I was before Eric died, and I will probably not end up being the person I am now, because I am ever changing.

One of the most difficult things I've had to do is sell Eric's car. It wasn't a great car, but it was his, and he loved it, but I didn't want to keep two cars for myself. I made the decision to sell his, trade in mine, and get the car I always wanted—a VW Cabriolet convertible.

The decision was difficult because I was having a hard time realizing it was okay to do something nice for myself. Once I realized it was not only okay, but was what Eric wanted, the decision became easier.

As I drove the car home from the dealer, with the top down, in the middle of March, I could just feel Eric smiling right along with me.

Eric and me.

MY BEST FRIEND, MY BROTHER—
HARRY BEAN'S STORY

TRANSCRIPT FROM VIDEOTAPE OF HARRY'S READING IN AVON, INDIANA, ON APRIL 26, 2002

LYSA: I feel like your brother knew he was about to die, but not like when a person is sick, has cancer. He made a comment to you weeks before about you doing something if he dies. . . . This make sense to you?

HARRY: A couple of weeks before he died, out of the blue, Jason says to me, "Hey, if I die before you, do me a favor. Don't let them bury me. I want to be cremated and have my ashes spread in the forest, where I belong." With him being only seventeen and me being nineteen, I laughed and told him halfheartedly, "You got it, bro, but only if you do the same for me."

What I Remember Most About Jason is how much he loved life and helping people, especially his family. He loved the freedom of the open road, the feeling of being in the woods, surrounded by home, as he would say.

Jason was always cracking jokes, always playing pranks on me, laughing at silly stuff, and though Jason was younger, and shorter, than me, I always looked up to him.

He was passionate about living to the fullest, while I was more of the serious, "gotta-do-it-now" type of guy. Jason wanted me to slow down, **enjoy** the smell of the roses, the color of the sky, and realize life was short, and though we could not change the past, we could look forward to the future, and enjoy this gift called the present.

LYSA: I am getting a message from someone who calls himself "a little man." He calls himself this because he has lived many lifetimes in his short one. He's saying he'd be good to take along on my tour. He's skilled at getting into places and finding ways to do stuff and live for free, without money.

HARRY: Yes, that's him. He traveled across the country with no job and no money and always found a way to make it work. He was my "little man," loving life all the time.

LYSA: (touching my neck) I'm not sure what I'm doing here. He is racing you, making a necklace or . . .

HARRY: My brother and I used to make necklaces to sell at Grateful Dead concerts. We'd have races to see who could bead the best necklace the fastest.

There we were—Jason, our two friends, and me—driving along the open road, laughing, talking, thoroughly enjoying each other's company, and out of nowhere, in the blink of an eye, a semi-truck comes toward us, too fast for me to get out of the way, too fast for anyone to react. As the truck smashes into our vehicle, I hear a hideous crashing sound, and I'm out, unconscious.

I awaken in a hospital room surrounded by family and friends. My first thought is, "Jason! Is he okay?" I ask my mom. She assures me he's fine, in the next room, recovering nicely.

"What about the others?"

I am told they are fine. I was the only one seriously injured.

I lay on my pillow, feeling thankful everyone is okay.

A week later, I am told the truth.

The semitruck driver was indeed, unharmed.

My brother, Jason, and our two friends, were killed—instantly.

Within a matter of seconds, my entire world collapses, and I lose all reason for wanting to live. My parents admit they didn't tell me the truth because they feared I'd slip back into a coma and give up my fight for life if I'd heard too soon. They're probably right.

I believe Jason led me to my reading. I found out about Lysa's Barnes & Noble tour an hour before her event in Avon, Indiana, and decided there wasn't enough time to find a sitter, get ready, and make it there. But something inside kept pushing me to go. No, forcing me actually. It was a strange feeling, so at the last minute, my wife and I decided to go.

I had no expectations of any reading or anything of the sort. Mainly, I told myself I was going with my wife because she'd lost her father a few months earlier and was grieving immensely.

Lysa gave my wife an astonishing reading and was about to wrap up her book signing when out of nowhere she called me out of the crowd. She said she had a spirit who wouldn't leave her alone until he said what he needed to say. She proceeded to tell me about Jason's life, as I sat there open-mouthed and in shock.

When she started speaking of Top Gun and headphones, I had no clue what this meant. I thought she was off-base or confused or something. On the way home, it hit me like a ton of bricks. "The captain 'O' fan club through Boy Scouts!" I shouted. My brother and I worked our butts off all summer selling greeting cards to save points for prizes. At the end of the summer, we pooled our points and bought Top Gun headphone walkie-talkies! When I remembered this, I cursed out loud and scared my wife, who thought something was wrong.

Nothing was wrong. Everything was right.

I am a completely different person now. I am learning to lighten up and not to take life so seriously. I have learned how to deal with overwhelming grief and don't like hearing people say Jason is "gone but not forgotten." He is neither "gone" nor will he ever be "forgotten." His spirit remains with me through every decision, throughout every day.

Although some people tend to pull away when grieving, isolating themselves in a private hell of misery, I became closer to my loved ones, wanting to seize the moment and never again miss the chance to tell someone how much I love them, especially my best friend, my brother, *Jason*.

Jason.

MY BEAUTIFUL SON—
RITA MURPHY'S STORY

Rita Murphy remembers it clearly:

"Hi, Mom." My twenty-one-year-old son, Peter, smiles as he lifts the groceries from my car.

"Aren't you going to be late for class?"

He kisses me on the forehead, his way of telling me not to worry. He gathers his things and walks toward the door. As I begin putting away groceries, I hear Peter yell something, and automatically yell back, "Okay, honey," even though I have no idea what he said.

My other son, Jamie, who's seventeen, comes out of his room. "Did you say something to me, Mom?"

"Peter yelled something I couldn't hear. I don't want him to be late for school so I'll just ask him when he gets home."

By ten o'clock, Peter always returned from night school, so when I didn't hear from him by eleven, I got worried and left several messages on his cell phone. I knew if he could've called, he would've, which meant whatever news I would receive wouldn't be good.

DAY ONE: I wait for the phone to ring. It never does. I call my sister Kathie and her husband, Ray Sr., who starts calling the hospitals and police stations. There are no accidents reported. Peter isn't at the hospital. There are no signs of his car.

DAY TWO: His college confirms he attended class last night, but didn't show up for his class this morning. I report Peter missing to the police. The troopers tell me Peter is probably out partying. He'll be home soon. I know my son. He'd never go out partying without telling me.

DAY THREE: Peter's best friend and cousin, Ray Jr., gathers Peter's friends and starts a search party. My sisters-in-law create missing person posters and put them up at every store and establishment from town to town. My brother, John, sets up a command center and calls every police officer and contact he knows.

DAY FOUR: Friends and family are coming with food to feed the growing search parties. Even though Peter's disappearance makes our local paper, his story is overshadowed by Ground Zero and since local troopers are doing little to find Peter, Ray Jr. decides to go to Mt. Kisco, where Peter grew up, to see if his childhood friends have heard anything. He goes to Mt. Kisco police department and meets Detective Maria Palazzetti, our guardian angel.

DAY FIVE: Detective Palazzetti helps Ray Jr. search out every lead, every tip. She promises to stay with the case and do whatever she can until we find Peter.

DAY SIX: Not a word or break in the case. We are all exhausted and out of ideas. It is Sunday, so we decide to go to church, and right before we leave, the doorbell rings.

"Is Ms. Murphy at home?" asks one of the two state troopers standing at my front door.

I send everyone, except my brother, John, out of the room. He wraps his arms around me, as we await news we do not want to hear.

"There was a one-vehicle accident," the trooper begins. "I'm sorry, . . . your son is deceased."

For six long days, I'd kept myself under control. Now, I lose it.

I replay the words "your son is deceased." I cry. I scream. I go into shock.

When I'm coherent enough, I find out Peter's car accident occurred ten minutes from where we live. He'd lost control of his car on Highway 684, skidding off the road into the only part of the median that doesn't have a guardrail and contains trees, which is why we didn't see his car. Since it was autumn, it took six days for enough leaves to fall from the trees to be able to notice it. I think of how many times we passed him, driving right by, not knowing my son was tucked beneath those trees.

I now pass the skid marks from Peter's car every time I go to work.

What I Remember Most About Peter is everything. Every detail from his birth, his toddler years, his youth, his teens, his young adulthood; I don't want to forget anything.

On the six-month anniversary of his death, my sister, Kathie, and I went to the zoo, thinking if we walked until we couldn't walk anymore, maybe we'd finally get a full night of sleep. We walked through the Bronx Zoo for five hours, and afterward, I got into the car, looked at Kathie, and said, "No matter what, Peter is still dead."

I went home and felt a depression falling over me that I had been fighting for six months. Now, I had no fight left. I was ready to give up. I tried so hard to be there for Jamie, but I just couldn't do it anymore. I was done.

I was sitting at my desk at work contemplating all of this when Kathie called to tell me an amazing story. She said my niece, Liz, was at work when her boss asked if she wanted to come along to Barnes & Noble in Mohegan Lake to a signing for a book called *Conversations with the Spirit World*. Liz said, "Sure, why not."

Peter came through that night.

I was smiling as Kathie was telling me this.

The next night, I drove two hours to see Lysa speak, and the first thing she said to me was Peter wanted me to know his spirit left the accident scene immediately. He got out fast. She described things the way Peter would describe them and told me things only he and I knew. I had a phone session with her where she talked about Peter's brother taping up a poster of Peter's favorite movie. Jamie had just done that in honor of his brother. Peter pointed out the photo of his brother and him with missing teeth, which made me laugh because I put this photo on our refrigerator the day before.

It feels good to know Peter is here pointing out what we're doing, aware of how much we miss and love him.

That night, I had the first full night sleep since Peter went missing.

My reading saved me from going into a depression. It gave me back hope and the knowledge I will see my son again one day. I still grieve for him, but whenever I get overwhelmed, I listen to the tape of the reading and it gives me comfort.

—Love, Rita Murphy

Jamie, me, and Peter.

LOSING MY LITTLE GIRL—
DAWN GREGORY'S STORY

I am not a nutcase.

I am a mom who lost her little girl and didn't want to live without her, so I admitted myself to a psychiatric ward. There, I met Lysa's mom, Linda, a therapist who happened to be filling in for another therapist, which could either be called a fluke, or, as I prefer—fate.

RECORDED TRANSCRIPT FROM DAWN'S IN-PERSON READING
ON AUGUST 31, 2001

LYSA: I feel like I am convulsing, uncontrollably. Do you understand this?

DAWN: Yes.

LYSA: A little girl, very young, two or three . . .

DAWN: She was three.

LYSA: She shows me the bathroom, something with the bathroom connected to her crossing.

DAWN: Yes.

LYSA: Now, she shows me her toothbrush. . . . This is gross. She is cleaning the toilet with her toothbrush.

DAWN: (laughs) Yes, she did. I brought her toothbrush here with me today.

LYSA: She shows you with her in the bathroom. You leave and come back and she is gone.

DAWN: (crying) I was giving her a bath. . . . My son called me. I left her in a tub of water barely up to her belly. I was gone less than five minutes. When I came back, she was facedown in the tub. Not breathing.

LYSA: No matter how many times you beat yourself up, it won't change a thing. I know that sounds harsh, but you have a beautiful son sitting next to you, and your daughter is saying to me, *"Mommy, quit it."* No matter how many times you wish you never left the bathroom, it won't change that you did. You cannot undo what is done. I know you realize this intellectually, but you can beat yourself up until the day you cross over, and all you'll have done is missed out on both your sons' lives. . . . No matter how guilty you feel, no matter how much regret you carry with you, it won't bring your daughter back.

What I Remember Most About My Daughter, Cassandra is her spirit, her fearlessness, and her big beautiful soulful eyes and wide-open smile. I remember her desire to take in as much as possible, as fast as possible, and her attempts to emulate her older brother whenever she had the chance. I remember her ability to scream loudly and give great hugs and how she would take my face in her hands and just look at me and sing "Wish Upon a Star."

I don't want to forget anything about her, and sometimes fear I will.

From the age of six months, Cassandra had frequent seizures, some lasting thirty minutes. She would have three to four seizures a week, yet doctors could not figure out what was wrong.

I hadn't told Lysa's mom anything about Cassandra, yet when I sat down for my reading, Lysa told me many things regarding her physical appearance, personality, the way she died, and her prior health condition, she could not have known other than by communicating with Cassie.

I'd had so much guilt surrounding her death. It was horrible, finding her facedown in the bathtub, realizing it was my negligence, trying to give her CPR, knowing she was already gone, talking to the police, going to the hospital, having to tell her father what happened, and watching her stay alive, hooked up to machines for fourteen hours, knowing she wasn't really there.

Then, having hospital personnel ignore me, facing my family and my ex-husband's family, holding her hand, watching her little heart finally give up, knowing I'd never see her smile or hear her mischievous laugh again, leaving the hospital without her.

Cassie contributed to my life in countless ways. Even though she was only three, her fearless nature and take-life-by-the-balls attitude totally cracked me up. She was a character who taught me to live each moment with ferocity and vigor.

Her crossing forced me to slow down and appreciate my loved ones. I've learned that terrible, devastating things can happen at any time and any place, and that life is short and unpredictable, so it's important to never take one moment, or one person, for granted and never compromise your values or who you are as a person.

After my reading, I felt better, especially after Cassie commented on my all-consuming guilt and said she was going to help me learn how to let it go. Cassie said it was her choice and her time to go and it would have happened regardless.

As humans, we cannot control every situation, or save every person. Life takes its course whether or not we agree with what happens. There are good moments, for sure, even though the bad seem to hit harder, which is why I now actively focus on the positive, knowing I want to see and do so much before my time in this life is up. I want to make my little girl proud.

Cassandra, I love you.

A Poem About Life

by Lysa Mateu

First I was dying to finish high school and start college.

And then I was dying to finish college and start working.

And then I was dying to stop working and get married.

And soon after, I was dying to have children.

And then I was dying for my children to be old enough to go to school

so I could return to work.

And soon after, I was dying to retire from work.

And now, I am Dying.

And as I sit back and survey my life,

I suddenly realize I forgot to do one enormously important thing...

I Forgot To Live.

SEPT/OCT '98

-Malibu Chronicle

A poem I wrote, published in the *Malibu Chronicle* in 1998.

Open the Door to the Other Side

Sign Up for Your Private Channeling/Psychic Session with Lysa Mateu
You will connect with your loved ones who have crossed over and learn how to tap
into your intuition, preserve and replenish your soul. Lysa puts you in touch with the
choices you have made and offers you the opportunity to experience the truth about
who you are and why you are here. The result is clarity, inspiration and a renewed
sense of purpose for your life.

YOUR APPOINTMENT IS WAITING FOR YOU

Call 310-820-0711
Or sign up online at
www.channelingspirits.com
www.psychicdiaries.com

*Lysa does 98 percent of her sessions over the phone and your receive a
free recording of your session.*

PSYCHIC DIARIES GIFT PACKAGE

You will receive a personally signed copy of Lysa's inspiring book

CONVERSATIONS WITH THE SPIRIT WORLD
&
SECRETS OF PSYCHIC DEVELOPMENT

Your amazing psychic development CD, recorded by Lysa, teaches you how to
know spirits are around, how to tell the difference between a psychic message
and your thoughts, how to contact and identify your spirit guides, and
how to employ easy-to-use techniques to heighten your intuitive
and psychic ability to use in your everyday life.

This is a specially discounted package 30% off retail price

☐ YES, I want ____ Psychic Diaries Package(s) for $25.00 each, including *Conversations
with the Spirit World* ____Book or 3-CD Set____ (check one) PLUS *Secrets of Psychic
Development* on CD____ or Cassette____

Name_____
Address_____
City_____ State____ Zip_____ Phone _____
E-Mail: _____(For Confirmation)
(We accept Visa, M/C & American Express)

Credit card type _____ Card #_____ Expiration date _____

To order by phone, call 310-820-0711, or to order by mail: Send check or money
order for $25.00 per Psychic Package & $4.95 S/H (add $2 for each additional set) to:

CHANNELING SPIRITS
P.O. BOX 11454
FORT LAUDERDALE FLORIDA 33339
lysa@channelingspirits.com
(You can also send letters to Lysa at this address!!)